JANE AUSTEN

Jane Austen

Reflections of a Reader

Nora Bartlett

Edited by Jane Stabler

OpenBook Publishers

https://www.openbookpublishers.com

ISBN Paperback: 9781783749751
ISBN Hardback: 9781783749768
ISBN Digital (PDF): 9781783749775
ISBN Digital ebook (epub): 9781783749782
ISBN Digital ebook (mobi): 9781783749799
ISBN XML: 9781783749805
DOI: 10.11647/OBP.0216

Cover image: Ivan Kramskoy, *Woman Reading. Portrait of Sofia Kramskaya* (after 1866), Wikimedia, https://commons.wikimedia.org/wiki/File:Ivan_Kramskoy_-_Reading_woman_(portrait_of_artist%27s_wife).jpg

Cover design: Anna Gatti.

Contents

Preface

Jane Stabler

Nora Bartlett (1949–2016) was an inspirational teacher of nineteenth- and twentieth-century fiction at the Universities of Oxford and St Andrews. Among her many areas of expertise, she was a superlative reader of Jane Austen, whose novels she first enjoyed at the age of six and carried on reading and re-reading almost every year for the rest of her life. After her death from an aggressive and terrifyingly swift oesophageal cancer at the age of only sixty-seven, her husband, the historian Robert Bartlett, gathered her Jane Austen papers and identified a press that would publish them. They were to appear as Nora had delivered them, written in an informal oral register for a general audience. Nora was well aware of recent Austen scholarship, but she recognised that for the vast majority of Austen's readers who were not academics, the shared pleasure and sometimes frustration of reading the novels themselves and their relationship with what Nora called 'the texture of reality' was what should be at the heart of any literary discussion.[1] Her Austen talks are presented here as she left them, with minimal editorial intervention to identify quotations and provide the necessary critical context that Nora would have given in extempore asides to her audience. Nora knew Austen so well that she usually quoted short passages from memory and she drew other allusions freely from her extensive reading across all periods of literature and film. Her occasional creative reimaginings of Austen are the effect of Austen's immediacy, a process of readerly response Nora describes in her first talk ('we speak in our heads lines she never wrote'), which is often revealing in a different way from

---

1   Nora Bartlett, 'An Excerpt from my Unpublished Writing', in *On Gender and Writing*, ed. by Michelene Wandor (Boston: Pandora, 1983), pp. 10–16 (p. 11).

      https://doi.org/10.11647/OBP.0216.14

an accurate quotation. Where this is the case and Nora's distinctive inflection serves as a vehicle for a motif in the talk as a whole, her gloss on Austen or other authors has been left intact and the original reference is given in a footnote.

These talks were written over several decades, and delivered on separate occasions to Jane Austen Society of Scotland gatherings, undergraduate literary societies, book clubs, to her students in continuing education programmes and the occasional academic symposium. Some of them subsequently appeared as blogs, generously donated to former students; some sections were eventually published as parts of more academic articles in journals such as *Persuasions*.[2] Nora's insights about the significance of mourning at the start of *Sense and Sensibility*, for example, appeared in a Festschrift for the legal and literary scholar, William Ian Miller.[3] Across all these talks, readers will recognise the way Nora circled around particular themes, studying them from a variety of angles and turning them about so that her regular audience could appreciate different facets of apparently familiar plots.

The final versions of all the talks that follow were selected by her husband. They exemplify Nora's deep but lightly worn erudition, her sense of humour and her generosity of spirit. We can savour her quizzical observations of family life, forbearance of more egotistical members of the academic community, concern for the young men and women who were her students and how they might flourish, an American concern about British standards of healthcare (mediated by her sister, who remained living in Rochester, New York, where Nora grew up), relish of tray bakes and a wonderful capacity for fellowship with others. Nora was a tireless correspondent, managing to sustain an astonishing number of multi-stranded conversations through text, email and shared *New Yorker* cartoons. Like Austen, Nora enjoyed a strong epistolary connection with her sister, who was a confidante and the alibi for her stringent observations of human foibles; unlike Austen, Nora shared her

---

2   Nora Bartlett, 'Deaths and Entrances: The Opening of *Sense and Sensibility*', *Persuasions On-line*, 32.2 (2012), http://jasna.org/persuasions/on-line/vol32no2/bartlett.html?

3   Nora Bartlett, 'Silence as a Weapon of Self-Defence in *Sense and Sensibility*', in *Emotion, Violence, Vengeance and Law in the Middle Ages: Essays in Honour of William Ian Miller*, ed. by Kate Gilbert and Stephen D. White (Leiden: Brill, 2018), pp. 344–50, https://doi.org/10.1163/9789004366374_019

intellectual life with her husband for whom she was the first and best reader of all he wrote.

These are the critical essays of someone who was clearly herself a novelist. In 1983 when she was in her early thirties, Nora published a wryly self-deprecating article on what it was like to be an unpublished novelist. Some of the insights she articulated courageously and unself-sparingly in that short but very powerful piece of writing help to explain her close attention to Austen's sense of herself as a writer. Nora described her own writing life as 'a pattern of continual interruptions'.[4] Unlike Austen, it was the experience of motherhood at the age of twenty-four that propelled her into writing her first novel: 'nothing in my life', she wrote, 'ever surprised me so much as what happens to women when they have children'. She continued:

> At the time I found it awful, or mostly awful, but now it seems to me as if my previous life had been a dim, flat, verbal thing, a spoken monologue that ran on and on in my head detailing the elements of existence as they presented themselves to me. My son interrupted that, and the way that interruption feels, still, is that he gave me the world.[5]

Although it came from a different source, it was this profound capacity for curiosity, warming to interest in other existences that made Nora and Jane Austen into like-minded novelists. Nora's explanation of the difference her first son made to the way she looked at and interacted with the world captures what it is that draws people to read and to write fiction:

> What he kept on teaching me was that he was a different person from me, separate, with a different body and mind and imagination. Not just that his sex was different but that he was quite other, and this made me begin to wonder, as I never had before, what other people's experience of the world was like.[6]

Nora's novels were not unread, but she remained unpublished. *First Impressions*, Jane Austen's first novel to be submitted to a press, was rejected unread and despite having three novels in a state of near completion when she moved to Chawton, Austen remained unpublished

---

4   Nora Bartlett, 'An Excerpt from my Unpublished Writing', p. 11.
5   Ibid.
6   Ibid.

for the best part of a decade. Nora was acutely alert to the effects of being able or not to try out a narrative voice with a readership; her own 'shame and misery' about publishers' rejections sharpened her perceptiveness about the different stages of Austen's writing career and the significance of her shift from being unpublished to being read by a larger audience than the family circle.[7] It was Nora who first drew my attention to the way in which Austen's work on her mature novels was braided so that she was likely to have been working on *Pride and Prejudice* and *Mansfield Park* at the same time; preparing *Mansfield Park* for the press at the same time as beginning work on *Emma*, and writing *Persuasion* while *Emma* was in the press. To be able to hold such different works in her head at the same time is a sign of Austen's creative genius; it is also a variety of multi-tasking that Nora would recognise as an integral part of quotidian domestic existence. For Nora, the connection between Austen's fiction and lived experience is vital, and this is evident in her approach to the novels. 'Emma in the Snow', for example, grew out of at least two real-life events: an email exchange with a fellow American about the dismal paucity of snow in the UK and (during the same winter) a day when an unusually heavy night's fall of snow in Fife meant that the editor of this volume was snowed-in in a hill-top hamlet waiting for the local farmer's tractor to clear the road so that she could get into St Andrews to teach a morning seminar on *Emma*. Digging had commenced at first light, but after two hours, the communal spade-work of several households had only removed a few feet of the snow drift across the lane. Nora telephoned shortly after 8 a.m.; she lived on the main road in the west end of St Andrews and had already (like Mr. Knightley) walked into town and back to ascertain whether it was possible to get to the grocery store. Solicitous and animated as ever, she enquired if I would like to borrow her now grown-up children's sled for my son and whether she could call on the local taxi firm for an estimate of when the inland road to my village would be clear. I explained my anxiety about the 10 a.m. *Emma* class; if I was still stuck, would she be able to take the class for me?—Nora almost whooped with joy, said that she had just been re-reading *Emma* for something else and that she would gladly step in. Four hours later, when I finally managed to inch my car down

---

7   Ibid., p. 15.

to the main road and into town, Nora was waiting with an exuberant account of how, following the student presentations, the lesson plan had been put aside and the whole seminar devoted to a discussion of the significance of the snow in *Emma*. She had also made brownies for the class, and gave me some to take back with the sled.

Nora's unfailing kindness and resourcefulness made her a wonderful teacher; she always found something good to extract from even the most dismally truncated exam script and her willingness to listen attentively marks her readings of Austen. In the following extracts from the fragmentary 'Pauses in Jane Austen', readers can hear what made her such a great explicator of Austen's artistry. Nora focuses on *Pride and Prejudice* and *Persuasion*; her pairing of textual examples, with sideways glances across Austen's works always throws light on what her friend, Caroline Walker Bynum brilliantly calls 'dissimilar similitudes'.[8] To examine the pauses in these two novels, Nora begins with the 'short pause' after Mr. Collins's proposal to Elizabeth Bennet in *Pride and Prejudice*:

> This is a strong example of how Jane Austen uses the 'pause' to create comedy, as in *Persuasion*, where in Chapter iii Sir Walter Elliot shows his ignorance of the world, the law, and his own dire economic straits by declaring loftily that he is 'by no means' certain 'as to the privileges' attached to the tenancy of Kellynch-hall—the tenant may be limited in his access to Kellynch's 'pleasure-grounds [...] shrubberies [...] flower gardens.'
>
> After this preposterous statement there is 'a short pause' while his steward, Mr. Shepherd, is clearly biting his tongue to keep either from laughing or from replying with the sharpness which the comment deserves: he knows more than anyone what a jam the Elliots are in and how much they need this tenant, and he knows the law—but he is used to crawling to Sir Walter, has become of necessity what the Scottish call a 'sook,' or suck-up, and will reply, as his clever daughter Mrs. Clay will always reply to the patronizing comments of Sir Walter and Miss Elliot, diplomatically, flatteringly. They are playing a long game with their short pauses.
>
> So, the 'pause' is often a moment when a character is suppressing a laugh, or an angry reply: it stands for a rebellion that does not take place,

---

8   Caroline Walker Bynum, *Dissimilar Similitudes: Devotional Objects in Late Medieval Europe* (New York: Zone Books, 2020), https://doi.org/10.2307/j.ctv15r5dvj; the book is dedicated to Nora.

or takes place only internally. But there are other types of pause also, and one occurs in *Pride and Prejudice* a little later, in Chapter xxi, when Jane Bennet has received, and relayed to Elizabeth, the distressing news of the Bingley party's sudden departure from Netherfield. Elizabeth is listening, and forming her own opinions of, the 'high-flown expressions' of Miss Bingley's letter. She knows, however, that Jane's view of the sisters is different from hers, so replies carefully, 'after a short pause,' not showing her own sense that the female Bingleys are treacherous snobs and false friends, because she knows that that would both hurt the tender-hearted, trusting Jane, and alarm her about their brother. Instead she is, like Mr. Shepherd, tactful: 'may we not hope that [...] the delightful intercourse you have known as friends, will be renewed with yet greater satisfaction as sisters.'

In that 'short pause' Elizabeth was thinking what to say: and though Jane Austen presents her characters' thoughts with incomparable depth and subtlety in her use of free-indirect discourse, where the narrative mingles with the character's thoughts, here she allows the reader to invent or imagine what kind of thinking has gone into those 'short pauses': Mr. Shepherd wants to move the topic on to a more realistic plane, and wants not to lose his job; Elizabeth wants to give her beloved sister the kind of comfort in this unexpected turn of events that she believes is genuinely appropriate to the situation. Both characters, in highly contrasting circumstances, are taking care with their speech.[9]

This extract illustrates quintessential Nora Bartlett: penetrating analysis of a moment, warm colloquial summary of the situation (Sir Walter being 'in a jam'; Mr. Shepherd being 'a sook'), and the affirmative recognition of an unspoken act of kindness. Perhaps most the most striking trait of all is Nora's identification of patterns of behaviour in Austen's fiction, an incisive recognition which can only come from years of immersion and deep contemplation of the novels. Her quick eye unerringly picked out the recurring motifs that create the rich texture of relationships in Austen's fiction, such as the pattern of maternal absence and a male mentor, or a mother favouring the child who most resembles her, or the different ways in which the act of attending or attention is refracted across members of the same family. Nora's inside-out knowledge of the texts also alerts us to Austen's innately dramatic presentation of dialogue, enabling readers to recognise and assess points of contrast and progression—as when Nora points out that Henry Crawford

---

9   Nora Bartlett, 'Pauses in Jane Austen', unpublished material from lecture notes.

realizes that he could 'so wholly [...] confide' in Fanny in the same room in the Parsonage in which he and Mary callously planned to make 'a small hole in Fanny Price's heart' (*Mansfield Park*, II xii 341; II vi 267). As well as her formidable grasp of plot devices, Nora was also attuned to the sound of Austen's prose. Again, Nora skilfully links this to her audience's experience of navigating the everyday:

> But the pauses also produce a kind of realism in the rhythms of speech as Jane Austen's novels display it: we all know from our own experience of conversation, formal or informal, that we are often required to pause before speaking—like Mr. Shepherd and Elizabeth, we are deciding what to say next. In *Pride and Prejudice*, despite the 'sparkling' reputation of its dialogue, there are many such pauses—even with Mr. Wickham, so easy to talk to that a clever young woman ought to be more on her guard, there are 'many pauses' and 'trials of other subjects' while Elizabeth tries to maintain her composure as she and Wickham mount their joint attack on Mr. Darcy's character. And in her talk with Mr. Darcy, there are so many pauses that one is tempted to wonder if Jane Austen is thinking of the famously tongue-tied heroine created by her beloved Fanny Burney in *Evelina*, who, dancing with her high-born admirer at her first London ball, can say nothing at all.
>
> Elizabeth, not quite so simple, nevertheless experiences in her first dance with Mr. Darcy, 'a pause of some minutes,' and is forced to blurt out—here abandoning tact—that there are 'no other two people in the room who have less to say for themselves.' Later, in Mr. Darcy's first, unsuccessful proposal at the Rosings parsonage, there will be 'a pause' on his part, in which his thoughts are embodied in physical reactions that Elizabeth cannot help seeing and experiencing—'his complexion became pale with anger, and the disturbance of his mind was visible in every feature'—this 'pause was to Elizabeth's feelings dreadful.' She does not realize, but the reader probably does, how much her feelings are already blending with Darcy's: the reader can feel the intensity of her erotic response to Darcy—amidst all her resentment and rage—in that 'dreadful pause.'[10]

'She does not realize, but the reader probably does', is Nora's characteristic way of sharing her perceptions. She is pointing out something that not all readers will have noticed—certainly not all first-time undergraduate readers—but at all stages, her critical commentary embraces and carries with it everyone in the room, generously extending textual exploration

---

10   Ibid.

to all those present instead of the more common and disingenuous use of 'the reader' which, in a lot of criticism, tends to mean 'me'. In the last paragraphs of her drafted talk on pauses, Nora returns us to one of the eleven pauses in *Persuasion,* which she considers 'the briefest and greatest of her novels':

> I have looked at one comic [pause] and want to end with one luminous and serious one, complicated by its being heard not only by those in the conversation, but overheard by the silent, pensive Anne. This is Captain Wentworth and Louisa Musgrove, nutting and flirting in the hedgerows in Chapter x while Anne is left alone, neglected by all, feeling no connection with anything but the melancholy autumnal landscape. Louisa, that healthy, lively, commonplace young girl, is expressing her resentment of her sister-in-law Mary's snobbishness:
>
> 'She has a great deal too much of the Elliot pride—we do so wish that Charles had married Anne—I suppose you know he wanted to marry Anne?'
>
> After a moment's pause, Captain Wentworth said, 'Do you mean that she refused him?'
>
> 'Oh! Yes, certainly.'
>
> 'When did that happen?'
>
> Louisa is not imaginative enough to wonder at this abrupt shift, this surprising interest in Anne, on the part of a man who has been studiously ignoring her for weeks, but the reader thinks his or her way deep into that pause: later Captain Wentworth, referring to that refusal of Charles, tells Anne, 'I could not help thinking, "was this for me?"' But there is more—as in the later moment when he responds to Mr. Elliot's admiring glance at Anne on the Cobb at Lyme, he is suddenly seeing Anne again as she had once appeared to him—young and beautiful and desirable, stepping toward him beckoningly, freed from the ghastly nun-hood of the years between. There are many moments in the novel which show the ways in which these two cannot get away from each other, but here, as often, it is displayed in a pause, spoken in silence.

Here, as so often in her talks, Nora allows her listeners to linger over the cadences of an Austen novel and to let the resonances of the scene ripple out in the minds of the listeners. She had a lovely reading voice and beautifully articulated quotations were at the heart of all her talks. Nora always preferred to plant questions rather than hammer out a thesis, she is a skilful interpreter both of what is said and what is unsaid, but she never presses too hard on the unsaid, being wary of the egotism involved in much 'against the grain' critical theory, which drowned out the voice of the writer with strident polemic. A tolerant and humane feminist and former Trotskyist herself, she could be acerbic about academic books with loud titles, 'which achieve their real influence on people who do not have to read them, who get all they need out of the title'.[11] Instead, her talks on any given topic always set out to 'think about it with you' and to 'help us to see it better'. Like all teachers, she was concerned about the correction of error, but she preferred to do this through a mutual appreciation of nuance: seeing clearly and accurately was part of Austen's art, and reflection on that art was a way of inculcating the clear and accurate perception which is always the necessary first step toward social amelioration.

One of the advantages of being published, Nora wrote, was that it would enable her 'to yell more'.[12] Her work on Jane Austen evinces a strong sense of political purpose and if one were pushed to categorise her methodology, it would be 'close reading with an agenda'. Her feminism, inflected by left-wing Catholicism, comes through in her attention to Austen's depiction of how families work (or not), and especially how women perform the roles of being sisters, mothers and grandmothers. She explores perennial women's questions such as women's involvement in their own oppression, how dangerous the world is for unprotected women, and how to recognise and guard against the particular threat of the predatory, but attractive male. Her aesthetic and moral sensibility led her to weigh continuously what she called the 'education and miseducation of the heart', the importance of scrutinizing behaviour, of being aware of the existence of others beyond the borders of the self, and the bleak moral paradox that proper delicacy about the feelings of others more often than not leads to characters being alone. The modern existential problem of loneliness is one of the unrecognised features of Austen's world that Nora brings into focus as well as being one of the issues that she sought to combat in her life and work.

After Nora's death, one of her former tutees, Mark Liddell, posted a witty, moving account of her determination to correct a tutorial group's

---

11   Obituary of Mary Ellmann, whose work 'has the disadvantage of needing to be read' (Nora Bartlett, 'Mary Ellmann', *The Independent* (June 7, 1989), p. 18).
12   Nora Bartlett, 'An Excerpt from my Unpublished Writing', p. 15.

failure to appreciate the greatness of the film *It's a Wonderful Life*.[13]
Mark used a line from the film as an epitaph for Nora: 'Strange, isn't it?
Each man's life touches so many other lives. When he isn't around, he
leaves an awful hole, doesn't he?'. The angel Clarence speaks here of a
male character and, apposite as those words are, it is keeping with the
spirit of this book to pair his epitaph with another, which celebrates the
difference made by female character. Nora had an effect on those around
her of the kind George Eliot describes on the last page of *Middlemarch*,
where we are told about the 'incalculably diffusive' effect of a good
woman. It is one of the hallmarks of Nora's Austen talks that, like her
life, they have a far-reaching after-life. 'She was a great loss, greater than
I recognized until now', as one of the peer-reviewers of this volume
observed: *Reflections of a Reader* allows us to see just that.

---

13 'Nora Bartlett', *Mark Liddell* (November 24, 2016), https://liddellmark.wordpress.
    com/2016/11/24/nora-bartlett/

A Note on Texts

All quotations from Jane Austen's published fiction and manuscripts have been keyed to the Cambridge University Press edition of the *Works of Jane Austen* (General Editor, Janet Todd). Parenthetical references are to volume, chapter and page number for the major novels and letter or chapter number and page number, or just page number for shorter works. Jane Austen's letters are quoted by page number from the Oxford University Press edition, collected and edited by Deirdre Le Faye (3rd edition). Every effort has been made to track and trace all the references to other literary critics and other literary works, which were usually unattributed in the scripts of Nora's talks. The editor will gladly restore and acknowledge any outstanding attributions in future printings.

1. Reading *Pride and Prejudice* over Fifty Years

I gave another talk about *Pride and Prejudice* earlier this year to the student literary society we have at St Andrews, and in the discussion that followed one student said something very memorable; we were talking about the Keira Knightley film version and, as seems to be usual, almost everyone in the room except me hated Keira Knightley, which I find fascinating, but the comment the student made was even more fascinating: she mentioned the continual little smug smirk on Keira's face and said in some exasperation, 'when movies want to show that a girl is smart, the only thing they can think of is to have her sneer at everybody!' I thought that was very illuminating, and not only about the film but the book: Elizabeth Bennet is clever and she knows it. We don't all, automatically, like or identify with people who think they are clever.

I want to talk today about some of the techniques Jane Austen uses to enable readers to feel through, to feel with, to identify with, her characters. Identification within the novel can change over time, particularly over long periods of time. A few years ago, I realized that I had been reading *Pride and Prejudice* for fifty years, since I was six and found the book on my grandfather's bookshelf. What I actually understood I cannot of course remember, but it seemed to present no problems to my understanding. I was never bewildered. I read the novel in a state of high excitement, and then I read it again. This has been happening ever since, several times a year. I have had this novel as a companion through almost every stage of my life.

So, that is one part of what I would like to talk about today: the way in which one's reading changes at different stages of life. The other is the role which silence, and listening, play in Jane Austen's novels, even in this one, so famed for the brilliance of its dialogue. I am going to

 https://doi.org/10.11647/OBP.0216.01

try to interweave these two themes, and because my notion of stages of a reading life began as stages of a woman's reading life, I would like to weave in also a third strand, which is a question about whether the novel is seen as presupposing, or addressing, a female reader. This has been made more apparent to me recently by discovering David Miller's short, strange book, *Jane Austen, or the Secret of Style*, which interrogates that assumption by positing a young *male* reader and describing his predicament. In her reading, according to Miller, a young female reader, 'had done what a female not only would, but ought' but 'the same discovery that [...] made the girl a good girl, made the boy all wrong'.[1]

Professor Miller is trying to assess the effects of what many seem to assume about the gender of the narrative voice in Jane Austen's novels: that is, though there is seldom the intrusion of an 'I' and never an invented, named narrator as there is in, say, the novels of Sir Walter Scott, somehow the voice that speaks is a female voice. Miller explores the possibility that the young boy who uses his own inner voice to speak the narrator's words in a Jane Austen novel is somehow 'getting himself into trouble'. This question came very pointedly into my mind when I recently gave a version of this paper to a student group in Scotland, a group I have addressed before on twentieth-century topics and therefore *know* includes both young men and young women, to find that for *Pride and Prejudice* I had drawn a larger audience than usual, but composed exclusively of young women. I am going to be talking about how the novel effects an identification between the reader and Elizabeth, but I would like to raise the question of how and whether the novel genders the reader as female, and does so through the narrative.[2]

This is related to a question which has been debated among writers on Jane Austen for at least a century, which is how completely the novel's narrative point of view is identified with that of its central figure. Some writers seem to see the novels as 'thought experiments' in the depiction of a single point-of-view of the sort that we find in, say, Virginia Woolf, in that departures from that viewpoint are read as lapses, to be found more often in the early novels, or in a novel like *Persuasion* that was not

1   D. A. Miller, *Jane Austen, or the Secret of Style* (Princeton and Oxford: Princeton University Press, 2003), p. 3.
2   For further discussion, see Joe Bray, *The Female Reader in the English Novel from Burney to Austen* (New York: Routledge, 2009), https://doi.org/10.4324/9780203888674

fully revised.³ My own sense—I want us to look at this—is that while the novels work to make you identify with the central figure (in *Pride and Prejudice* with Elizabeth), the narrative as a whole is not participating fully with that process, but is offering us a comment on it, is not even, as consistently as is often suggested, fully sympathetic with her viewpoint. I think it is a markedly cool eye that watches Elizabeth at the novel's very end, acting efficiently to exclude her mother from 'the comfort and elegance of their family party at Pemberley' (III xviii 426). I believe it is the late American feminist critic Carolyn Heilbrun who commented on this passage, 'Never trust a Daddy's girl'.⁴

I have been struggling for some time to find ways of characterizing Austen's narrative voice/voices, and gender is only one aspect of its elusiveness. There is moral ambiguity, as well. But here, in *Pride and Prejudice*, not the first novel published but often the first one read, is there a sense of its addressing the reader as female, possibly colluding, two females, together? Is that how we experience this famously understated, enigmatic, but also colourful and melodramatic narrative? My own reading was once a 'girl's' and is now a 'woman's', but also on multiple re-readings finds traces of a speaker who is eerily untethered and ungendered, like an angel un-voiced, like a countertenor. The unsatisfactory term critics have found for this is 'irony', but I would like to find another. Miller, whom I mentioned earlier, is worried we might need to use the term 'neuter', which he doesn't like, and I don't like either, since it reminds me of *lost* gender.⁵ Might it not be possible to look for something more thrilling, comparable to the cartwheeling exuberance about gender one finds in Shakespeare's comedies?⁶

---

3   For Austen and cognitive explorations, see Susan Morgan, *In the Meantime: Character and Perception in Jane Austen's Fiction* (Chicago: University of Chicago Press, 1980); Alan Richardson, *British Romanticism and the Science of Mind* (Cambridge: Cambridge University Press, 2001), pp. 101–11.

4   Source unidentified. In a 1988 study, Heilbrun commented on the 'perfunctoriness' of the endings of Jane Austen's novels, including *Pride and Prejudice*: 'Elizabeth [...] says of Darcy at the end that he is not yet ready to be laughed at, or with, and there is no woman with whom to share laughter. Austen probably laughed a good deal with her sister and her nieces, but laughter did not mark the high point of any of her adventures or the adventures of her heroines'. See Carolyn G. Heilbrun, *Writing A Woman's Life* (London: The Woman's Press, 1989), pp. 129–30.

5   Miller, *Jane Austen*, pp. 33–38.

6   Something like this emerges in Claudia L. Johnson, *Equivocal Beings: Politics, Gender, and Sentimentality in the 1790s* (Chicago and London: University of Chicago Press,

I don't want you to let go of the sense that there is something stranger going on, and that Jane Austen's novels, read rightly, have something of an uncanny quality. We might want to think of Jane Austen as the author of a set of six strange novels that could be known under the collective title, *Being Female*—acknowledging the full complexity of the way that the first voice that spoke inside my head, when I began reading Jane Austen, was something like a woman's. Though her nieces and nephews read her novels and gave her advice about them while in their teens, I don't think she was herself producing 'early readers' in the manner of, say, Dr. Seuss, and at six I was younger than the reader Jane Austen had in mind. Nevertheless, I'm going to start by boldly suggesting that I was one kind of ideal reader at that very early age; I am suggesting that my youth and absolute inexperience was an odd kind of equipment for one sort of reading. Jane Austen acknowledged that she expected her readers to 'like' Elizabeth; I worshipped her, wanted to be her; I shared and accepted, as a reader with even a little experience could not, I think, the accuracy of her 'first impressions' of all the new people and places to which the novel's lively opening pages introduces her—and *First Impressions* was, of course, the novel's working title.

It has become a critical commonplace to suggest that almost all of Jane Austen's novels in some way enact 'the Cinderella theme with the fairy godmother omitted'.[7] I think the fairy tale element gave a shape to my readings and re-readings throughout childhood: the two very beautiful and impoverished heroines, the rich and handsome heroes, pairs of wicked sisters, gnomes and trolls and wicked sprites, and even a bad fairy in the form of Lady Catherine de Bourgh. At age six, actual fairy tales made up much of my other reading, and this was but a gratifyingly longer fairy tale, a fairy tale with conversations in it, an important qualification, which I will talk about in a moment.

As a little girl and for a long time afterwards, I identified with Elizabeth Bennet. But the identification with Elizabeth which Jane Austen so skilfully engineers produces at this age and perhaps at any, or at most, *first* readings of the novel, some moments which can't be

---

1995), pp. 191–204.

7   D. W. Harding, 'Regulated Hatred: An Aspect of the Work of Jane Austen', *Scrutiny*,
      8 (1939–40), 236–62; reprinted in *Jane Austen: Critical Assessments*, ed. by Ian
      Littlewood, 4 vols (Mountfield: Helm, 1998), II, p. 292.

reproduced at later readings. One important one, which no reader is likely to forget, is Elizabeth's wide-eyed, mesmerized acceptance of Mr. Wickham's life story, the story of how Mr. Darcy has, out of pure jealousy, ruined his boyhood companion's life and prospects. This takes place, all will recall, at an evening party at the house of well-meaning but vulgar Aunt Phillips (the frequent fate of older women is to lapse into vulgarity) where Mr. Wickham's inability to play whist has placed him, with a powerful foreshadowing of later events, between Elizabeth and Lydia. Earlier in the day, Elizabeth has seen a mysterious exchange of glances between the charming young officer and the hated Mr. Darcy; and she is curious. She leads Mr. Wickham to talk of their relationship, after—oddly impulsively, don't we think?—revealing to a complete stranger, her own dislike of the man. And Wickham, after a little coy hesitation, tells his tale of Mr. Darcy's vindictiveness and breach of promise to someone '"connected with his family [...] from [...] infancy"' (I xvi 86). Wickham is also, of course, talking to a complete stranger.

The staging of Elizabeth's responses here is worth our taking time to notice: when Wickham is talking about Mr. Darcy she finds 'the interest of the subject increase'; she 'listened with all her heart; but the delicacy of it prevented farther inquiry' (I xvi 88). Her sense of delicacy, we note, extends only to her own behaviour and not, memorably, to any sense of Mr. Wickham's, who tells her—one imagines his look of conscious self-restraint, the bitten lip, the shake of his head as he says, '"Till I can forget his father, I can never defy or expose *him*"' (I xvi 89) Elizabeth does not seem to notice—not for many months, and until forced to by incontrovertible evidence—that he says these words *while* exposing Mr. Darcy. Aged six, I did not notice this, either; but Elizabeth is almost twenty. Neither does she notice that Wickham's story is a nest of cliché: Darcy's father '"was one of the best men that ever breathed and the truest friend I ever had"'; he has been left with '"a thousand tender recollections"' of this dear friend (I xvi 88). Elizabeth, smart, well-read, but young, does not realize that his conversation combines the scandalous with the fatuous—he must be so good-looking! And so impenetrable. Miller suggests that it is impossible for the reader to see the action from Wickham's point of view, to get into the shoes of this young soldier.[8] One of *Mansfield Park's* many experiments is an exploration of the inner world of a predatory male, but that is not allowed here.

What Jane Austen demonstrates instead here is the spellbinding power of a sexually opportunistic and very attractive man to produce this blinkered response in a young woman. A girl of high intelligence, but relatively little experience of men, responds to Wickham's gambit as naively as did I at six, a young child with absolutely no experience of much outside family life. The Cinderella story here is as full of power and danger as any true folk or fairy tale: Elizabeth, seated excitingly, as I have said, playing Lottery Tickets, with its prizes and forfeits, next to the entrancing Wickham, who has Lydia on his other side, Lydia, who 200 pages later will pay the ultimate forfeit to this heartless and dissolute charmer's desire for easy money, and easy sexual conquests. We might just note here that Lydia's flirtatiousness, and her being 'a most determined talker', almost prevented this private conversation; she is distracted from Wickham only by her absorption in the game (I xvi 86). We see her 'making bets and exclaiming after prizes'—how dangerous for a woman to have such excessive energy; how ambivalent Jane Austen is about it (I xvi 86). Lottery Tickets is a noisy 'round game', all luck and no skill—poor Lydia! And we might note how cool, how askance, is the narrative's composure while watching its beloved heroine responding over-excitedly to the man: 'Elizabeth honoured him for such feelings, and thought him handsomer than ever as he expressed them' (I xvi 89).

Cleverly selective, the novel does not give us much more in the way of demonstrations like this one of Wickham's charm. Little more of his conversation is presented in these early chapters; we are only told about his favourable effects on the Bennet parents, and on discerning Aunt Gardiner who likes him so much. His speech is not depicted again until many chapters later, until the much later scenes in Chapter xli in which he attempts to revive Lizzy's interest, and then, like the disenchanted Lizzy, we detect 'an affectation and a sameness to disgust and weary' (II xviii 258). Even in this early novel, drafted before the nineteenth century began, and 'lopt & cropt' ten years later, the balance of who talks, whose

---

8   This is a gloss on Miller's brief discussion of the cross-dressing episode in which
     Lydia Bennet helps to dress the young soldier, Chamberlayne, in women's clothes
     and the other men, including Wickham, 'did not know him in the least' (Miller, *Jane
     Austen*, p. 3).

dialogue is quoted and whose isn't, and when, is very important.[9] Jane Austen's family read plays as well as novels aloud to each other after dinner, and before the family left her childhood home at Steventon parsonage, they put on plays themselves in a small way. Some of the pieces of Jane Austen's surviving juvenile writing are very short, very funny plays. She is interested in dialogue, good at it and knows when *not* to do it.[10] Sometimes in re-reading Jane Austen you look for a bit of dialogue you think you remember and find it isn't there, it has only been suggested by the narrative and then re-imagined, as speech, by the reader: we speak in our heads lines she never wrote.

The exchanges we *do* hear in *Pride and Prejudice*, and famously, are those between Elizabeth and Darcy—erotically charged, but also sharp and convincing, and I would like to look at one exchange to demonstrate the character of some of these conversations, the 'light & bright & sparkling' surface that, like the fairy-tale plot, provokes delight in the reader.[11] We might just pause, first, though, to look at the way in which Mr. Darcy, in Volume I of the novel, is becoming more and more attracted to Elizabeth. The direction this attraction takes him in is interesting, and we might want to note that, having boorishly described her as '"tolerable; but not handsome enough to tempt *me*"' in Chapter iii, he finds it 'mortifying' in Chapter vi to find himself finding her 'pleasing' (I iii 12; I vi 26). He is watching her; his next move is, intriguingly, to *listen*: 'as a step towards conversing with her himself, [he] attended to her conversation with others' (I vi 26). Elizabeth notices this: '"What does Mr. Darcy mean," said she to Charlotte, "by listening to my conversation with Colonel Forster?"' (I vi 26). Keep this listening in mind; we want to be thinking, as we read Jane Austen, not only about who is talking and what they are saying but about who might be listening.

The next passage of dialogue I have chosen, from Chapter xxxi, is interesting in this regard, for it is set at Rosings, the home of Lady Catherine de Bourgh, the daughter and sister of an Earl, who ought, technically at least, to be the arbiter of taste and breeding her chaplain Mr. Collins thinks her, but who proves herself with every speech and

---

9   *Letters*, p. 202.
10 For further discussion, see *The Talk in Jane Austen*, ed. by Bruce Stovel and Lynn Weinloss Gregg (Edmonton: University of Alberta Press, 2002).
11 *Letters*, p. 203.

every action to be ill-bred and ill-mannered. The scene takes place after dinner; Lady Catherine and the parsonage party are at a little distance. If this were a play they would be 'upstage right', and Mr. Darcy and his cousin Colonel Fitzwilliam have drifted 'downstage left' to hear Elizabeth play the piano. Darcy, having been separated from Elizabeth for more than ten chapters, is clearly beginning to warm himself again in the pleasure of her company, to remember what he feels like when he is with her. Elizabeth tells him and his cousin that she has information to give about him that will '"shock your relations"', toying inwardly with what she *thinks* she *does* know about him, his wrongs to Wickham, but nevertheless behaving in such an 'arch' way as unwittingly to attract him: '"I am not afraid of you,"' he says, 'smilingly' and almost affectionately (II viii 195–96). His cousin is told that he refused to dance at the Meryton Assembly but not that Elizabeth was the woman with whom he did not dance. There is some inconsequential, rather intimate, banter. '"Well, Colonel Fitzwilliam, what do I play next?" she asks: '"My fingers wait your orders."' (II viii 196). Diffidently, but with the obstinacy which Mrs. Gardiner will eventually locate as his defining characteristic, Darcy interrupts: he is still responding to her teasing accusation. '"Perhaps," said Darcy, "I should have judged better, had I sought an introduction, but I am ill-qualified to recommend myself to strangers."' (II viii 196). Note the grammar here: the conditional predominates—'perhaps I should [...] had I sought', closing with the apparently shy but perhaps proud or reserved admission: 'I am ill qualified'.

Elizabeth's response, interestingly, does not cue the reader to her inner state. There is no lead-up to her swift and smart rejoinder, which apparently comes from a sudden confidence. '"Shall we"', she begins— *we*, to the son of an Earl whom she has known for a day or two (it is worth noting that the Austen family had a wide acquaintance among the gentry and counted many baronets among their associates, but had little contact with the nobility)—'"Shall we ask your cousin the reason of this?' said Elizabeth, still addressing Colonel Fitzwilliam. '"Shall we ask him why a man of sense and education, and who has lived in the world, is ill-qualified to recommend himself to strangers?"' (II viii 196). *Shall we*, she brightly suggests. As readers, we remember that Lizzy has been described from the story's opening as having 'wit'. '"Lizzy has something more of quickness than her sisters"', her intelligent father has said, to her far less intelligent mother (I i 5).

But perhaps the smoothly confident, witty address to the Colonel would not be equally smooth if made to the object of her witticism? Elizabeth presents herself here as if she were being straightforward and direct; she lightly characterizes Darcy as hidden, reserved. But she is using indirection herself here, by addressing Fitzwilliam. Here we see both potential lovers, one unsuspecting, one beginning to be certain of his fate, simultaneously tongue-tied, bashful, both, in the mode of lovers, in that he speaks hesitantly, and she addresses a third party, and yet both are warmly competent at self-revelation.

> 'I certainly have not the talent which some people possess,' said Darcy, 'of conversing easily with those I have never seen before. I cannot catch their tone of conversation, or appear interested in their concerns, as I often see done.'
> 'My fingers,' said Elizabeth, 'do not move over this instrument in the masterly manner which I see so many women's do. They have not the same force or rapidity, and do not produce the same expression. But then I have always supposed it to be my own fault—because I would not take the trouble of practising. It is not that I do not believe *my* fingers as capable as any other woman's of superior execution.'
> Darcy smiled and said, 'You are perfectly right. You have employed your time much better. No one admitted to the privilege of hearing you, can think anything wanting. We neither of us perform to strangers.' (II viii 197)

It seems important for the surface sparkle that we do *not* see Elizabeth searching through the confusion she often feels in Darcy's presence for the right words here. She is fluent, almost without the slight hesitation that would be produced by commas. And Darcy picks up some of that fluency, that confidence. They have both, briefly, the right words, they have mastered the sort of exchange in which their capacity for intimacy is revealed through their simultaneous recognition of, and reserve about, one another. I don't intend to endlessly quote witty dialogue. In recent re-readings of the novel I am struck more by how often, between Elizabeth and Darcy, there is a *failure* to be witty, an appealing failure, a sense of mutual difficulty, of conversation being blunted or even utterly scuppered by an undertow of real emotion neither is prepared to acknowledge.

As a sort of background to this discussion, here is a short passage from *Evelina* by Fanny Burney, one of Jane Austen's favourite novelists. The title character is describing her first adult ball and her first dance with a man:

> He seemed very desirous of entering into conversation with me; but I was seized with such a panic, that I could hardly speak a word, and nothing but the shame of so soon changing my mind prevented my returning to my seat, and declining to dance at all.
>
> He appeared to be surprised at my terror, which I believe was but too apparent: however, he asked no questions, though I fear he must think it very odd, for I did not choose to tell him it was owing to my never before dancing but with a school-girl.
>
> His conversation was sensible and spirited; his air, and address were open and noble; his manners gentle, attentive, and infinitely engaging; his person is all elegance, and his countenance the most animated and expressive I have ever seen...[12]

When she wishes simply to sit down, she is urged, '"But you must speak to your partner first."' Evelina confesses: '"However, I had not sufficient courage to address him; and so away we all three tript, and seated ourselves at another end of the room."'[13]

This novel, written in 1778, published, like Jane Austen's first novel, 'by a lady', is an obvious influence not only on Jane Austen but on most nineteenth-century novels about women. 'The History of a Young Lady's Entrance into the World', it is filled to the brim with uncouth and unwanted admirers, ill-bred older women, and of decent, loyal (and rich, and well-born) suitors. It is a novel full of embarrassment, which is a topic I would like to address in a minute. But I would like to move on via tongue-tiedness. The *Evelina* passage is excruciating because, though Lord Orville, her lovely dancing partner, makes every courteous effort to speak, unlike Mr. Darcy, Evelina, unlike Lizzy, cannot say *anything* at all. Nothing. Not a word. We know that Jane Austen found this scene very funny; and I think we see an intriguing rewriting of it at the ball at Netherfield, where Elizabeth and Darcy finally—indeed, for the only time in the novel—dance.

---

12   Fanny Burney, *Evelina: Or the History of a Young Lady's Entrance into the World*, ed. by Edward A. Bloom (Oxford and New York: Oxford University Press, 1968; repr. 1990), p. 30.
13   Ibid.

This is back in Chapter xviii. We will all remember that the ball at Netherfield is a kind of turning point. The next day, the Netherfield party decamp to London and Jane is left, for a time, deserted by Bingley, and the novel is left without the stimulation of the growing Darcy-Elizabeth relationship. Though there are compensations: the next chapter opens with Mr. Collins's proposal. At the Netherfield ball, Elizabeth, who has earlier promised her mother never to dance with Mr. Darcy, is taken by surprise and forced to accept him as a partner. Elizabeth is at first determined to share Mr. Darcy's silence, then decides that 'to oblige him to talk' will be to torture him even more (I xviii 102). They discuss the dance itself, the equivalent of talking about the weather. They discuss, in a way that embarrasses both of them, Wickham. They are disastrously interrupted by Sir William Lucas with his blundering remarks about the approaching marriage between Bingley and Jane. And they discuss each other. While still in a state of some self-possession Elizabeth has said, with deliberate preposterousness, that she has '"always seen a great similarity in the turn of our minds"' and Mr. Darcy has mumbled something back (I xviii 103). Later on, when they are both trying to get back on to their conversational feet after Sir William's interruption, things get even more hopeless. They stagger along, saying things they do not mean, trying to follow one another through a mire of almost *non sequiturs*. Elizabeth tries to converse, for convention's sake—they are in public, they barely know each other, they are turning each other through space in time to music, after all, so touching one another, if barely, and they have to behave themselves. She tries to 'shake off her gravity' and *keep talking* (I xviii 105). Darcy also determinedly struggles on as they weave and wind through oceans of unacknowledged feeling:

'What think you of books?' said he, smiling.

'Books—Oh! No.—I am sure we never read the same, or not with the same feelings.'

'I am sorry you think so; but if that be the case, there can at least be no want of subject.—We may compare our different opinions.'

'No—I cannot talk of books in a ball-room; my head is always full of something else.'

'The *present* always occupies you in such scenes—does it?' said he, with a look of doubt.

'Yes, always,' she replied, without knowing what she said, for her thoughts had wandered far from the subject, as soon afterwards

appeared by her suddenly exclaiming, 'I remember hearing you once
say, Mr. Darcy, that you hardly ever forgave, that your resentment once
created was unappeasable. You are very cautious, I suppose, as to its
being created?'
    'I am,' said he, with a firm voice.
    'And never allow yourself to be blinded by prejudice?'
    'I hope not.'

Here it seems to me that one of the perfections of the novel is in this very
imperfect, mutually unsatisfactory, mutually embarrassing exchange,
which, if it leaves Elizabeth's mind (we don't know) stays in Darcy's.
For months.

Something I think is very important here—I note it in *Persuasion*
also—is that though Jane Austen's novels do feature both witty, and
comically witless, speakers (Mr. and Mrs. Bennet immediately leap
to mind), very often, and easy to miss, characters' wits fail them
in the dialogue. They are, like Evelina, tongue-tied. Think of Darcy
and Elizabeth outside Pemberley in Chapter xliii, talking 'with great
perseverance' about Matlock and Dove Dale (III i 284). But these
presented failures are framed, in the narrative, by such rhythmic prose
that the sense of sparkle and vibrancy is maintained. There are pauses
that are like pauses in music. There is a wonderful one in *Pride and
Prejudice* where, having demanded some professions of envy and
admiration of his lifestyle from the departing Elizabeth, Mr. Collins
walks about the room 'while Elizabeth tried to unite civility and truth
in a few short sentences' (II xv 239).

From Mr. Collins it is but a short step to the social embarrassment
that many critics have noted is *Pride and Prejudice's* great theme. David
Miller describes the second-order awkwardness, for the young male
reader, of such profound identification with a young woman, 'enjoying,
or imagining enjoying, the happy ending of a plot that, except in this
mode of writing, one never could perform'.[14] For the young girl, the
awkwardnesses presented even in this 'light & bright & sparkling' text
were increasingly highlighted for me as a reader as I grew older and
continued to reread the novel, and naturally reached their peak during
the period of life when embarrassment seems to be the most crucial of
human experiences. Adolescence is the period when the reader of *Pride*

---

14   Miller, *Jane Austen*, p. 34.

and Prejudice is approaching the same age as that of her heroines, which I think of as sort of 'Stage II' of reading Jane Austen. In this stage there is more suffering for the reader whatever his or her sex.

Jane Austen is sometimes spoken about as if she were not a very 'physical' novelist, as if she did not attend much to physical sensation in her characters.[15] I would dispute this in general, but surely even those who hold that mistaken view must agree that she is the Poet Laureate of the blush—that physical sensation so well known to children and adolescents, rarer in adults.[16] It would be interesting to count the blushes in *Pride and Prejudice*, not only Lizzy's, but Jane's, of course, and Charlotte Lucas's, and then of course to count the blushes that do *not* occur. Lydia and Wickham in their triumphant return to Longbourn as young marrieds do not blush, though they cause blushes and the other ritual responses of embarrassment and chagrin: the eyes lifted heavenwards, the shudders and shrugs. Here it is siblings and their spouses who cause the embarrassment, but more often, in keeping with the spirit of adolescence, it is parents and parent-figures. Many adults are ludicrous in the novel—Sir William Lucas, Lady Catherine and, of course, Mr. Collins, who, though young, seems from his profession and his pomposity to belong to an older generation—but it is Elizabeth's parents and particularly her mother who exhibit, in Mr. Darcy's wounding phrase, 'that total want of propriety so frequently, so almost uniformly betrayed by herself' (II xii 220).

The reader knows all about this from the beginning, of course. Mrs. Bennet's foolish, embarrassing obsession with marrying her daughters, which is, of course, shared by the novel, and does, of course, prove in the end to be appropriate to the situation and the tale. It is the basis on which we become acquainted with the family. But the people of Meryton and of the Bennets' part of Hertfordshire are probably used to Mrs. Bennet's silliness. It is in contact with the newcomers at Netherfield that her improprieties cause her daughter the full agonies of embarrassment. In Chapter ix when Jane, with her fateful cold, and Elizabeth as her

---

15 For a full-length study devoted to countering to this view, see John Wiltshire, *Jane Austen and the Body* (Cambridge: Cambridge University Press, 1992; repr. 2004).

16 See K. Halsey, 'The Blush of Modesty or the Blush of Shame? Reading Jane Austen's Blushes', *Forum for Modern Language Studies*, 42 (2006), 226–38, https://doi.org/10.1093/fmls/cql015

nurse, have been for some days at Netherfield, they receive a morning visit from Mrs. Bennet and the three younger girls, and Mrs. Bennet, mistaking Caroline Bingley's 'cold civility' for real friendliness, speaks of her gratitude, and Jane's beauty, at too-great length (I ix 46). When Lizzy and the gallant Bingley attempt to turn the conversation, she, Mrs. Bennet, wonderfully, fears that *Lizzy* is behaving embarrassingly: '"do not run on,"' she cries noisily, '"in the wild manner that you are suffered to do at home."' (I ix 46). Then begins a wonderfully loyal display of comradeship from Bingley and even from Darcy, in an attempt to quiet Mrs. Bennet:

> 'I did not know before,' continued Bingley immediately, 'that you were a studier of character. It must be an amusing study.'
>
> 'Yes; but intricate characters are the *most* amusing. They have at least that advantage.'
>
> 'The country,' said Darcy, 'can in general supply but few subjects for such a study. In a country neighbourhood you move in a very confined and unvarying society.'
>
> 'But people themselves alter so much, that there is something new to be observed in them for ever.'
>
> 'Yes, indeed,' cried Mrs. Bennet, offended by his manner of mentioning a country neighbourhood. 'I assure you there is quite as much of *that* going on in the country as in town.'
>
> Every body was surprised; and Darcy, after looking at her for a moment, turned silently away. Mrs. Bennet, who fancied she had gained a complete victory over him, continued her triumph.
>
> 'I cannot see that London has any great advantage over the country for my part, except the shops and public places. The country is a vast deal pleasanter, is not it, Mr. Bingley?'
>
> 'When I am in the country,' he replied, 'I never wish to leave it; and when I am in town it is pretty much the same. They have each their advantages, and I can be equally happy in either.'
>
> 'Aye—that is because you have the right disposition. But that gentleman,' looking at Darcy, 'seemed to think the country was nothing at all.'
>
> 'Indeed, Mama, you are mistaken,' said Elizabeth, blushing for her mother. 'You quite mistook Mr. Darcy. He only meant that there were not such a variety of people to be met with in the country as in town, which you must acknowledge to be true.'
>
> 'Certainly, my dear, nobody said there were; but as to not meeting with many people in this neighbourhood, I believe there are few

neighbourhoods larger. I know we dine with four and twenty families.'
(I ix 47–48)

The *rate* at which the young people speak to silence their elder, their attempt to create a small, young-adult, civilized space—a linguistic community—which will exclude the old, and the teenaged, Bennet hoydens fails; it costs Elizabeth a blush, and, interestingly, a defence of the enemy, Mr. Darcy. But her mother's rigorously adhered-to stubbornness and stupidity carries the day. Even kindly Bingley has to stifle a laugh, and his sister's conspiratorial glance at Darcy does not escape Elizabeth.

At this point we realize the impossibility of counting blushes: they are too many to count. And the chapter closes with an early demonstration from Lydia, who is here first described—'a stout, well-grown girl of fifteen' with 'high animal spirits'—demanding the ball which will so definitively close the first part of the novel (I ix 49). As her mother and sisters leave, Elizabeth escapes also, back to her sister, but in her attendance on Jane's sickbed she is probably accompanied by a thousand embarrassing recollections, those sickening after-blushes so familiar to adolescents.

We've seen Elizabeth embarrassed early on, of course, and crucially, when she overhears Mr. Darcy's famous comment on her looks and her wallflower status at the Assembly in Meryton in Chapter iii where they meet; and there we see her defence against embarrassment, which is to turn it into comedy: 'She told the story however with great spirit among her friends' (I iii 12). This defence she has learned no doubt from her father, who has used it for a quarter of a century as a protection against the shame of living with her mother. I quote from Chapter xlii: 'to his wife he was very little otherwise indebted, than as her ignorance and folly had contributed to his amusement.' (II xix 262). Mr. Bennet's sense of humour has probably saved his marriage—if it has been saved—and his sanity. He has bequeathed that sense of humour to Elizabeth in particular. This shared sense of humour provides the father-daughter pair with many delicious moments: at dinner with Mr. Collins in Chapter xiv, Mr. Bennet needs nothing more than 'an occasional glance at Elizabeth' to augment his enjoyment of Mr. Collins's absurdity (I xiv 76). And nothing demonstrates their affectionate complicity more than his mock-serious treatment of her Chapter xix proposal from her ridiculous cousin: '"From this day forward you will be a stranger to one of your parents..."' (I xx 125). Even in the moment, in front of her howling Mama, Elizabeth cannot help smiling.[17]

And yet. When young, with living parents and ludicrous suitors of one's own, one might sit as a reader squarely with Elizabeth and her father. Mrs. Bennet is impossible. She is even immoral, in her lack of care for Lydia's fortnight as Wickham's common-law wife. She has no judgement; she prefers Lydia to Elizabeth! But look back over that scene again not as a Stage II reader, but with the perspective of a later stage, of a reader many years older than Elizabeth, or older than Mrs. Bennet, who cannot be more than forty-five or -six. Examine the prelude to the scene: in Chapter xix Mr. Collins proposes. In Chapter xx a distraught Mrs. Bennet invades her husband's library to beg for his support:

> 'Oh! Mr. Bennet, you are wanted immediately; we are all in an uproar. You must come and make Lizzy marry Mr. Collins, for she vows she will not have him, and if you do not make haste he will change his mind and not have *her*.'
>
> Mr. Bennet raised his eyes from his book as she entered, and fixed them on her face with a calm unconcern which was not in the least altered by her communication.
>
> 'I have not the pleasure of understanding you,' said he, when she had finished her speech. 'Of what are you talking?'
>
> 'Of Mr. Collins and Lizzy. Lizzy declares she will not have Mr. Collins, and Mr. Collins begins to say that he will not have Lizzy.'
>
> 'And what am I to do on the occasion?—It seems an hopeless business.'

No one can read his words of 'calm unconcern' without smiling, and he has had, as we are often reminded, twenty-five years of Mrs. Bennet's flutterings and palpitations, her 'nerves'. But for 'calm unconcern' here, read also 'heartless indifference'. The entail of his estate which makes the early marrying off of daughters such a frantic concern is not Mr. Bennet's fault, but his improvidence, the family's 'living up to its income' at least partly is. The literary historian Alistair Duckworth has shown

---

17 The original passage reads '"From this day you must be a stranger to one of your parents"'. In her quotation, Nora has interwoven the phrasing from the marriage service in the Book of Common Prayer: 'To have and to hold from this day forward, for better for worse, for richer, for poorer, in sickness and in health, to love and to cherish, till death us do part'.

compellingly how very little money the widow and five unmarried daughters will have to live on should he die: the interest of five thousand pounds, at best at the time about £50 per annum for each daughter.[18] For the impoverished and homeless Bennets, had not the older girls made those good marriages, real destitution would have followed Mr. Bennet's early death. But Mr. Bennet, whatever he may experience on the occasions when as he later puts it, he allows himself to feel '"how much I have been to blame"', treats this very serious situation as a joke. Mrs. Bennet treats it, in her way, seriously, but her way is treated by the novel as a joke (III vi 330).

There is no doubt that we are kept at a distance from Mrs. Bennet. But we are, less consistently, distanced from Mr. Bennet also. Many chapters later, at a point where Mr. Bennet is unwittingly wounding Elizabeth's feelings by suggesting that Mr. Darcy is indifferent to her, he asks, '"For what do we live, but to make sport for our neighbours, and to laugh at them in our turn?"' (III xv 403). Elizabeth does not demur, but she may recall, as the reader may also, that those unlovable Bingley sisters were described early in the novel as having 'considerable' powers of conversation, which included the capacity to 'laugh at their acquaintance with spirit' (I xi 59). It is not an admiring description. Whatever fun she has with her father—and remember that Lydia has fun with her mother—Elizabeth's predicament with regard to both parents is not an enviable one.

It is notable that, as female readers and critics of Jane Austen age, they become less dismissive of Mrs. Bennet and of what a great early critic, Mary Lascelles, called 'stupid middle-aged women'.[19] The narrative, in some ways so unequivocal about Mrs. Bennet—the first chapter states near its close, 'She was a woman of mean understanding, little information and uncertain temper'—begins to seem, in its ready sneering, to be pointing at its own insufficiency (I i 5). The withdrawal of sympathy seems, on rereading, too drastic not to be, perhaps, a gesture we are meant to notice. I have referred already to the chilly tone of the close, and its apparent removal of Mrs. Bennet from the

---

18 Alistair M. Duckworth, *The Improvement of the Estate: A Study of Jane Austen's Novels* (Baltimore: Johns Hopkins Press, 1971), pp. 3–4n.

19 Mary Lascelles, *Jane Austen and Her Art* (Oxford and New York: Oxford University Press, 1939; repr. 1983), p. 150.

guest list at Pemberley. The older reader regards young Elizabeth with a motherly solicitude, then stiffens and wonders, is this how mothers are treated in this world? Once the marriages are made, are those who insist on their making to be brushed aside and abandoned? And since the novel itself has been busy fulfilling Mrs. Bennet's wishes, that is, 'the business of her life was to get her daughters married', and Jane Austen cheerfully commented to her nieces that the other sisters, too, eventually married, does this not further complicate the narrative's—and the reader's—distance from/and closeness to that 'stupid woman'? (I i 5). The closeness we *feel*, of course, is to that clever girl, who presents us, over and over, with the vertiginous pleasures of that happy ending, in which both heroine and hero's complete happiness is presented as an undoubted and permanent fact: '"I am the happiest creature in the world"' (III xviii 424). So, while it may be the case that, as Marilyn Butler suggests, older women characters get a rough deal from Jane Austen, who sadly did not live to be very old, to older readers she is really very generous.[20]

---

20 Marilyn Butler, *Jane Austen* (Oxford: Oxford University Press, 2007), p. 69: 'Certainly her family would have conceded that Jane, like Emma, had a dutiful regard for the parish's old ladies'.

2. Sense and Sensibility

It is a special pleasure to be talking to you today about *Sense and Sensibility*, because it is my own particular favourite among Jane Austen's novels—for a number of reasons, I think. One is that, like *Pride and Prejudice*, it treats love between sisters, and, unlike *Pride and Prejudice*, it also treats the difference and difficulty between them, silences between them, secrets on both sides.[1] That two-sidedness is important. Because *Pride and Prejudice* has only one heroine, Lizzy, only one sister has secrets, but *Sense and Sensibility* has two heroines. As I grow older and reread the novel, I am more and more convinced of that: two heroines, two sisters, living side by side, for much of the novel sharing a bedroom, and sharing a deep silence about the things that are most important to them.

Those silences are a part of what I want to talk about today, but first I would like to talk about another reason why I am so fond of *Sense and Sensibility*, and that is because it was Jane Austen's breakthrough novel, the first to be published. I like to think it made her very happy. It was published in 1811, but written for the most part much earlier. It started as an epistolary novel, *Elinor and Marianne*—note that the two sisters are there from the beginning—was recast, with a new title, suggestive of the antithesis she wanted the novel to deal with, in the late 1790s, then put aside, along with the future *Pride and Prejudice* and *Northanger Abbey*, during the long, difficult, disappointing years of the first decade of the nineteenth century, the peripatetic years which took the Austens to cramped rented rooms in Southampton and Bath. Biographers believe that one of the first things Jane Austen did after settling with her widowed mother and her sister Cassandra into the cottage at Chawton

---

1   For a recent discussion of sibling relationships in Austen's fiction, see Peter W. Graham, 'Born to Diverge: An Evolutionary Perspective on Sibling Personality Development in Austen's Novels', *Persuasions On-line*, 25.1 (2004), http://www.jasna.org/persuasions/on-line/vol25no1/graham.html

       https://doi.org/10.11647/OBP.0216.02

in Hampshire that would be her home for the rest of her life (after setting up, like Marianne, the piano with which she liked to begin her day, and which she had lived without for years) was to take out the manuscript of *Sense and Sensibility* and begin final revisions.

In 1810 her brother Henry successfully negotiated a contract with the publisher Thomas Egerton, although the Austens received nothing for the novel, and indeed paid for its publication. Like many other books by women in the period, it emerged anonymous, 'By a Lady', in 1811. It was quickly something of a sell-out, the whole print-run, probably 1000 or less, being off the publisher's hands in a few months. When *Pride and Prejudice* emerged in 1813 it was advertised as 'By the Author of "Sense and Sensibility"'. Jane Austen referred to *Pride and Prejudice* as 'my own darling Child' and loved hearing people praise both novels, particularly in the period when her authorship was not known.[2] *Pride and Prejudice* was, as it has remained, the bigger hit, but *Sense and Sensibility* was praised by such figures from English high life as Lady Henrietta Bessborough, the sister of the Duchess of Devonshire, and poor little Princess Charlotte, daughter of the Prince Regent, who thought Marianne was 'much like herself'.[3] The novel brought Jane Austen a profit of £140, possibly the first money she had ever earned. Cassandra had a small legacy from her dead fiancé, but Jane had subsisted up to the age of thirty-six on pocket money.

I want to leave the moment of publication now and re-enter the novel through the writing, but I want to note in passing that, like *Northanger Abbey*, *Sense and Sensibility* remains something of a stepchild for critics. Harold Bloom takes the position that Jane Austen 'wrote four great novels', and Frank Kermode in an article in the *London Review of Books* comments on the 'crudeness' of its plot, its 'stilted, improbable conversations', its 'stark contrasts' and calls it 'easily the weakest of the six'.[4] I will take up some of those issues, especially contrast and

---

2   *Letters*, p. 201. Austen wrote of *Sense and Sensibility* that 'I can no more forget it, than a mother can forget her sucking child' (*Letters*, p. 182).

3   *Letters of the Princess Charlotte 1811–1817*, ed. by A. Aspinall (London: Home and Van Thal, 1949), p. 26: 'I think Maryanne & me are very like in *disposition*, that certainly I am not so good, the same imprudence, &c, however very like'.

4   Harold Bloom, *How to Read and Why* (New York: Touchstone, 2000), p. 158; Frank Kermode, 'Too Good and Too Silly', *London Review of Books*, 31.8 (2009), https://www.lrb.co.uk/the-paper/v31/n08/frank-kermode/too-good-and-too-silly. Kermode writes of *Sense and Sensibility* that 'It is the weakest of the six principal

conversation, in due course, but I would like to look at the question of crudeness right away.

Some of Jane Austen's juvenile writings, such as *Love and Freindship*, the collection of fictional letters and a bit of a play from the section of her juvenilia unceremoniously called 'scraps', date from her mid-teens, so not long before she began to produce the fictional letters that would eventually be transformed into *Sense and Sensibility* and *Pride and Prejudice*, and the wry commentary on Gothic novels that would become *Northanger Abbey*.[5] Claire Tomalin in her biography has a wonderful picture of a moment in the later 1790s when Jane Austen has the rapidly growing manuscripts for all three great novels hidden away somewhere, to be rewritten in moments stolen from her busy family and social life.[6] But it is the role of the early manuscripts in that family life I want to look at for a moment. We know that Jane Austen read her juvenile works, and her novels, out loud in the family circle. They were typical of lively, bookish, middle-class families of their time in that reading aloud constituted much of their entertainment. Jane Austen's family were certainly luckier than most, and when we read the juvenilia, with its hearty laughter at subjects such as murder, incest, alcoholism and adultery, we realize that, since they enjoyed this, their staple diet cannot have been sermons, nor even very genteel novels. We can allow something for the toleration a family might extend to a beloved and precocious youngest daughter, but a glance at *Love and Freindship*, with its catalogue of wild-eyed co-incidences, sudden death and disinheritances, all carried off in a very high style ('"Yes, cold and insensible Nymph, (replied I) that luckless Swain, your brother, is no more, and you may now glory in being the heiress of Sir Edward's fortune"'), will show,

---

novels', though he notes that it 'makes an unexpected contribution to feminist and other good causes'. Kermode's objections are to the 'bookish' nature of the dialogue and the hackneyed 'disinheritance novel' genre: 'Can it be that the force which prevents this novel from slipping into oblivion like those earlier "disinheritance novels" is the buoyancy provided by its fellows in the canon?'.

5   This section of *Volume the Second* is labelled as 'scraps' by R. W. Chapman in Volume VI (*Minor Works*) of his edition of Austen's works. The Cambridge edition of the *Juvenilia*, edited by Peter Sabor does not classify the same section in this way.

6 ⸳ Claire Tomalin, *Jane Austen. A Life* (London: Penguin, 1998; repr. 2000), p. 169: 'Everything was set for her to put in a little more work perhaps on the three manuscripts [...] find a publisher [...] and start on a new novel. This did not happen. Instead she fell silent'.

it seems to me, a sheer pleasure in the sorts of exaggeration to which fiction gives license.[7] This novelist justly famed for her subtlety also enjoyed crude, broad humour, melodrama and gore.

Before we leave the juvenilia, we should note that several of her 'scraps' were plays. Recent Jane Austen criticism has focussed interestingly on these plays, and the other plays she and her family acted out and read around the fire (since, unlike her later heroine, Fanny Price, Jane Austen participated in private theatricals).[8] Their role in her writing was important and I will be referring to this dramatic or dramatized quality, which I find especially strong in the early novels, *Sense and Sensibility* in particular, which can be seen as a comedy of errors.

I am going to be talking chiefly about who knows what, and when, in the novel, but I would like to start with one famous comic scene from Volume I, Chapter ii. This scene (particularly well done in the Ang Lee film)[9] pictures Mr. and Mrs. John Dashwood, newly ensconced as master and mistress of Norland, working out the terms of their responsibilities to John Dashwood's stepmother and stepsisters. Everyone remembers this scene, which occupies a whole chapter to itself, and, in a tour de force of dialogue, shows their blindingly selfish progression from something to nothing. After Fanny has ruled out money gifts to the girls and an annuity to their mother, John suggests,

> 'A present of fifty pounds, now and then, will prevent their ever being distressed for money, and will, I think, be amply discharging my promise to my father.'
>
> 'To be sure it will. Indeed, to say the truth, I am convinced within myself that your father had no idea of your giving them any money at all. The assistance he thought of, I dare say, was only such as might be reasonably expected of you; for instance [...] helping them to move their things, and sending them presents of fish and game, and so forth, whenever they are in season. I'll lay my life that he meant nothing farther; indeed, it would be very strange and unreasonable if he did. Do but consider, my dear Mr. Dashwood, how excessively comfortable

7   *Juvenilia*, ed. Sabor, p. 134.
8   See, for example, Paula Byrne, *Jane Austen and the Theatre* (New York and London: Hambledon, 2002) and Penny Gay, *Jane Austen and the Theatre* (Cambridge: Cambridge University Press, 2002).
9   See Penny Gay, '*Sense and Sensibility* in a Postfeminist World: Sisterhood Is Still Powerful', in *Jane Austen on Screen*, ed. by Gina Macdonald and Andre F. Macdonald (Cambridge: Cambridge University Press, 2003), pp. 90–110.

your mother-in-law and her daughters may live on the interest of seven thousand pounds, besides the thousand pounds belonging to each of the girls, which brings them in fifty pounds a year apiece, and, of course, they will pay their mother for their board out of it. [...] what on earth can four women want for more than that?—They will live so cheap! Their housekeeping will be nothing at all. They will have no carriage, no horses, and hardly any servants; they will keep no company, and can have no expences of any kind! Only conceive how comfortable they will be!' (I ii 13–14)

Frank Kermode comments that this scene could be based on the scene in *King Lear* in which Regan and Goneril whittle Lear's attendants down to one and then to nothing, and, while the Shakespeare play that is talked about in this novel is not *King Lear* but *Hamlet*, one can imagine Jane Austen reading *Lear*, with its bad parenting and its bloody excesses, with relish.[10]

Note Fanny's reliance on words such as 'reasonable', which she repeats. In the novel's terms, Fanny represents 'sense' and not 'sensibility', an exaggeration of a certain kind of sense, with a strangled-at-birth absence of real feeling. Real feeling is suggested, however, in a shadowy way, by where and when the conversation happens. The undeniable funniness of this sequence is set against a death: this conversation is taking place *because of* a deathbed promise, and within days of the death. This juxtaposition of grief and savage humour is something we'll see more of in the novel, but I would like to concentrate for a moment on that death. Mr. Dashwood's is the only deathbed scene in Jane Austen's novels, and though it is very faint, only two paragraphs of Chapter i, with no reported speech, it shows us the father's anxious feeling, pleading for his wife and daughters, 'with all the strength and urgency which illness could command', and John's more-than perfunctory response: 'he was affected by a recommendation of such a nature at such a time' (I i 5). To stir John to even a momentary flicker of financial generosity, this unexpected death must have been moving indeed. And it is not the first death recorded in the novel. Though the tone of *Sense and Sensibility* is here quite different from the juvenilia, it does polish off two Dashwoods

---

10 Kermode, 'Too Good and Too Silly'. Kermode writes: 'The little scene sounds like a parodic reminiscence of the scene in *King Lear* when Goneril and Regan reduce Lear's retinue from 100 knights to none'.

in the first three pages. Perhaps the Austen family, listening to the opening words of *Elinor and Marianne* around the tea table in the late 1790s, became only gradually aware that they were not meant to *laugh* at these deaths—that Norland was indeed a house of mourning.

Jane Austen does not make a great deal of fuss about mourning rituals, but we all remember from *Persuasion* that, at least in baronets' families, mourning was worn for quite distant relatives, and Mr. Elliot, a widower, cannot think of marrying for at least a year after the death of his unloved wife. But when we think about the tone of life at Norland as we first encounter it, we should remember that the Dashwood girls have been in mourning, first for their uncle, and then for their father, for some time. This in part must account for the solitary quality of their life: Elinor, at nineteen, can have been to few balls during this mourning period, Marianne, at seventeen, probably to none at all. When they leave Norland, though they miss it terribly, they do not seem to miss any friends or any society beyond their own family. Life for the Dashwood girls at Norland, even in the happy times before their father's death, seems very different from life among the Bennet girls, with all its shopping and flirting and dancing. Some critics find the early conversations among the Dashwood women stilted and sententious, and they do lack the funniness and flash of the conversations between Elizabeth and Jane— not, I think through incompetence: they were written, and re-written in the same two periods. The Dashwood girls are temperamentally more bookish, less sociable, less socially experienced. Marianne certainly has—and perhaps Elinor has too—that sense of superiority to others, to outsiders, that is sometimes found in thoughtful and bookish children who are not much used to mixing with others.

We hear about Elinor in Chapter i and are told a whole paragraph of things about her:

> She had an excellent heart;—her disposition was affectionate, and her feelings were strong; but she knew how to govern them: it was a knowledge which her mother had yet to learn; and which one of her sisters had resolved never to be taught. (I i 7)

This introduces us, of course to Marianne. It is interesting that the first term given to her is 'sensible', a word which straddles the 'sense' and 'sensibility' of the title:

> She was sensible and clever; but eager in everything: her sorrows, her
> joys, could have no moderation. She was generous, amiable, interesting:
> she was everything but prudent. The resemblance between her and her
> mother was strikingly great. (I i 7)

More of Mrs. Dashwood, and of that resemblance, later. I want to
concentrate on the two sisters, who are introduced here as in part
contrasts to one another, not, actually, in quality of feeling, because
both are described as tender-hearted, but in control of feeling, even a
little more qualified, in terms of desire for control of feeling. Marianne
does not wish to learn the skill which Elinor has somehow (how, one
wonders? Possibly all that waiting on her bothersome rich uncle?)
taught herself.

Many readers have noted that the three early novels depict heroines
who have close and mutual ties of love with more than one member of
their family: Catherine in *Northanger Abbey* simply comes from a happy
family, Elizabeth has her father and Jane, and Elinor has Marianne and
her mother, whereas in the later novels there is distance or difficulty, even
if only in the form of Emma's superiority of intelligence to her father and
sister. But in this most sisterly of novels—for all of *Sense and Sensibility*
the sisters remain together, whereas in *Pride and Prejudice* they are for
much of the novel separated—there is another kind of division, caused
by another paradox. In this novel, this novelist so skilled in dialogue
condemns her two main characters to a profound mutual silence. The
novel is all about the things they cannot or do not tell each other. It is all
about secrets.[11]

Most of the novel is told from Elinor's point of view and it is through
her that we experience most of the events in it. However, if we look back
at that reprehensible conversation in Chapter ii between John and Fanny,
we should note that it remains unknown to any of the Dashwood women
and is known in fact only to the reader. Mrs. Dashwood knows about
the deathbed promise and expects for a long time (three chapters) that
it will be fulfilled, though she has to give it up in the end, since John's

---

11   See also Angela Leighton, 'Sense and Silences: Reading Jane Austen Again', in *Jane
     Austen: New Perspectives*, ed. by Janet Todd (New York and London: Holmes and
     Meier, 1983), pp. 128–41; John Wiltshire, 'Elinor Dashwood and Concealment', in
     The Hidden Jane Austen (Cambridge: Cambridge University Press, 2014), pp. 28–50,
     https://doi.org/10.1017/cbo9781107449435.004

conversation is so full of money worries that it looks as if he might want to borrow money rather than give her or her daughters any! But she does not know the process of infinite regress by which the promise was talked away, and it is important that she does not. Though we see them occasionally talking of money (Margaret, who is thirteen, at one point wishes they would all be given a large fortune) and expense is from time to time mentioned among the mother and daughters, they cannot be shown having the sort of calculating conversation that characterizes Fanny and John. Indeed, already in *Sense and Sensibility*, her first novel, Jane Austen has established the rule, so important in her novels, that concern about details, of money, food, clothing or health, renders characters ridiculous or bad or both.

It is in Chapter iv that Elinor becomes the character through whom we experience the events of the novel. Though we are sometimes in Marianne's mind, it is never for long, and this has led, I think, to a slightly too Elinor-centred reading of the novel. Later I would like to consider the extent to which this is also Marianne's book, but I think it makes sense to start with Elinor. It is through Elinor that we know most of what we know, and also through Elinor—because, all the way through the novel, there are things that Elinor does not know—that we receive most of the surprises which the novel features.

I think in my own first, adolescent, reading of the novel I found Elinor a bit bloodless and correct, and I am always surprised to find, at the beginning, that she is only nineteen and that therefore the gap between her and Marianne is only two years. That makes her the same age as Elizabeth Bennet and younger than Emma—does she not seem older? Of course, she is an eldest child, and, though we know nothing of the girls' relations with their father except that his temper was 'cheerful and sanguine' (I i 5), we can perhaps imagine, since Elinor seems to know how to manage accounts, and to have a more realistic sense of household economy than her mother, that he was at least a bit 'sensible' and that she spent some time in his company, and that perhaps while Mrs. Dashwood and Marianne were reading Cowper together, Elinor was covering scraps of her father's ledger paper with promising doodles.

But we become familiar with Elinor as a viewpoint as she is presented to us, at nineteen, as a heroine of romance: one of Mrs. Dashwood's few accurate perceptions is the recognition, in Chapter iii, of 'a growing attachment between her eldest girl and the brother of Mrs. John Dashwood' (I iii 17). Mrs. Dashwood takes this recognition and runs with it: 'No sooner did she perceive any symptom of love in his behaviour to Elinor, than she considered their serious attachment as certain, and looked forward to their marriage as rapidly approaching' (I iii 19). This is Mrs. Dashwood we are talking about, not the thirteen-year-old Margaret. She shares this confidence (in both sense of the word) with Marianne: '"In a few months [...] Elinor will in all probability be settled for life"' (I iii 19). Marianne is only partly gratified by this—Edward is a bit stiff, reads aloud without skill (we will revisit this question of his reading skills)—but not because she has any doubt of the outcome.

Of course, as is often the case with the perceptions of unwise people in Jane Austen, they turn out to be right, though, as with Mr. Bingley and Jane, of which Mrs. Bennet was so confident, it takes a little longer for these witless prophecies to work themselves out. The reader coming to *Sense and Sensibility* after *Pride and Prejudice*, as most people do now (though remember that the original readers would have gone the other way), is perhaps startled by how swiftly, and with how little dancing and conversation—Edward does not, in fact, say a word until he re-enters the novel in Chapter xvi—the romance is in train, and worries whether, with all this certainty, there will be any pleasurable waiting and wondering of the *Pride and Prejudice* type.

But Elinor is uncertain, not of her own feelings, but of Edward's, and of the future. In such uncertainty, it is painful for someone of her strength of feeling even to talk of the future, but she allows herself to praise Edward to her mother in Chapter iii and then, in Chapter iv, to speak of him with unguarded warmth to Marianne:

> 'his mind is well–informed, his enjoyment of books exceedingly great, his imagination lively, [...] his taste delicate and pure. [...] At first sight, his address is certainly not striking; and his person can hardly be called handsome, till the expression of his eyes, which are uncommonly good, and the general sweetness of his countenance, is perceived. At present, I know him so well, that I think him really handsome; or, at least, almost so. What say you, Marianne?'
>
> 'I shall very soon think him handsome, Elinor, if I do not now. When you tell me to love him as a brother, I shall no more see imperfection in his face, than I now do in his heart.' (I iv 23–24)

This is truly dreadful for Elinor, who does not share her mother's confidence, nor, after this one mistake, much of her tendency readily to confide. Though Marianne and Mrs. Dashwood do not use the vulgar terms to which the girls will be treated at Barton Park, their imaginations have run away with them down the same route that Sir John's and Mrs. Jennings's go, and their more elegant terminology, as closer to the language of Elinor's own deepest wishes, may be more painful than Sir John's talk of 'setting their caps' or Mrs. Jennings's of 'getting husbands' (I ix 53; I vii 40; II iv 186).

I'd like to draw your attention again to Edward's silences in the opening chapters. One effect of this is that we don't ever hear him tell a lie. We never see him speaking, as he must have to, evasively, only hear about his occasional 'want of spirits', which the first-time reader doesn't understand but the re-reader recognizes as a result of his embarrassment about his engagement, his secret engagement, to Lucy (I iv 25). Here is the state of things at this early stage of the novel: Elinor is in love with Edward, and Edward with her, but he is engaged to Lucy, which Elinor does not know. She will not find it out until the end of Volume I, and she will learn it in a particularly ghastly way, which we will look into in a moment. What is important, I think, is that Edward has a secret that neither Elinor, nor the reader, knows, and that, because of that, his entrance as a speaker—his being given, in dramatic terms, a speaking part—has to be delayed until his arrival at Barton Park, when, suffering under the burden of his secret as he has for half a year, he is presented as almost broken-down. It seems important that Edward should never be presented to the reader as a glib liar. Although he must be behaving, if not dishonestly, certainly evasively, we don't have to hear and judge it, any more than we have to suffer through his lustreless reading aloud.

Willoughby, who enters much more dramatically in Chapter ix, reads aloud beautifully, and we have a great deal of his speech, though as we, the readers, are in the same position as Elinor, sitting on the outside, looking on from a distance at his romance with Marianne, we never hear any of his private speeches to Marianne, except when they are made, 'in a lowered voice', in public (I xiv 86). Willoughby is a complex character, much more so than fellow cad Mr. Wickham from *Pride and Prejudice*, whose thinness and insipidity is apparent after the first reading—and I would like to look at Willoughby again later—but let us examine, in the same way as we did with Elinor and Edward, the genuineness of the understanding between him and Marianne. Marianne is in love with Willoughby, has been almost from the first, and he, though he was only amusing himself with her at the start, realizes before they part in Chapter xv that he is in love with her too, though he does not say so. He means to say so, but delays, and then events prevent his speaking. But what he knows, that Marianne doesn't, is that he is deeply in debt, means to marry for money, has at least a glimmer of an understanding with the rich Miss Grey, and has recently seduced and abandoned a sixteen-year-old girl in Bath. He claims, later, not to have known she was pregnant, and perhaps he does not. But this is the man who is hesitating over offering his heart to Marianne, while taking hers—these are his secrets.

When he leaves, Marianne knows however that 'except in her heart' they are *not* engaged (I x 58; II vii 214).[12] As Elinor tells Mrs. Jennings later, '"he has broken no positive engagement with my sister"' (II viii 222). But Marianne's mother and her sister do not know that, and that lack of knowledge, along with Mrs. Dashwood's 'delicate' refusal to inquire, to ask the question that will at least penetrate the aura of isolation which quickly grows around the desolate and self-absorbed Marianne, this all places a distance between the two sisters, which subsists for many, many chapters (I xvi 98).

This is perhaps the moment to speak of Mrs. Dashwood, one of Jane Austen's many foolish mothers and mother-figures, just as Willoughby is one of her cads, but as with Willoughby there is a difference, the important difference that as a personality she is attractive: she is an intelligent woman, and a loving mother, but her actions and her inaction are disastrous. She is cut off from her daughters by a purely fantastic sense of delicacy and honour ('"I should never deserve her confidence again"' (I xvi 98)) that refuses the maternal prerogative of eliciting trust, as if it would be as vulgar for her to ask her daughters a direct question

---

12   The relevant passages are: 'In hastily forming and giving his opinion of other people, in sacrificing general politeness to the enjoyment of undivided attention where his heart was engaged, and in slighting too easily the forms of worldly propriety, he displayed a want of caution which Elinor could not approve, in spite of all that he and Marianne could say in its support.' and '"I felt myself," she added, "to be as solemnly engaged to him, as if the strictest legal covenant had bound us to each other."'

as it is for Mrs. Jennings and Mrs. Palmer to do so. One wonders if there isn't an element of cowardice in her refusal to confront Marianne, as there is, it seems to me, in her willingness to believe, as time passes, that Elinor can forget about Edward. When she is brought, at the novel's end, to a dramatic realization of how much she has erred, it is gratifying, but perhaps more gratifying than plausible. One might make allowances for a recent widow; I'm not sure Jane Austen does.

So, as the first volume heads towards its close, Elinor is ignorant, not of Marianne's feelings but of her true situation; Marianne is too wrapped up in her suffering to think of Elinor's situation or her feelings; their mother is ignorant of both. If one glances sideways here, at *Pride and Prejudice*, one finds at about the same point that Jane and Elizabeth have decided mutually not to discuss Mr. Bingley any more, as it is too painful for Jane. This is not the case, of course, with Mrs. Bennet. Mothers don't seem able, in Jane Austen, to get it right.[13]

In *Sense and Sensibility*, however, once they get to Devonshire, the Dashwood women are surrounded by talkers, Sir John and Mrs. Jennings, who are also ignorant of the feelings they may be injuring, who have no secrets of their own and can imagine no secrets that will not be better for sharing. '"Come, come, let's have no secrets among friends"' (II iv 186), Mrs. Jennings says eagerly to Colonel Brandon, a man with secrets and not a talker. These talkers are two of Jane Austen's finest minor characters.[14] Particularly interesting is the way in which they, Mrs. Jennings especially, reveal their decent, if not very intellectual, qualities. One aspect of the novel's being told from mild, tolerant Elinor's point of view rather than irritable Marianne's, is that their essential good will is gradually demonstrated, and the reader realizes that, though these figures possess neither sense nor sensibility, they are not part of the cold world inhabited by Mrs. Ferrars and her daughter and son-in-law. Because we see these figures, and less important ones such as Mr. and Mrs. Palmer, through Elinor's critical, but not unforgiving, point of view, they remain droll but decent people, capable of generous and unselfish acts even while remaining '"ridiculous"', as Mrs. Palmer says, with unwitting accuracy, of her husband (I xix 124). Seen through other eyes than Elinor's, the two unequal marriages that Mrs. Jennings's

---

13   Nora discusses problematic mother-daughter relationships in the next Chapter.
14   Nora discusses Mrs. Jennings in Chapter 4.

daughters have made might seem not comic but tragic, in their lack of shared interests, or even shared topics of conversation. Jane Austen likes to set up patterns of contrasting pairs, especially in these early novels, and Lady Middleton and Mrs. Palmer are another pair of sisters, another set of mother and daughters, though with all the talking at Barton Park, when Lady Middleton speaks to her mother it is usually an attempt to shut her up, and Lady Middleton and Mrs. Palmer do not seem to speak at all—another sort of silence between sisters.

Just before the end of Volume I, a third pair of sisters is introduced at Barton Park: the accurately named Steeles, Mrs. Jennings's cousins. Mrs. Jennings has many virtues but almost no judgement and she cannot see past Lucy's prettiness and her polite manners, though Elinor and Marianne can, and the reader can, taking Lucy at first to be a kind of Mrs. Elton figure, unpleasant but not much to do with the plot. Marianne sees her in this way for much of the novel, but Elinor, for good reasons, cannot.

The two scenes at the end of Volume I and the beginning of Volume II, the scenes in which Lucy forces her confidence—her secret—on Elinor, are central to the way the novel works, and I want to examine them in some detail.

Lucy and her sister Anne are introduced in a series of effective comic vignettes which reveal them as flatterers and sycophants, fawning on the higher status of the family at Barton Park, but also show them as sharp and rather desperate young women, the older sister pathetically *jeune-fille* in her manner, the younger eagerly attentive to her own interests. They are some years older than Elinor and Marianne, and Elinor initially pities them. She is also made curious by their appearing to have some previous acquaintance with Edward Ferrars. Marianne, of course, lost in her daydreams of Willoughby, takes no interest in them, and no part in their conversation, but Elinor is polite and Lucy more than polite: she 'missed no opportunity of engaging her in conversation, or of striving to improve their acquaintance by an easy and frank communication of her sentiments.' (I xxii 146).

The first serious 'communication' comes on a walk from Barton Park to Barton Cottage. Lucy asks Elinor, utterly unexpectedly, whether she knows Edward's mother. This approach is significant, because it is Edward's mother, who holds the purse-strings, that interests Lucy most. It is Edward's mother, whom in hardness of heart and mercenary motives she resembles, with whom in the end she builds the closest relationship. Startled, Elinor replies truthfully that she does not.

> 'I am sure you think me very strange [...],' said Lucy, eyeing Elinor attentively as she spoke; 'but perhaps there may be reasons [...] I hope you will do me the justice of believing that I do not mean to be impertinent.' (II xxii 147)

Let's look at those attentive eyes. The walk from the Park to the Cottage is said to be full of natural beauty, but Lucy's eyes are all for Elinor as she continues to produce her carefully prepared, but artfully hesitating, tale:

> 'the time *may* come [...] when we may be very intimately connected.' She looked down as she said this, amiably bashful, with only one side glance at her companion to observe its effect on her. (I xxii 148)

Note the glance to the side: Lucy is acting a part. Elinor, here utterly astonished and unprepared, is not. She grasps blindly at possibilities. Can Lucy have some connection with the younger brother, Robert?

> 'No;' replied Lucy, 'not to Mr. *Robert* Ferrars—I never saw him in my life; but,' fixing her eyes upon Elinor, 'to his elder brother.' (I xxii 148)

Keep an eye on those eyes: she is watching the effect she is having. And it takes all of Elinor's considerable reserves of strength—one thing we see happening through the novel is a series of enormous demands on that strength—to hold on to her 'astonishment' and 'incredulity' as Lucy produces the miniature of Edward which is the first of a series of tokens, of props, by which she proves the truth of what she is saying (I xxii 148–49). Elinor ventures only one earnest look at the other girl, trying to see if she is lying. But, though completely disingenuous, she is completely truthful too, and, sinkingly, Elinor must acknowledge it. As Lucy's bits of stage business, the handkerchief, the plea for advice, the letter, proliferate, demonstrating the truth of her claims, Elinor is only barely able to hold onto her composure before circumstances relieve her of her companion—or her assailant, for Lucy means to crush her rival, treating her as 'Edward's sister', as 'an indifferent person' (I xxii 149; II ii 172), treating her indeed, as if she were the younger girl and Elinor an elderly spinster. And Elinor is very nearly crushed: 'She was mortified, shocked, confounded. [...] Elinor was then at liberty to think and be wretched' (I xxii 155). That is the close of Volume I.

When they next meet, however, Elinor is better prepared. When they next speak together, at an evening party at Barton Park, both of the young women are acting, and the scene is like a stage set. They are seated opposite one another at a work-table, making a filigree basket for a spoilt little girl. Upstage left, the others play cards, and their noise covers the girls' conversation. The spotlight is on Elinor and Lucy. Elinor starts the subject, for more reasons than one:

> She wanted to hear many particulars of their engagement repeated again, she wanted more clearly to understand what Lucy really felt for Edward, whether there were any sincerity in her declaration of tender regard for him, and she particularly wanted to convince Lucy, by her readiness to enter on the matter again [...] that she was no otherwise interested in it than as a friend. (II i 162)

I am not exactly sure what filigree work entails, whether there are any sharp implements involved or not, but in this exchange there is more than one steely young woman seated with busy hands at that work-table.

> 'Indeed you wrong me,' replied Lucy with great solemnity; 'I know nobody of whose judgment I think so highly as I do of yours; [...] if you was to say to me, "I advise you by all means to put an end to your engagement with Edward Ferrars [...]," I should resolve upon doing it immediately.'
>
> Elinor blushed for the insincerity of Edward's future wife, and replied, 'this [...] raises my influence much too high; the power of dividing two people so tenderly attached is too much for an indifferent person.'
>
> ''Tis because you are an indifferent person,' said Lucy, with some pique, and laying a particular stress on those words, 'that your judgment might justly have such weight with me. If you could be supposed to be biased in any respect by your own feelings, your opinion would not be worth having.' (II ii 171–72)

Lucy's feral savagery seems more than matched by Elinor's determination not to be overpowered. In a fair fight, in fact, I'd back Elinor, but Lucy, of course, isn't fair.

What has happened now is that Edward's secret is known to Elinor, and one imagines that an early missive from Lucy, in that correspondence licensed by even a secret engagement, informs Edward of the fact. His misery at this time can be imagined, too, and is, by

Elinor, but she can tell no one because she has been sworn to secrecy by Lucy: real, positive, dramatic secrecy, instead of the numb and wounding silences she is living through with Marianne. Lucy, in fact, is a grotesque counterpart to both Elinor and Marianne, a sort of twin in a dark mirror: an impecunious dependent cousin, who must marry to survive, just as Elinor and Marianne must. Her sniping relationship with her sister Anne, which like Lady Middleton's with her sister, consists of suppressing her vulgarity, is also an exaggerated version of Elinor's frequent moves to cover for Marianne's flouting of convention. But by forcing this undesired confidential relationship onto Elinor, just as Marianne is withholding her confidence, she becomes a taunting version of Marianne, while, engaged to Edward, she is also standing in place of Elinor.

Lucy is symbolically ubiquitous but also physically ubiquitous—consider the scene near the end of Volume II when Edward arrives at Mrs. Jennings's to find her sitting with Elinor—and, as she is a genuinely malicious character, worse in her way than either Fanny or Mrs. Ferrars, this ubiquity is frightening and terrible, as well as ferociously comic. With her sister, poor Miss Steele, with her talk of '"smart beaux"' and her delusions about '"the Doctor"', she forms a brilliant comic duo (I xxi 142–43). Recall the scene in Volume III when Miss Steele fills Elinor in on the details of a tender scene between Edward and Lucy, after the exposure of their secret engagement, only to reveal to Elinor that she acquired her information by listening at the keyhole. Again, the squalidly intimate, openly quarrelsome, but also quarrelsomely open, relations between these two, contrast with the Dashwood inhibitions. Later Lucy will make off with Anne's last penny when she is running off with Robert. This is all grotesquely dissimilar to the mutual delicacy of Elinor and Marianne, but it is that mutual delicacy that leaves them both, at times, alone.

I would like to return to Elinor before we close, but now I want to talk about Marianne for a while. A standard way of reading the novel is to note that both young women—it's stated in Chapter i—have sense and sensibility in different proportions, but that over the course of the novel there is some shifting of those proportions. In that reading, Marianne is taught by Elinor's example to become, broadly speaking, more sensible, while Elinor's clinging to her early romantic feeling for Edward, proves her sensibility, but the bulk of the learning is done by Marianne, who is the sister who most needs it. I am not entirely happy with that. There is, certainly, a narrative tone at times that is very critical, almost exasperated with Marianne, as in Volume I, Chapter xv: 'She was without any power, because she was without any desire of command over herself' (I xv 95). This is in obvious contrast with Elinor's hard-won, and truly admirable, self-command, which is commended, there is no doubt, throughout. But does this anti-Marianne voice prevail, I wonder? It seems close, to me, to what seems the only real weakness in the novel, which is an occasional tendency to glib sermons, as when, during the stunning Gothic-style encounter with a night-time, desperate, but still glamorous Willoughby, Elinor proses on internally about 'the irreparable injury which [...] idleness, dissipation, and luxury' had made on him, without making him, one feels, a whit less sexually attractive to her or her sister! (III viii 375).

I think we see Marianne, as the novel really sees her, in her escapades of quixotic kindness, as when in Volume I she embarrasses Elinor by staring at her when 'leaving their hearts in Sussex' (I vii 40) is mentioned by Mrs. Jennings, or when in Volume II she takes up Elinor's pieces of artwork after they have been rejected by Mrs. Ferrars, in order 'to admire them herself as they ought to be admired' (II xii 268). Or when she barges into the awkward threesome of Lucy, Edward and Elinor, greets Edward so warmly, and assures him in a noisy aside that Lucy won't be staying long. Marianne is both a wonderful comic character, and a nearly tragic one, and it is this knife-edge of her presentation that gives the novel its peculiar character—there are two women in this book. The brilliance of the novel is that, though one is seen almost exclusively through the eyes of the other, both are there.

Consider Marianne's 'mad scene'—recall that she and Willoughby were reading *Hamlet* (had they got to Act IV, scene 5?)—which takes place, as all will remember, at a party given by a friend of Lady Middleton's, another brilliantly staged scene. Elinor sees Willoughby first, talking to his fiancée, and he sees her and gives a distant nod. It is a few moments before Marianne, sunk in gloom, notices him: 'At that moment she first perceived him, and her whole countenance glowing with sudden delight, she would have moved towards him instantly, had not her sister caught hold of her' (II vi 200). That spontaneity, particularly when it is contrasted, not with Elinor's restraint, which is moved by protective love, but with Willoughby's distant courtesy as he crosses to her slowly and greets her stiffly, speaking the dialect of 'sense' which his straitened circumstances have forced him to learn: 'after saying, "Yes, I had the pleasure of receiving the information of your arrival in town, which you were so good as to send me," turned hastily away with a slight bow' (II vi 202). His 'slight bow' rebuffs Marianne's '"Will you not shake hands with me?"' (II vi 201). The reader is not inside Marianne's shocked, hurt, disbelieving thoughts, but knows what she is feeling, wonderfully, through Elinor, who, herself disappointed in love, feels Marianne's pain as her own. Elinor still, at the end of that scene, does not know the story, does not know there was no engagement, but she knows what Marianne is experiencing, and, through her, the reader does. Even those whose hearts have been hardened by Marianne's many insufferable and thoughtless remarks, will feel her 'silent agony, too much oppressed even for tears' on the long carriage ride back to Mrs. Jennings's house, because Elinor does (II vi 203).

Elinor is also the reader's entry point to the scene in Volume III, Chapter vii, in which Marianne lies, at Cleveland, near death from a fever. This scene is so beautifully constructed that, though I have read the novel many times and I *know* Marianne gets better, I cannot stop reading until the night is over and the apothecary had made his second visit in twelve hours (those were the days) and 'About noon [...] she began—but with a caution—a dread of disappointment, which for some time kept her silent, even to her friend—to fancy, to hope she could perceive a slight amendment in her sister's pulse' (III vii 355).

Now that we know it is going to come out all right, let us look back at the previous night:

> Elinor remained alone with Marianne.
>
> The repose of the latter became more and more disturbed; and her sister, who watched with unremitting attention her continual change of posture, and heard the frequent but inarticulate sounds of complaint which passed her lips, was almost wishing to rouse her from so painful a slumber, when Marianne, suddenly awakened by some accidental noise in the house, started hastily up, and with feverish wildness, cried out— 'Is mamma coming?'—

'Not yet,' replied the other, concealing her terror, and assisting Marianne to lie down again, 'but she will be here, I hope, before it is long [...]'

'But she must not go round by London,' cried Marianne, in the same hurried manner, 'I shall never see her, if she goes by London.' (III vii 351)

Marianne's almost infantile whimper, and Elinor's 'terror', convey the uncanny quality of delirium: Elinor is afraid *of* Marianne for a moment as well as *for* her, and that moment of vulnerability in Elinor is almost frightening for the reader, who relies, as everyone else does, on her strength. What will we do, we think, if *she* breaks down?

There will be one more such moment, which I want to close by looking at, but I want to move towards it via some of the moments of comedy, in particular of comic misapprehension, that mark this novel, whose subject is really neither sense nor sensibility. Like *Pride and Prejudice* and also like *Northanger Abbey*, its subject is the education and miseducation of the heart. Its characters learn, even Elinor learns, through error. There is a pattern, discernible throughout, of misapprehension. Colonel Brandon, that decent and deeply romantic man to whom I haven't paid sufficient attention, is thought by Mrs. Jennings, presumably also by the Middletons, to have a natural daughter. Though there is no evidence that these three read novels, or read anything, they have evidently heard of the novelistic convention by which 'ward' means 'illegitimate child'. Mrs. Palmer thinks Colonel Brandon wanted to marry her; she also, like Marianne, thinks him dull—'"He is such a charming man, that it is quite a pity he should be so grave and so dull"' (I xx 133). If Mrs. Palmer thinks it, it can't be true, so if the reader finds Colonel Brandon dull, the reader is wrong. On several occasions Marianne mistakes the Colonel, when he knocks or when his step is heard on the stair, for Willoughby. On another occasion she mistakes Edward for Willoughby—but then Edward and Willoughby, those unstable lovers, those men with secrets, have, superficially, much in common. But towards the end of the novel, Elinor mistakes Edward for Colonel Brandon. Lucy seems to have mistaken Edward for Robert, or Robert for Edward, as she is engaged to one but marries the other. Mrs. Ferrars has sometimes two sons, sometimes one, sometimes none, and Robert, though born later, somehow becomes permanently the older son. John and Fanny, who are full of sense, but always wrong, think Edward or

Robert will certainly marry Miss Morton; they think Colonel Brandon is in love with Elinor. But then, Edward thinks Colonel Brandon is in love with Elinor, and Mrs. Jennings is so certain he is in love with Elinor that there is a hilarious (though structurally odd, since it entails a sudden shift to her point of view) scene in which she imagines the Colonel is proposing and wonders why he is saying, '"I am afraid it cannot take place very soon." "Lord! what should hinder it!"', she almost cries out, in an ecstasy of error (III iii 319).

The misapprehensions which are not at all comic, of course, are those of Elinor's mother, with respect to Elinor as well as Marianne. She has had to concentrate on Marianne and has done so by convincing herself that Elinor is indifferent to Edward. At the news that '"Mr. Ferrars is married"', her daughters' shocked reactions, Elinor's pallor and Marianne's fainting fit, force Mrs. Dashwood to see what Elinor has been living with for half a year (III xi 400).

I would like to close with a consideration of Edward's announcement, because, while it presents an absolutely vertiginous plot movement which is at once astounding and convincing, it also brings together the almost unreconcilable extremes of comedy and feeling which this novel contains. And, of course, it features that characteristic trope of mistaken identity. Edward has appeared unannounced. Through gritted teeth, Mrs. Dashwood asks after 'Mrs. Ferrars'. Edward stutters,

> 'Perhaps you mean—my brother—you mean Mrs.—Mrs. *Robert* Ferrars.'
>
> 'Mrs. Robert Ferrars!'—was repeated by Marianne and her mother, in an accent of the utmost amazement;—and though Elinor could not speak, even *her* eyes were fixed on him with the same impatient wonder. He rose from his seat and walked to the window, apparently from not knowing what to do; took up a pair of scissors that lay there, and while spoiling both them and their sheath by cutting the latter to pieces as he spoke, said, in an hurried voice, 'Perhaps you do not know—you may not have heard that my brother is lately married to—to the youngest—to Miss Lucy Steele.' (III xii 407–08)

Notice that change of emphasis: Edward, though beside himself, is not going to risk any further mistakes.

> 'Yes,' said he, 'they were married last week, and are now at Dawlish.'

At which the careful reader, remembering Robert's yearning to go to Dawlish, must explode, but only for a moment, because in the next line comes Elinor's acute, her agonized, response, the break in her iron self-control:

> Elinor could sit it no longer. She almost ran out of the room, and as soon as the door was closed, burst into tears of joy; which at first she thought would never cease. (III xii 408)

The others see, they hear, her emotion, but for once she doesn't care. More than a year of suffering is about to end, and it will end soon, for both sisters. Marianne does not speak again in the novel after that echoed '"Mrs. Robert Ferrars"', does not even play the piano, and this silence is perhaps the source of some readers' dissatisfaction with the conclusion of the story. But I do not accept the notion that the meaning of the title is reversed in the end, and that Marianne's marriage is a sensible one. I think that in the way in which Edward realized when he met Elinor that he was mistaken about Lucy, and that, comically and viciously, Lucy realized that she was making a mistake about Edward, Marianne realizes when she finally learns to know Colonel Brandon, that he is the real, romantic match for her. They will read Shakespeare together, though they may never get around to finishing *Hamlet*. The comedy of errors is brought to a perfect conclusion.

3. Mothers and Daughters in Jane Austen

None of Jane Austen's heroines becomes a mother in the course of the novels, which take them, usually, only to the altar and not beyond, but all are daughters, with at least one parent. And all of them, even Anne Elliot of *Persuasion*, at twenty-seven the eldest heroine, are, at the beginning of the novels, living at home with their families, though families of very different shapes. Jane Austen does not write, as the Gothic novelists did and as many novelists of the later nineteenth century did, about orphans or foundlings who did not know who their parents were. She was interested in how families operated,[1] and though sometimes it seems as if her heroines exist only to show how unlike parents a child can be, all are affected by their relationship with their mothers, even when, as happens more than once, those mothers are absent, or dead.[2]

I thought in the first half of my talk I would go quickly through all the novels to outline the mother-daughter situation that is central to each one, and then, because I can't do justice to all six, concentrate on two in particular: the two most popular and widely read, *Sense and Sensibility* and *Pride and Prejudice*. These are both, alas, novels in which mothers fail their daughters but they do so in different ways, and it will be interesting to examine the differences. What they also have in common—and I think this is relevant to the topic—is that Jane Austen

---

1   For previous discussion of this topic, see Juliet McMaster, 'Jane Austen's Children', *Persuasions On-line*, 31.1 (2012), jasna.org/persuasions/on-line/vol31no1/mcmaster. html? and Christopher Ricks, 'Jane Austen and the Business of Mothering', in *Essays in Appreciation* (New York and Oxford: Oxford University Press, 1998), pp. 90–113.

2   For a full-length study of absent mothers in the fiction of Austen's time, see Susan C. Greenfield, *Mothering Daughters: Novels and the Politics of Family Romance, Frances Burney to Jane Austen* (Detroit: Wayne State University Press, 2001).

          https://doi.org/10.11647/OBP.0216.03

wrote the earliest versions of them when she was very young and very close to the age of her heroines, and perhaps at a time when her view of mothers was that of a girl in her late teens and early twenties. When she revised and published the novels she was in her late thirties, but as you probably know she had continued to live with her parents, and after her father's sudden death, continued to live with her mother, and did so until the end of her life—and I will say just a little before I close about her mother, about Mrs. Austen.

First, though, let us go through the six major novels in order of publication. These novels were written over a long period, and rewritten, and in some cases published long after they were written, and the last novel published was actually one of the first written, but since that novel, *Northanger Abbey,* is the only novel to feature a sensible and successful mother, I thought it would be nice to build up toward that cheerful apex of good parenting, before we look at the sorry spectacle of mothering in the two novels in the second half of this talk.

Sense and Sensibility, published in 1811, begins, uniquely for Jane Austen, with a death, the death of the father of the three Dashwood girls, who are by that death made poor, dowryless, and homeless all at a single stroke. Because their family was a close and loving one, they are also made wretchedly unhappy. Deaths don't always have that effect in Jane Austen, and she is at times almost scandalously honest about how the death of a parent or other elderly relative might be very much wished for. But the Dashwood girls, Elinor, Marianne, and the very much younger girl Margaret, have a mother who is affectionate, intelligent, loyal and charming. But all these qualities do not, as we'll see, make her altogether a good mother: one of the tensions in this novel is between being a fond mother and a good mother. Mrs. Dashwood is always the former, always loving and affectionate, and good company, too; she has so many attractive qualities! But while she neither—intentionally— neglects her daughters, nor spoils them, her ideas about how the world works, her belief in sensibility over sense, endangers both of them.

Pride and Prejudice, published in 1813, has in Mrs. Bennet probably the most famous mother in Jane Austen, perhaps in all fiction:

> *Her* mind was less difficult to develope. She was a woman of mean understanding, little information, and uncertain temper. When she was

discontented she fancied herself nervous. The business of her life was to get her daughters married; its solace was visiting and news. (I i 5)

That character assassination in Chapter i is never really countered by anything else we learn about her, and yet, as Mrs. Bennet anxiously hovers over the marital prospects of her five daughters, who, should their father die as the Dashwoods' does, in this era of high mortality, would be much poorer than the Dashwoods, as she struggles with that situation we might want to spare her a sympathetic thought. One of the very few good additions to the dialogue made by the film of 2005 in which Keira Knightley was so miscast as Elizabeth Bennet, was an exchange between the scornful Elizabeth and her mother in which Elizabeth storms, 'why do you think so much about marriage!' and the mother snaps back, 'so will you, when you have five daughters!'.[3] The fact that the exchange would not happen in Jane Austen's world and is out of character for both speakers seems less important here than that this is the fundamental dilemma: as another impoverished unmarried daughter says in one of Jane Austen's unfinished novels, '"you know we *must* marry...'".[4] All of Jane Austen's heroines are husband-hunters, though none would like to admit it, even to themselves: it is only by the Mrs. Bennets of her world that this fact is mentioned.

Mansfield Park is the next to be published, and that novel begins by listing the marital fortunes of the three sisters from Northampton who will become Lady Bertram, Mrs. Norris and Mrs. Price. Mrs. Norris, cold and stingy, has no children (luckily for the children) but indolent Lady Bertram is the mother of two daughters, Maria and Julia, and slatternly Mrs. Price of several, of whom the reader's concern is with Fanny. I said earlier that Jane Austen didn't write about orphans or foundlings, but Fanny in a way is both, because she is adopted away from her impecunious family in Portsmouth to be brought up in the Bertram home alongside, but not in equality with, her cousins. Abandoned by her own mother—she is the child who can be spared by a woman who adores

---

3   *Pride and Prejudice*, dir. by Joe Wright (United International Pictures, 2005). See the special issue of *Persuasions On-line*, 27.2 (2007), which was dedicated to discussion of the film, and the review by Susan Fraiman, 'The Liberation of Elizabeth Bennet', *Persuasions On-line*, 31.1 (2010), http://www.jasna.org/persuasions/on-line/vol31no1/fraiman.html

4   *The Watsons*, in *Later Manuscripts*, ed. Todd and Bree, p. 82.

her sons and neglects her daughters—Fanny does not find a mother-substitute at Mansfield Park, but as often happens in Jane Austen novels, mysteriously brings herself up, with the guidance of one sympathetic, though often obtuse, male, her cousin Edmund. We might want to note right now that this pattern of relative maternal neglect, or absence, and a male mentor figure, occurs more than once in these six novels. In *Pride and Prejudice*, *Emma* and *Northanger Abbey*, the central young women learn valuable lessons from the men they will marry.

Emma is the next novel, and Emma's mother is dead. In a way which suited eighteenth-century minds, in a period when so many women died in childbirth or died young from other illnesses, we're told that her mother had died too long ago for Emma to have more than 'an indistinct remembrance of her caresses', and that her place was amply filled by the governess Miss Taylor. But Miss Taylor arrived when Emma was five, and presumably she came very soon after Mrs. Woodhouse's death. The loss of a mother at five is not really a minor loss, according to our thinking now, is it? So we might want to link motherless Emma Woodhouse, Emma who likes playing lady bountiful with other characters, whom she treats as if she were a little girl and they were her toys,[5] Emma who is the cleverest but also the least mature, in some ways, of the central figures in Jane Austen, with our next heroine, motherless Anne Elliot, who certainly does remember the death of her mother and mourns her loss, since it happened when she was thirteen.

One of the first things we know about Anne Elliot is that her mother has died, because as you'll remember the novel begins with Anne's silly, vain, snobbish father, Sir Walter, indulging in his favourite book, the Baronetage, which tells the history of his family and includes his own marriage and children. One of the many distinctive things about *Persuasion* is that everything in it is given a date: we know Anne's birthday, very unusual for a fictional character, and we know the year of her mother's death. Later on, that death will be alluded to as the reason she was unhappy at school, and the reason why, except for her brief youthful engagement with the appreciative Frederick Wentworth, no one for a long time has cared much about her considerable musical ability (Anne is a talented pianist, like several of Jane Austen's heroines and

---

5   Nora discusses the relationship between Emma and Harriet in Chapter 8.

Jane Austen herself.). Her over-reliance, at nineteen, on the bad advice given her by her friend Lady Russell, who was also her mother's friend, the catastrophic, and plot-igniting, advice to break the engagement to Wentworth, might be read as a symptom of her gratitude, as a girl whose sisters and father offer her little or no warmth or support, to someone who was 'in the place of a parent' (II xi 267–68). A kind and honoured mother-substitute has, in the word that echoes through the novel, 'persuaded' her to make a terrible mistake, one which, wonderfully, the novel corrects.

In *Northanger Abbey*, written early but published posthumously along with *Persuasion*, the last motherless girl is not quite a heroine. The heroine of the novel is in fact the very young Catherine, who is a bit giddy and impressionable, but comes, unusually in Jane Austen, from a large, healthy, fairly well-off family with a pair of live, and reliable, parents at its centre. Catherine's mother is one of the few really sensible mature women whom Jane Austen writes about. But Catherine meets, in the course of her own very naïve husband-hunting, with Eleanor Tilney, the sister of Henry, the young man with whom Catherine has fallen in love. Eleanor is not a heroine but is a very important secondary figure, and she takes us in a circle back to Jane Austen's early work, for like Elinor in *Sense and Sensibility*—and like Emma Woodhouse and Anne Elliot—Eleanor in *Northanger Abbey* is motherless. Her mother has died like Anne's when she was in her teens, leaving her like Anne with a cold and selfish father. She has no vain and self-absorbed sisters, it is true, but also no permanent companion at home, for her brothers, one selfish like her father, the other the charming, warm, funny, affectionate Henry, lead the lives of middle-class boys of that time and go away to school and university. Eleanor probably had, like Emma, a governess, but she is long gone, and when Henry is away she has only the rather empty role of playing at presiding over her father's household, again, like Emma, but Emma really does run the house whereas Eleanor is 'but a nominal mistress of' Northanger Abbey (II xiii 232), really thought of by her father as a beautiful possession like his pictures or china, and as a counter in the marriage games he wants to play with his children's lives, as he plans wealthy alliances for them.

We are talking about mothers today, not fathers, but General Tilney is one of the most unpleasant fathers anywhere in Jane Austen. The way in which his presence checks laughter and natural behaviour is wonderfully depicted, and the fun Catherine and Eleanor have when he is briefly away, lingering late in the dining room, as if they were gentlemen, is dramatized also, as is the exchange Eleanor has with Catherine about her mother's death and how she misses her. This conversation has the important plot function of planting in Catherine's mind the idea that the General is a murderer (he's bad, but not quite that bad) but it is also there to give us a sense of the loneliness and suffering of even a well-off, beautiful, confident young woman like Eleanor Tilney, if she loses her mother before she grows up. '"A mother would have been always present. A mother would have been a constant friend"', she laments (II vii 185).

But if losing a mother is tragic, we shall see that having one can be a problem, too, especially in the two early novels I want to spend time with now. I'll go again in order of publication and look first at *Sense and Sensibility*, which has many mother-daughter sets, starting with the least important and also the least attractive, that is Fanny Dashwood, the selfish, cold and avaricious sister-in-law of the Dashwood girls, and her equally cold and avaricious mother, Mrs. Ferrars, who is also the mother of Edward Ferrars, the young man with whom Elinor, the heroine through whose eyes we see most of the novel's action, is in love. Mrs. Ferrars is extremely rich. She has inherited all of her husband's money and uses it to alternately indulge and bully her children. We never find out how that money was earned, but one or two country estates are mentioned, though never visited in the novel. Presumably Mrs. Ferrars, who really cares for nothing but money, keeps them making money for her by renting them out. They are spoken of only as sources of income. Sometimes in the novel they are dangled over Edward as a bribe to make him do something that will make his mother proud of him. By choosing to live in London, being an absentee landlady who does not live on her own land, but turns it into money, she reduces her attraction for country-loving Jane Austen. But dislikeable though she is, we cannot say that all of her money comes from trade—we see money from trade in the situations of other characters in the novel, and in *Pride and Prejudice*. Income from trade alone is always thought by the more snobbish characters in the novels as something to be ashamed of, but Jane Austen is more up-to-date and understands that trade can also be an honest way to earn a living, and that it is the snooty characters' attitudes to it that are silly and outmoded. Her novels do, though, register a still-prevailing sense at the end of the eighteenth and the start of the nineteenth century that an income derived from the land, from agriculture, was more respectable, as a desire to live in the country rather than the town was usually a sign of a more stable set of values. Edward's worthiness to be a hero is indicated in part by his wishing to be ordained, and to take up a parish in the country. Mrs. Ferrars, who wishes her sons to 'make a name for themselves', to be 'public men' of some sort, or, failing that, to be the sort of playboy figure who careers around the metropolis from social event to social event in a barouche-landau (the very newest sort of coach, light and fast, able to hold four persons as well as the driver), shows nothing but the shallowest values, though seems respectable because she is so very dull: 'She was not a woman of many words', the narrative tells us, 'for, unlike people in general, she proportioned them to the number of her ideas' (II xii 265), a neat slap in two directions, at the noisy many as well as the silent Mrs. Ferrars.[6] Such ideas as she has, though, are all worldly: she will not allow her shy, thoughtful, well-meaning eldest son Edward to follow his own desires, because the clergy is '"not smart enough"', not flashy, not something about which she and her daughter can boast (I xix 119).

That daughter, Fanny, resembles her greatly, and we will see this pattern in the novel, of a mother having one daughter who resembles herself, and feeling special warmth, in a way of which the novel is not uncritical, toward that daughter. Toward Fanny, Mrs. Ferrars is, according to her lights, indulgent. She has given her a large dowry, as we learn in Chapter i, in this novel in which money is one of the main concerns, and she shares with Fanny, who is perhaps the eldest child (we don't know), all her hopes and schemes for her sons: Edward must be a great man, or Robert, his younger brother, must be; Edward (or

---

6   We are told, 'His mother wished to interest him in political concerns, to get him into parliament, or to see him connected with some of the great men of the day. Mrs. John Dashwood wished it likewise; but in the mean while, till one of these superior blessings could be attained, it would have quieted her ambition to see him driving a barouche. But Edward had no turn for great men or barouches. All his wishes centered in domestic comfort and the quiet of private life. Fortunately he had a younger brother who was more promising' (I iii 18). Later, Edward expresses the hope that his mother '"is now convinced that I have no more talents than inclination for a public life"' (I xvii 104).

Robert) must marry an heiress. Indeed, at different times they are meant to be marrying the *same* heiress.

When Edward turns out in the second volume of the novel not to be headed in that direction at all, but to have engaged himself, years earlier, to the impecunious nobody Lucy Steele, Mrs. Ferrars takes the extreme step of disinheriting him and transferring all the prerogatives of the eldest son to Robert, and all the income, too, enough to live on, the crucial £1000 a year which enabled a young couple to keep several servants, have dinner parties and a carriage. This despite the fact that she herself, and Fanny, are actually as attracted to Lucy's cold, ambitious and vulgar personality as they are repelled by Elinor Dashwood's quiet good manners.

Like mother, like daughter, then, and between Fanny Dashwood and her mother there is a kind of closeness based on similarity, though in fact in the novel we scarcely see them speaking to one another (there is a brief exchange while they both insult some of Elinor's artwork). However, John Dashwood, Fanny's husband, who adores both his wife and his mother-in-law (it is a credit to Jane Austen that here she can make a usually praise-worthy emotion, uxoriousness, and filial feeling toward a mother figure, so repellent as she does in the figure of John Dashwood) gives a triumphant description of a highly symbolic moment when his mother-in-law, on their arriving to visit her in London, '"put bank-notes into Fanny's hands to the amount of two hundred pounds"''(II xi 255). John gives this as an instance of Mrs. Ferrars's '"noble spirit"' (II xi 255), but the physicality of the description—the actual amount being *named*, and the picture of the hand-to-hand transfer—suggests both a grossness in the action, and the greedy materialism of both women. This is the stuff of their intimacy. Those of you who remember the novel's story well enough to recall how it turns out will know that in the end Lucy Steele, the penniless nobody from nowhere, the Becky Sharpe type figure driven entirely by mercenary motives, achieves the social rise she desires by tricking not Edward but Robert into marrying her, and that she becomes, in her own vigorous self-seeking, 'as necessary to Mrs. Ferrars'—*necessary* is a nice word—'as either Robert or Fanny' (III xiv 427). In short, Lucy becomes another daughter. But that is a domestic setting we are told about but don't see.

A mother whom we do see a great deal of, throughout the novel, is my own particular favourite, Mrs. Jennings, a character whom I think of as having great importance for the novel's overall shape and for its themes. For if the novel teaches impulsive, unguarded Marianne, Elinor's passionate younger sister, to be a little more sensible and self-controlled, it also teaches both Marianne *and* Elinor to have a value for Mrs. Jennings, whom they dismiss at first as 'vulgar', but whom the novel I think sees in a more complex way from the start.[7] Here is her introduction: 'Mrs. Jennings [...] was a good-humoured, merry, fat, elderly woman, who talked a great deal, seemed very happy, and rather vulgar' (I vii 40). Okay: she *is* vulgar. She is nosy and noisy and more interested in enjoying herself than in how the way she enjoys herself appears to other people. But the shape of the sentence there is interesting, for 'good humour', a very important category in Jane Austen, is the first quality named, and 'rather vulgar' the last. Elinor and Marianne, nicely brought up, about as far themselves from vulgarity as it is possible to get and still be alive, place more emphasis on that last quality perhaps than the narrative does. I won't say too much more about vulgarity now—it's a characteristic that was obviously very significant in the social world Jane Austen lived in and wants to describe—but it is worth keeping that introduction to Mrs. Jennings in mind when we get on to that other vulgar mother, Mrs. Bennet in *Pride and Prejudice*.

Mrs. Jennings has two daughters: one, Lady Middleton, married to Sir John, the man who provides the Dashwood family with their new home in Devon, Barton Cottage, the setting of much of the first part of the novel, is her antithesis. Lady Middleton was probably one of those girls whose education has raised her enough above her parents' manners so that she feels horror and embarrassment at them, and who lacks the intelligence and good sense to make her, as she gets beyond the teen years, revise that early judgment. Lady Middleton's beauty and elegant clothes and superficial good manners have enabled her to marry a baronet, and she is not going to admit her own origins. All the Jennings's money, which seems to be considerable, was earned in trade and in the City and the Jennings girls grew up a step or two away from the warehouses where their merchant father's goods were stored while the money was

---

7   For a detailed consideration of Mrs. Jennings, see Chapter 4.

piling up. While Lady Middleton tolerates her mother, Sir John, her husband, *adores* his mother-in-law, who is like him in her boisterous good humour and her pleasure in society; there are wonderful scenes in the novel of the good fun that mother and son-in-law have together, well captured in the 1995 film with Emma Thompson.[8] But, as for Mrs. Jennings and Lady Middleton, there is no intimacy between them; Lady Middleton spends all her time 'humouring her children' and trying to control her husband's sociability and her mother's speech, without too much expenditure of energy (unlike her mother she is indolent except where her children are concerned).[9] When Mrs. Jennings learns from twelve-year-old Margaret Dashwood, who is an active but unmalicious gossip (Mrs. Jennings is always winkling out information from children and servants) that Elinor's suitor's name 'begins with an F', Marianne anticipates the 'raillery' that will follow and tries 'with great warmth' to silence Margaret (I xii 72). There is then a neat pincer movement as Lady Middleton and Colonel Brandon, she from squeamishness, he from a kind wish to spare Elinor embarrassment, try to change the subject to the weather 'and much was said on the subject of rain by both of them' (I xii 72). I think—this is an early work, and it is not quite perfect, perhaps, but it is wonderfully economical with dialogue—that there is not a single example in the novel of an exchange between Mrs. Jennings and her eldest daughter.

With her younger daughter, though, with plump, pretty Charlotte, now married to Mr. Palmer, a rising MP, she is much more intimate. Here is a second example of a daughter being like her mother, and this similarity bringing them close: Mrs. Palmer's likeness to her mother is expressed as a complete *dis*similarity to her older sister, Lady Middleton, who is 'totally unlike her in every respect' (I xix 123). Here are mother and daughter together:

---

8   *Sense and Sensibility*, dir. by Ang Lee (Sony Pictures Releasing, 1995).
9   In Volume I, Chapter vii, Austen briskly accounts for different ways of spending time: 'Sir John was a sportsman, Lady Middleton a mother. He hunted and shot, and she humoured her children; and these were their only resources. Lady Middleton had the advantage of being able to spoil her children all the year round, while Sir John's independent employments were in existence only half the time' (I vii 38). Later, in Chapter xxi, we are told that the Miss Steeles also devote a lot of time to humouring Lady Middleton's children: 'With her children they were in continual raptures, extolling their beauty, courting their notice, and humouring all their whims' (I xxi 138).

Mrs. Jennings, in the mean time, talked on as loud as she could, and continued her account of their surprise, the evening before, on seeing their friends, without ceasing till every thing was told. Mrs. Palmer laughed heartily at the recollection of their astonishment, and every body agreed, two or three times over, that it had been quite an agreeable surprise.

'You may believe how glad we all were to see them,' added Mrs. Jennings, leaning forwards towards Elinor, and speaking in a low voice as if she meant to be heard by no one else, though they were seated on different sides of the room; 'but, however, I can't help wishing they had not travelled quite so fast, nor made such a long journey of it, for they came all round by London upon account of some business, for you know (nodding significantly and pointing to her daughter) it was wrong in her situation. I wanted her to stay at home and rest this morning, but she would come with us; she longed so much to see you all!'

Mrs. Palmer laughed, and said it would not do her any harm.

'She expects to be confined in February,' continued Mrs. Jennings. (I xix 124)

Mrs. Palmer is about six months pregnant, at a time when pregnancy was beginning to be an awkward subject in mixed company.[10] The Dashwoods, though not encouraging, are polite about this, but 'Lady Middleton could no longer endure such a conversation', and struggles to change the subject, while her younger sister laughs and her mother chatters inextinguishably on (I xix 125). In this novel about sisters which uses dialogue so carefully, there is, again, not a single exchange of dialogue between this pair of sisters: Lady Middleton says not a word to either of the women with whom she spent her childhood and adolescence. Although, unlike her mother and sister, Lady Middleton is not a great comic figure, comedy arises in the novel from time to time because, though the Dashwood sisters have quickly found that Lady Middleton is so 'cold and insipid' that it is impossible to get to know her, her icy good breeding is sometimes welcome just as a relief from the noise and innuendoes of Mrs. Palmer and Mrs. Jennings.[11] I'll say more

---

10   For further discussion of the awkwardness of pregnancy, see Jenny Davidson, *Reading Jane Austen* (Cambridge: Cambridge University Press, 2017), https://doi.org/10.1017/9781108367974, pp. 124–25.

11   Austen's summary is: that 'the cold insipidity of Lady Middleton was […] particularly repulsive' to the Dashwood sisters (I vii 41). Interestingly, Elinor believes that Marianne's warmth forces her to project these characteristics onto Edward Ferrars: '"You decide on his imperfections so much in the mass," replied Elinor, "and so

about the way Mrs. Jennings's good qualities, and even Mr. and Mrs. Palmer's, gradually become apparent, as we look at the more important mother and daughters in the novel, the Dashwoods.

Because I love Jane Austen's heroines, I especially love *Sense and Sensibility*, in which you get two. As well as the entertaining minor figures we've been looking at, there is the beautiful, bereft, grieving Dashwood family, two teenage sisters and one little girl, and their attractive, charming, sensitive mother, a widow in her early forties, for as I've already said, *Sense and Sensibility* begins with a death, the death of Mr. Dashwood, a death which leaves his wife and children—and the novel makes no bones about this—nearly impoverished, homeless, living on the income of ten thousand pounds. Dying, Mr. Dashwood extracted a promise of aid for them from his son from his first marriage, John, but the reader learns as soon as Chapter ii that that promise means just nothing, which is what John and Fanny will do for 'half blood' or 'half sisters' (I ii 9–10). Since we have already discussed how Fanny can gleefully countenance the disinheriting of her actual brother, Edward, we should not be surprised that half-sisters don't rate a share of her scanty goodwill: '"They will have no carriage, no horses, and hardly any servants; they will keep no company [...] Only conceive how comfortable they will be!"' she purrs contentedly (I ii 14).

We spend most of the novel with the two Dashwood sisters, and especially with Elinor, but how did two sisters so close in age, so fond of each other, so alike in intelligence and refinement and sensitivity (this is not the kind of contrast we see in the Bennet family, where the younger daughters seem to have come from a different gene pool), how did these two close, affectionate sisters, come to be such different beings? Let's backtrack: Elinor, at nineteen, is the advisor to her mother, whose 'eagerness of mind' means that at forty or so Mrs. Dashwood 'had yet to learn' that self-governance Elinor has acquired: 'The resemblance between [Marianne] and her mother was very great ' (I i 7).

---

much on the strength of your own imagination, that the commendation *I* am able to give of him is comparatively cold and insipid'" (I x 61). Coldness and insipidity, however, remain firmly attributed to Lady Middleton: 'Lady Middleton was equally pleased with Mrs. Dashwood. There was a kind of cold hearted selfishness on both sides, which mutually attracted them; and they sympathized with each other in an insipid propriety of demeanour, and a general want of understanding' (II xii 261).

This is the pattern we saw in the Jennings family, too, where the eldest daughter forms herself in contrast to her mother and the younger in similarity. Of course, the Dashwoods are serious and not comic characters, though I think there is comedy in them, also, in the mother's eagerness. Her rapid reactions, her disgust at Fanny Dashwood's arrogance, wonderfully combine a sympathetic presentation of a woman who has to see herself supplanted by another woman in her own home, and a satirical one, as she impractically starts to throw her things into a suitcase as soon as Fanny arrives, and almost every time Fanny's passive hostility turns aggressive, and has to be reasoned with by nineteen-year-old Elinor, who knows they have nowhere to go. Or Mrs. Dashwood's impulsive assumption that because Edward seems to like Elinor that they will be married; above all, her equally impulsive trust that, as the novel progresses, Marianne, who is sixteen going on seventeen, can make all her own decisions about her romantic life. This is both looked at with a kind of analytic concern—she is a likeable woman throughout—and made funny.

Let's look at her as Marianne's mother, then as Elinor's. Like Mrs. Ferrars and Mrs. Jennings, whom she does not resemble in other ways, she finds it easiest to sympathize with the daughter who most 'resembles her'. When Marianne, as is characteristic of her sixteen-year-old's self-absorption, murmurs, "'the more I know of the world, the more I am convinced that I shall never see a man whom I can really love. I require so much!'", Mrs. Dashwood responds encouragingly:

> 'Remember, my love, you are not yet seventeen. It is yet too early in life to despair of such an happiness. Why should you be less fortunate than your mother? In one circumstance only, my Marianne, may your destiny be different from her's!' (I iii 20–21)

More like a friend than a mother, Mrs. Dashwood does not seem to have the word 'caution"' in her vocabulary. Not a word is heard, between these pretty impoverished women, of anything practical about what might be desirable in a marriage partner in the way of profession, family or fortune; of course this means that nothing mercenary is ever said, either, and heroines in Jane Austen must walk a tightrope between their beliefs, in love and honour, and the cold facts of their need for financial security. Unlike Fanny Dashwood and her husband, who talk about nothing but money, they must manage this with only the faintest acknowledgement of their financial predicament.

When Marianne *does* meet a man who satisfies all that she requires, both she and her mother approve him without hesitation, but also without vulgar husband-hunting. Marianne meets Willoughby in the most romantic way possible—he rescues her after a fall on a storm-tossed hill and carries her home in his arms—and when the Dashwoods hear that he is '"very much worth catching"', Mrs. Dashwood disavows her daughters' desire to 'catch', not just Willoughby, but any man: '"It is not an employment to which they have been brought up. Men are very safe with us, let them be ever so rich"' (I ix 52–53).

Only Elinor has any reservations, and Elinor is uncomfortably aware her reservations about Willoughby might be founded in her own uncertainties about Edward and might even involve some envy that 'this was the season of happiness to Marianne', as she and Willoughby tear around the country in his gig, which has room only for two, and openly seek each other's company without reserve or hesitation (I xi 64). But Elinor is worried. She thinks it is wrong for them, with no official engagement, to show so openly their preference for one another; wrong for them to show, also quite openly, their indifference to the opinion of others and their sense of happy superiority to less glamorous figures such as Colonel Brandon, who also, quietly, unsuccessfully, loves Marianne. Mrs. Dashwood, though, at least a quarter of a century older and more experienced than Elinor, is not troubled: 'Mrs. Dashwood entered into all their feelings with a warmth which left her no inclination for checking this excessive display of them' (I xi 64). Even when Willoughby suddenly and inexplicably leaves for London, without making his intentions clear to Marianne or to her family, Mrs. Dashwood will not question Marianne as to whether they are engaged: '"I would not attempt to force the confidences of anyone, of a child much less"' (I xvi 98). Marianne will suffer in her self-imposed silence for months, will in fact nearly die of the after-effects of this suffering, and her mother will still cling to this sense of romantic delicacy about her daughter's feelings. And not only Marianne's: when it becomes evident that Elinor and Edward are not heading straight toward marriage, either, indeed, when it becomes known that he has long been engaged to another girl, Mrs. Dashwood is still too delicate-minded to bring up the subject.

We might want to ask, isn't there an element of cowardice in her not seeking more confidence from Marianne or from Elinor? What do we think about her maturity and responsibility as a parent? She never becomes an unsympathetic figure, never loses her charm, does she? But I feel the novel really wants us to scrutinize her behaviour here. I wonder whether, especially in the case of Elinor, there is not real neglect as well as cowardice. Even Elinor, so good at forgetting herself, wonders if her mother ever does remember her earlier hopes for herself and Edward. Though Elinor continually tries to play down her own sufferings, she is surprised at the ease with which her subterfuge succeeds at convincing her mother!

Throughout the novel there will be contrasts between the Dashwoods' extreme sensitivity to each other's feelings, a sensitivity which amounts to 'reserve', a quality Jane Austen is ambivalent about, does not wholly approve, and the boisterous openness of, on the one hand, Mrs. Jennings and Sir John ("'let's have no secrets between friends'") and, on the other, the two husband-hunting Steele sisters, who display an interesting combination of apparent openness—they know each other's secrets—and slyness—one way they know this is by listening at doors. But the combination in Mrs. Dashwood of unrestrained admiration for feeling as a guide, and restraint about investigating where that feeling has taken her favourite child, is very nearly lethal.

When Mrs. Dashwood finally becomes practical it is with a vengeance, as, after Marianne's illness she begins to plan her marriage to Colonel Brandon, which is accompanied by a shocking disregard for the facts of the past ("'there was always a something—if you remember,—in Willoughby's eyes at times, which I did not like'") and the earlier comment among the Dashwood women that "'thirty-five has nothing to do with matrimony'" is conveniently forgotten now (III ix 383; I viii 45). She continues the tunnel vision about Elinor's feelings for Edward. Having so much else to worry about, Mrs. Dashwood does not find it convenient to worry about Elinor, too, and when the supposed news of Edward's marriage to Lucy breaks upon them she sees, almost stunned, 'that in Elinor she might have a daughter suffering almost as much' as Marianne (III xi 403). There is a wonderful scene when Mrs. Dashwood and Elinor sit together in silence while Mrs. Dashwood takes in not only how much Elinor has suffered, but how much she has chosen to ignore that suffering.

Mrs. Dashwood, whether or not she is a good mother, is a marvellous creation on Jane Austen's part: a woman who aims at a kind of heroic, romantic closeness with her children but who is often prevented by her own powerful fantasies from being in any real contact with either of them. The happy ending that comes for both daughters is as much good luck for her and for them (as opposed to good sense) as are the happy endings of *Pride and Prejudice*. In that novel, published in 1813 'By the Author of "Sense and Sensibility"', we have one of the most famous mothers in literature: a mother not charming or clever, and floridly, vividly comic; and again a mother who has favourites among her children, and whose favouritism is even more dangerously bestowed than in *Sense and Sensibility*.

Mrs. Bennet, like Mrs. Jennings, is vulgar, and obsessed with marriage, but there the resemblance ends: for Mrs. Jennings is as happy as Mrs. Bennet is fretful and plaintive. In contrast to Mrs. Jennings's plump contentment is Mrs. Bennet's 'nervousness'. Mrs. Jennings has good sense: at the stage in the novel when everyone, with a variety of emotions, thinks that the disinherited Edward Ferrars is going to marry Lucy Steele, Mrs. Jennings is realistic about the fact that with an income of only a couple of hundred pounds a year they would only be able to afford 'a stout girl of all works', rather than the two or three servants that a larger income could maintain (III ii 314). Mrs. Jennings is thus commonsensical, in her way, but Mrs. Bennet is not. Mrs. Bennet is a lawyer's daughter who cannot be made to understand the nature of an entail, even though an entail was one of the commonest of legal arrangements for landed property, and she must have grown up hearing the term. As a companion, Mrs. Bennet is peevish (scolding one of her daughters for coughing); and as a neighbour she is competitive, boasting embarrassingly that her daughters are prettier, her drawing room larger, and her cuts of meat better cooked than those of the other inhabitants of Hertfordshire.

Because she is such an embarrassing mother, making it clear to everyone whom she meets how desperate she is to have her daughters married to rich and eligible men, it is the sensitive, discerning daughters, Elizabeth and Jane, whom one most often thinks of her as failing: she wishes Lizzy to marry the dull, plodding, silly and selfish Mr. Collins, whom she cannot love; she wants Jane to marry the man she does love, but only because he is rich; and yet, keen as she is for them to be married, it is her 'want of connection' as Mr. Darcy says, coupled with her 'total want of propriety', to quote Mr. Darcy once more, which again and again jeopardize their chances to marry anyone at all (II xii 220).

But then: let's think about marriage and mothers in both novels. In *Sense and Sensibility* there is a contrast between the romantic and delicate Mrs. Dashwood who has not brought her daughters up to be husband-hunters; but, since at the time it was almost impossible to bring them up for any other profession, it feels as if her thinking on the topic was insufficiently clear—even what is today called 'being in denial' and then was known as being deluded. Commonsensical Mrs. Jennings, having married off her two daughters, 'had now therefore nothing else to do but to marry all the rest of the world [...] she was always anxious to get a good husband for every pretty girl' (I viii 43). This generosity is in strong contrast to Mrs. Bennet's concern only with her own family of daughters. But Mrs. Jennings's situation is unusual in Jane Austen: most of the mothers we meet are anxiously looking out for husbands for their daughters even if, like Mrs. Dashwood, they pretend, most of all to themselves, that they are not.

The other mother with whom Mrs. Bennet most often compares herself is Lady Lucas, the wife of Sir William Lucas, and the mother of Elizabeth's friend Charlotte, and because the Lucas girls are so plain, and are often stuck in the kitchen making mince pies (and presumably learning how to run a household, which none of the Bennet girls has been taught), Mrs. Bennet feels securely superior in her relationship with Lady Lucas, who is not rich and is 'not too clever to be a valuable neighbour to Mrs. Bennet' and not likely to get the jump on her as mother of the bride (I v 19). With what horror, then, does Mrs. Bennet see Charlotte Lucas step into the breach left by Lizzy's refusal of Mr. Collins, becoming Mrs. Collins. Neither Mrs. Bennet nor Lady Lucas seems to see Mr. Collins's stupidity as a drawback, but then, unlike Mrs. Bennet, Lady Lucas is herself married to a very stupid man, and presumably knows it has its compensations, as Charlotte's later depicted contentment seems to suggest, and of course among those compensations, in this particular case, is that Charlotte will be Mrs. Bennet's successor as mistress of

Longbourn! Lady Lucas and her plain daughters are able to turn the tables very effectively on Mrs. Bennet and her pretty ones.

And there is that other 'her ladyship' in *Pride and Prejudice*, who is also the mother of a daughter: Lady Catherine de Bourgh. I am going to close with even more discussion of the weaknesses, as a mother, of Mrs. Bennet, but before I do let us examine Lady Catherine, also seeking a husband for her daughter, though Miss de Bourgh is independently wealthy and therefore has no financial need for one. Though more partial to, and more praising of, her only daughter than any other mother in Jane Austen, even doting Mrs. Dashwood or boastful Mrs. Bennet, Lady Catherine, continually makes remarks such as, '"Anne would have been a delightful performer, had her health allowed her to learn"' (II viii 197). This sort of daunting, inhibiting, exacting praise, it would seem, has crushed the life out of the poor girl—'thin and small [...] sickly and cross'—since in the novel this poor cipher never utters a word! (II v 180). Her mother does all the talking for her, and does almost everything else for her also, substituting her own prodigious energy for her daughter's lack of it, and one really has to wonder whether that volcanic maternal energy is not the source of the daughter's exhaustion? My own best wish for Miss de Bourgh is that she and Charlotte should form a close female friendship which will give some life to the poor dejected young girl and provide an outlet for Charlotte aside from pigs and poultry!

But it is worth making the comparison between Lady Catherine and Mrs. Bennet, for though Mrs. Bennet constantly shames her two eldest daughters she has not squashed them as Lady Catherine has hers. Jane and Elizabeth have somehow grown up intelligent, confident, and, what is more, morally discerning young women, who judge rightly (Elizabeth most of the time, Jane always) about the difference between right and wrong. However, Mrs. Bennet is not only the mother of Jane and Elizabeth, but of three younger girls, and I want to end by looking at those three girls as daughters, and in particular, since Kitty is something of a nonentity, a pale, coughing copy of Lydia, at two of them, at Lydia and Mary, those total opposites, who, it would seem, are equally the victims of their mother's, or their parents', bad parenting.

Lydia is another example, like the younger Jennings and Dashwood daughters in *Sense and Sensibility*, of a daughter who is prized because she is like her mother. And through Lydia we see what might have drawn Mr. Bennet to make his tragic error in marriage, for though Lydia is not a great beauty as Mrs. Bennet must have been—Jane has inherited that—Lydia is full of life and energy, *joie de vivre* and something the novel rather doubtingly calls 'high animal spirits' but we might want to call VA VA VOOM! (I ix 49). Ready to dance, to laugh, to lark about at the drop of a hat, impulsive and with little ability to control her impulses. Again, like Marianne, she is a very full portrait of one type of adolescent girl, but it's a type for which the world of Georgian England offers little scope aside from dancing and flirting. And, because her mother (and her father) have somehow left out of her education the fate that can befall a woman who takes flirting too far and risks engaging in sex outside marriage, that energy, that lack of self-control, could mean for her a terrible fate: without Mr. Darcy's intervention and his money, to make Wickham marry her, she would 'have come upon the town' as a camp-follower, a prostitute abandoned by her first lover (this does happen, and to a gentleman's daughter, in *Sense and Sensibility*) (III viii 342). Lydia's brush with ruin is as much due, as Mr. Bennet and his two thinking elder daughters know, to the fact that no one has attempted to instil any principles, or even any realistic dread of consequences, in her while she was growing up in a gentleman's family in the genteel south of England. Mrs. Bennet, who is delighted her daughter will be married at sixteen, to no matter whom or after no matter what an unseemly period of living together unmarried, and, as the narrative emphasizes, is more outraged that Lydia has no new clothes than that she almost had no husband, has no real principles; but Mr. Bennet has (III vii 343). He simply has not bothered to impart them to his younger children. Lydia has been allowed to bring herself up.

Mary, of course, full of 'observations of thread-bare morality' would seem to be the opposite case, but is she not equally neglected, particularly by her father? (I xiii 67). And not only neglected, but mocked and undermined as she attempts—and this is painful to the re-reader—as she is clearly attempting to gain her father's approval (it can't be her mother's!) by what the novel rather dismissively calls 'the solidity of her reflections' (I v 21). Mary is plain like the Lucas girls, but unlike them is not taught housewifely skills, and tries instead to shine via the dangerous arena of accomplishments. She doggedly practises the piano, reads worthy books, and (presumably) keeps a journal or a commonplace book no one else will ever want to look into, in order to record her reflections on what she reads, and probably to chalk up her hours of practice. But, as her father is also bookish, it seems unquestionable that what she wants is a little attention and approval from him—and this she never gets. At the novel's end she is left unmarried, uninvited to Pemberley or to Jane's house or even to the Northern army camps where Lydia has set up her tent, and has become, by default, her mother's companion and not her father's. The very last words about her in the novel contain a characteristic Mr. Bennet shrug: 'it was suspected by her father that she submitted to the change'—from the steady pursuit of accomplishments to the society of her mother and the 'world' of the Meryton neighbours—'without much reluctance' (III xix 428). Again, this is a talk about mothers and not fathers, but I am never quite sure whether the novel shares this lack of interest in Mary or condemns Mr. Bennet for it.

I'll end here by asking why, in Jane Austen's novels, there are so few sensible mothers? The thoughtful older women we meet are either, like Mrs. Croft in *Persuasion,* childless, or like Mrs. Gardiner in *Pride and Prejudice*, the parents of children not yet old enough to be on the marriage market. Mothers of marriageable daughters are in almost every case woefully inadequate at providing guidance for their daughters, and in the novels we have looked at closely they not only do no good but actually do harm to the daughters they profess to, or really do, love. I'll remind you again that Jane Austen did not become a mother herself, and just slip in the rather interesting fact that she was, like Elizabeth in *Pride and Prejudice*, something of a daddy's girl herself. Her father had such a belief in the first, epistolary, version of *Pride and Prejudice* that, though it was by his teenage daughter, he took it upon himself to send it off to a publisher—who sent it back by return of post. Mrs. Austen, once the business of bringing up children and running a large household was behind her, seemed to drift more and more into a rather vaguely defined invalidism, though of course it was her husband who died suddenly and unexpectedly, and then her gifted daughter who fell ill and died at just past forty. It is not certain, but it is sometimes suggested, that one of the reasons her sister Cassandra destroyed most of Jane Austen's letters could be that they contained—not unloving, probably, because the whole family was very close and affectionate, but perhaps unguarded—remarks about a mother who, because of her delicate health (though she survived her daughter by over ten years) commandeered the sofa in the drawing room at Chawton Cottage, while Jane Austen, writing *Sanditon,* and herself dying, was obliged to put up with an arrangement of 'two or three chairs'.[12] For those of you who have not read the wonderful fragments that are left of *Sanditon*, it is a satire about hypochondria.[13]

---

12 'Her reasons for this might have been left to be guessed, but for the importunities of a little niece, which obliged her to explain that if she had shown any inclination to use the sofa, her mother might have scrupled being on it so much as was good for her'. J. E. Austen Leigh, *A Memoir of Jane Austen by her Nephew* (London: Folio, 1989), p. 147. For further discussion of hypochondria, see Chapter 6.

13 For further discussion of *Sanditon*, see Chapter 13.

4. Mrs. Jennings

Books within Books

Before *Sense and Sensibility* was published in 1811, Jane Austen was an unpublished author; afterwards she was not. This seems a simple and obvious truth, but we shouldn't rush to think that we understand everything that is implied in the statement. Once she had published this novel, she was an author, its author, and the subsequent novels were known to be 'By the Author of "Sense and Sensibility"' and therefore raised certain expectations in publisher and reader. When she revised *Elinor and Marianne,* possibly an epistolary novel she had written first in 1795, rewritten in 1797 and finally revised for publication as *Sense and Sensibility* in the years between 1809 and 1811, no such expectations existed, and I think it is possible to assume a certain freedom in the revising of that novel, while not forgetting that Jane Austen had long aimed for publication, that her *Susan (Northanger Abbey)* had been accepted for publication in 1803, and that even earlier, in 1797, her father had sent off the epistolary *First Impressions* to a publisher, only to have it rejected unread. We can assume then that she was not a closet author in any way, not writing for therapy. But it is still significant that *Sense and Sensibility* shared with the juvenile writings that are collected in the manuscript notebooks, an intimacy with its readers, who were her family. Her family seem always to have been her first and perhaps her most important readers, even after 1811, but before that they might be, for all she knew, her only readers. I want to suggest a continuity between the rudeness and wildness that are such hallmarks of the juvenile writings, the tiny parody novels like *Frederic and Elfrida,* and the nature of the characterization, and some of the comedy, in *Sense and Sensibility*—and not only the comedy, but the distinctive blend of

https://doi.org/10.11647/OBP.0216.04

comedy and seriousness which Jane Austen is able to give to moments in her writing, and which is particularly exuberant and raw in the still pretty youthful *Sense and Sensibility*.

The 'novels' of the juvenile writing were often only a few pages long, though *Love and Freindship*, *Lady Susan* and the fragment *The Watsons* are much longer. But there is a charm to her willingness to give the name 'novel' to a three-page story such as *Henry and Eliza* and there is also, I think, a sense of how diverse might be the qualities that make a novel: how a long narrative such as she achieves in *Sense and Sensibility* is a drawing together of many such 'novels', all of which elbow each other appealingly in bids for the author's attention. Those who so wrongly find *Sense and Sensibility* unsatisfactory in any way (though they are fewer than they once were, a process to which the Cambridge editor Edward Copeland refers when he says the novel is no longer 'the red-headed stepchild' among Jane Austen's novels)[1] were perhaps responding to this bursting at the seams, this too-muchness of the novel.

One way to tame it, and a powerful way to read it, is to recognize the move forward Jane Austen makes in the construction of Elinor's as the novel's central experience, to see it as Elinor's book—belonging to its central character in a way that the epistolary *Lady Susan* did not— though that short novel, set aside a year or so before the first version of the *Elinor and Marianne* plot was begun, did contain more of Susan's words than those of any other persons, it is a book which displays the main character's vices and not her viewpoint, despite her liveliness and, in a way, her vulnerability as a woman on the hunt for a husband, like all Jane Austen's single women. But if *Sense and Sensibility* is Elinor's book it is also Marianne's book, and Lucy Steele's book—and not only the women: it is Colonel Brandon's book, and Willoughby's. Their stories are all given space, given room to breathe, in this ambitious, complex novel.

But I would like here to discuss the way in which it is Mrs. Jennings's book, in that no re-reader can fail to recognize the way the novel works to vindicate Mrs. Jennings's character and also to fulfil her wishes. The

---

1   'Unstable and shifting in its sympathies and issues, *Sense and Sensibility* has long been treated as disappointing and odd, the red-headed stepchild of the Austen canon'. Edward Copeland, ed., *Sense and Sensibility*, The Cambridge Edition of the Works of Jane Austen (Cambridge: Cambridge University Press, 2006), p. xxiv.

novel provides an amiably happy ending for both Dashwood sisters, but also a luxuriously happy one for Mrs. Jennings, who gets, as we shall see, all of her wishes, though sometimes in a comically topsy-turvy way.

Two Vulgar Women

To clarify the real complexity with which Mrs. Jennings's character is depicted and developed, it might be of value to compare her with that other vulgar, marriage-obsessed mother, Mrs. Bennet in *Pride and Prejudice*, whose character is presented with such acid dismissal at the famous end of Chapter i. The contrast there, the reader will remember, is with her apparently more ambivalently presented husband, that 'mixture of quick parts' whose wife will never understand him (I i 5). Her own character, however 'was less difficult to develope' (I i 5). Notice the loaded negatives: not 'much easier' but 'less difficult', giving a sense of the author presenting the character while, as it were, holding her nose; there is such aversion here. 'She was a woman of mean understanding, little information, and uncertain temper. When she was discontented she fancied herself nervous. The business of her life was to get her daughters married' (I i 5). Fifty words of neat character assassination— 'mean', 'little', 'uncertain', 'discontented', 'nervous'—from which only the most determined reading can rescue Mrs. Bennet. It is typical for long-term readers of Jane Austen to learn to see more from her point of view, since when one does the sums, the near-poverty of the family of five unmarried daughters, had Mr. Bennet died in Chapter ii instead of going to visit Mr. Bingley, shifts the emphasis on this 'business' of hers and makes Mr. Bennet's insouciance in the same chapter ('How so? how can it affect them?' (I i 4)) less charmingly offhand and more viciously irresponsible.

But there is no rescuing the character of Mrs. Bennet from the faults of her temperament or the vulgarity of her mind—her praising of her children in front of strangers, her sneering at the Lucas girls for their domestic skills, her cheerful acceptance of the prospect of a life of financial assistance from her hard-working brother—to say nothing of her moral indifference, and her social indifference also, to Lydia's having lived with George Wickham outside matrimony once matrimony has rescued the situation. One could go on: her virtues are few and her faults are many, and the novel does not work to minimize them, rarely lets her faults go un-noted, by husband, daughters or by the narrative. Her spirits, at the news of Lydia's patched-up marriage, are 'oppressively high', her reappearance at the head of her dinner table a source only of distress to her daughters (III viii 342). There is also, much earlier, in Volume I, the matter of her pressing Elizabeth to marry Mr. Collins with whom she could not possibly be happy. Though since it is also the one way in which the family can avert some of the consequences of the entail of the estate, that is not quite so clear-cut to a reader who has thought about the novel over time as it is to a new reader, reacting, along with Elizabeth, to Mr. Collins's drawbacks as a love interest. Nevertheless, even the most practically-minded reader will be shocked by the ill temper with which Mrs. Bennet greets the news of Mr. Collins marrying Charlotte Lucas instead, presented in her usual register of comic self-contradiction:

> In the first place, she persisted in disbelieving the whole of the matter; secondly, she was very sure that Mr. Collins had been taken in; thirdly, she trusted that they would never be happy together; and fourthly, that the marriage might be broken off. Two inferences, however, were plainly deduced from the whole; one, that Elizabeth was the cause of all the mischief; and the other, that she herself had been barbarously used by them all. (I xxiii 143)

This logical style of presenting her thinking dramatizes her own spectacular illogic, the illogic of a lawyer's daughter who can never be made to understand 'the nature of an entail', a legal commonplace that her own teenage daughters *can* understand (I xii 69). A careful reader might *feel for* this mother of five daughters who has 'no turn for economy' but teeters on the brink of poverty throughout the novel, but cannot *respect* her, anymore than—following her contemptuous husband's lead—her neighbours, or her daughters, can (III viii 340). Even tolerant Jane, that paragon, says once, '"Oh! that my dear mother had more command over herself..."' (II i 152). This lack of 'self-command', such a significant virtue for Jane Austen's endangered women, is all revealed in the opening chapters, and nothing in subsequent chapters rescues Mrs. Bennet from her failings. She provides much comedy, but she is always the 'woman of mean understanding [...] and uncertain temper' of Chapter i. The introduction opened, and closed, the book on Mrs. Bennet.

This is the introduction of Mrs. Jennings, on the other hand: she 'was a good-humoured, merry, fat elderly woman, who talked a great deal, seemed very happy, and rather vulgar' (I vii 40). Fat and elderly, unlike Mrs. Bennet who has been a notable beauty and is probably not much over forty-five when *Pride and Prejudice* begins, Mrs. Jennings could at first be a stock comic figure, and is that in part, but only in part. If her vulgarity is named, as Mrs. Bennet's is not, so is her happiness—it plays the role in her introduction played in Mrs. Bennet's by 'discontent' and 'nerves'. Long ago Mrs. Bennet captivated Mr. Bennet, not only by youth and beauty, but by 'the appearance of good humour' which youth and beauty can give but which in her is illusory (II xix 262). Not so in Mrs. Jennings. In the next chapter we learn that she:

> was a widow, with an ample jointure [she had married well] and had only two daughters, both of whom she had lived to see respectably married, and she had now therefore nothing to do but to marry all the rest of the world [...] she was always anxious to get a good husband for every pretty girl. (I viii 43)

What the reader might want to notice in all this is the openness of the language in which Mrs. Jennings, however 'vulgar' she is, is otherwise introduced ('good-humoured [...] happy [...] merry' versus Mrs. Bennet's crushing 'small information', etc. And the openness of her point of view: Mrs. Bennet (and this is understandable, she has five daughters and not much of a jointure to look forward to; Mrs. Jennings has her good marriage settlement and only two) thinks only of marrying her *own* daughters, and is shown again and again as being mean-spirited and competitive about the marriage opportunities of girls from other families; Mrs. Jennings on the other hand—that large-bodied, large-souled lady—is 'zealously active' in promoting 'weddings among all the young people of her acquaintance' (I viii 43).

Let's consider the meanings of that wish a little more: in a world in which marriage is the one attainable and desirable career option for women 'of small fortune' as Charlotte Lucas realistically reflects in *Pride and Prejudice*, how generous, how thoroughly good-hearted, such a set of aspirations as Mrs. Jennings's is, however embarrassing to the more refined—the Dashwoods and Lady Middleton and Colonel Brandon, all of whom would rather the case for the necessity of marriage were stated a little less baldly.[2] A deft move of the novel is that the more refined character to whom she is most often contrasted is her elder daughter, Lady Middleton, whose 'good breeding' (I vii 38) is sometimes more acceptable to the Dashwoods just because it is quieter, but who from the outset is described as insipid, and later as cold and selfish. (It is interesting that the novel's first volume introduces three pairs of sisters, and appears to foreground the vitality of the younger sister— Marianne, Mrs. Palmer, Lucy Steele—in each case.) Lady Middleton's cold selfishness is said to be a match for that of Fanny Dashwood— impressive! But the contrast between mother and daughter is not only between warmth and coldness, but between Lady Middleton's lack of interest in other people aside from her children, a lack of interest which is almost pathological. When the whole Middleton-Palmer-Jennings circle is in an uproar over Willoughby's mistreatment of Marianne in Volume II,

> Lady Middleton expressed her sense of the affair about once every day, or twice, if the subject occurred very often, by saying 'It is very shocking indeed!' and by means of this continual though gentle vent, was able not only to see the Miss Dashwoods from the first without the smallest emotion, but very soon to see them without recollecting a word of the matter. (II x 245)

She literally erases it from her memory, and it seems clear that no one but her children has any continuous existence in her thoughts at all. In contrast to this is Mrs. Jennings's assault on Colonel Brandon, meeting him weeks after his sudden departure for London in Volume I, with a volley of questions and demands which show that his mysterious trouble has been kept alive in her imagination, and her memory, all of this time: '"But, Colonel, where have you been to since we parted? And how does your business go on? Come, come, let's have no secrets among friends"' (II iv 186).

---

2   'Without thinking highly either of men or of matrimony, marriage had always been her object; it was the only honourable provision for well-educated young women of small fortune, and however uncertain of giving happiness, must be their pleasantest preservative from want' (I xxii 138).

The reader would be mistaken to think, as Marianne does, that this was a mere demand for gossip; the Colonel, who replies with 'his accustomary mildness' (II iv 186), does not think so, for surely it is a sense of her genuine goodness of heart, her care for her friends, that keeps the Colonel—a man, as we learn, as sensitive as Marianne and with much to be sensitive about—from being merely exasperated by Mrs. Jennings and her importunate questions and her misconception of his relationship with the younger Eliza. At some time previous to the opening of the novel, Colonel Brandon has learned to overlook Mrs. Jennings's vulgarity and to value her decency and humanity; and this is a lesson which the Dashwood sisters, thin-skinned and refined, like the Colonel, can learn also.

No one widely read in Jane Austen can fail to recognize that the capacity to retain a sympathetic sense of the existence of other people when not immediately confronted with them is of the highest importance to her. It has perhaps its finest and most warmly coloured expression in Anne Elliot's defence of women's loyalty to lost lovers near the close of *Persuasion* (Anne's longest speech in the novel, and one which not only moves Captain Wentworth to renew their engagement, but rouses the tender-hearted, grieving Captain Harville to cry, '"You are a good soul!"' (II xi 256)). This retaining of the imprint of others is one mark, in Jane Austen, of the 'good soul'. One of the ways *Pride and Prejudice* registers Mr. Darcy as a serious rather than an absurd character (though he is both at times) is at Rosings, where he demonstrates both that he has retained a strong sense of Elizabeth, and that he is willing to show it: '"I have had the pleasure of your acquaintance long enough to know, that you find great enjoyment in occasionally professing opinions which in fact are not your own,"' he says with some warmth as she sits at the piano with the—also somewhat smitten—Colonel Fitzwilliam (II viii 195). One might also mention here instances like Sir Thomas's remembering, in *Mansfield Park*, to have the fire laid in Fanny's room after their disagreement over Mr. Crawford, or his thinking to have Susan accompany her when she returns to Mansfield Park. A character with many weaknesses, pomposities, absurdities, who has made tragic errors in bringing up his own children, Sir Thomas is nevertheless marked more than once by this sense of the existence of others beyond the borders of the self, and of their continuous existence.

Such a sense marks Mrs. Jennings as a different kind of busybody
from, say, Miss Steele, who only wants to know how much the
Dashwoods' clothes cost them, or to have the whole story of Willoughby
and Marianne so that she can retail it to her friends. Mrs. Jennings *is* a
gossipy woman of course, and this proclivity produces much comedy—
'"Get it all out of her, my dear. She will tell you anything if you ask.
You see I cannot leave Mrs. Clarke"', she nudges Elinor when prevented
herself from talking to Nancy Steele after the big bust-up with the
Dashwoods (III ii 308). But she is much more: again and again, before
the reluctant Dashwood sisters (they are, after all, both teenagers) are
able to recognize her goodness of heart, the novel does so. In one of the
few instances in which Mrs. Dashwood behaves as if her experience of
forty years in the world had taught her anything, she describes Mrs.
Jennings to Elinor as 'a motherly good sort of woman'; Elinor, however,
squeamishly objects (while acknowledging her good heart) that '"she is
not a woman whose society can afford us pleasure, or whose protection
will give us consequence"' (II iii 177, 178). What Elinor refers to here is
that Mrs. Jennings is not a person of elegant manners or wide culture,
not the sort of reading, thinking, cultivated person that most Jane
Austen heroines admire and value and aspire to be. But this whole line
of discourse deserves attention. Later, when Elinor discovers to her
relief that 'excepting a few old city friends', Mrs. Jennings 'visited no
one, to whom an introduction could at all discompose the feelings of her
young companions', we might want to note that Elinor, the undoubted
centre of discernment and of emotional intelligence in the novel, is here
glancingly allied with the cold Lady Middleton (who regrets that the
old friends have not been dropped) (II v 191–92). Elinor also sounds
remarkably like Emma Woodhouse as that great snob muses absurdly
about how her sister Isabella's marrying into the Knightley family 'had
given them neither men, nor names, nor places, that could raise a blush'
(III vi 389).

Awareness of status, class, culture is nuanced in Jane Austen, and
every participant in the world of her novels must possess it in order to
survive, but Jane Austen thinks snobbishness is absurd even when it
is necessary—even when it is accurate. Elinor here is being observed
from a little distance, like Emma, as she weighs up the relative value
of 'consequence' and kindness. Just as the novel chooses to stand at a

slight, observant distance from the well-bred sisters when they refuse to gratify Mrs. Jennings's hospitable impulses on the journey to London, it distances Elinor here as she gives this relieved, but not entirely appealing, shrug at a near escape from the horrors of vulgarity.[3] That Lady Middleton is mentioned here is significant. The novel does not admire her, nor does Elinor. One of the effects of focusing in this way on Mrs. Jennings is that we can rescue Elinor from the charge sometimes made of her character, that she is too perfect: here we see that at nineteen—of course!—she still has much to learn.

And in the end Mrs. Jennings's real nobility of soul becomes impossible to miss, in a very rich harmonics of comic and serious strains, along with Elinor's, during Marianne's illness—it is their shared nursing of the terribly ill, beloved girl, which 'makes Elinor really love her' (III vii 348).[4] The reader is relieved that Elinor is finally catching up with how much real kindness, generosity, affectionateness and depth of feeling has always been present under the boisterous, unbeautiful exterior of the fat old woman. There is a section which moves from Elinor's consciousness, almost taking the free indirect style into Mrs. Jennings's head, as the older woman's own real anxiety over Marianne's danger is made explicit:

> Her heart was really grieved. The rapid decay, the early death of a girl so young, so lovely as Marianne, must have struck a less interested person with concern. On Mrs. Jennings's compassion, she had other claims. She had been for three months her companion, was still under her care, and she was known to have been greatly injured, and long unhappy. The distress of her sister too, particularly a favourite, was before her;—and as for their mother, when Mrs. Jennings considered that Marianne might probably be to *her* what Charlotte was to herself, her sympathy in *her* sufferings was very sincere. (III vii 354)

---

3   'Mrs. Jennings on her side treated them both with all possible kindness, was solicitous on every occasion for their ease and enjoyment, and only disturbed that she could not make them choose their own dinners at the inn, nor extort a confession of their preferring salmon to cod, or boiled fowls to veal cutlets' (II iv 182).

4   This moment stands in marked contrast to the novel's other more staged mentions of 'real love': at the end of Vol. I, Chapter iii, Marianne is convinced she might 'never see a man whom I can really love' (I iii 21) and in Vol. III, Chapter viii, Willoughby poses the rhetorical question to himself: ' had I really loved, could I have sacrificed my feelings to vanity, to avarice?' (III viii 363).

The whole-heartedness of this passage is distinctive: no Austenian irony, even, I think, in the unlikely comparison between Marianne and Charlotte. The novel is crying out here, like Captain Harville to Anne, 'you are a good soul!' and the index of this kind of soul-goodness is, as with Anne, the holding onto the feelings and thoughts—the lives—of others. Mrs. Jennings is thinking of Marianne's whole story, of Elinor's sisterly love, of Mrs. Dashwood's feeling for her younger daughter, and measuring it against the strongest heart-feeling of her own emotional life, her love for silly, good-natured Charlotte.

But the writing of the whole section which includes Marianne's illness and her recovery is simultaneously direct and emotionally powerful—and observant and, just glancingly, comic, even as it drives toward possible tragedy. A sharply painful segment of a long comic arc in which the girls' growing closeness to this absurd and improbable figure is observed. It is beautifully staged: Mrs. Jennings thinks that Marianne will die and surely her expectation, withheld from Elinor through an uncharacteristic tact, but communicated in her more usual incontinent fashion to her maid, is part of the brilliant presentation of Marianne's illness, in which the steep rise of her suffering and delirium, the depiction of Elinor's terror when Marianne becomes irrational and babbles incoherently about their mother and London all has to be attended to closely by the reader, for whom after however many readings Marianne's recovery is always an achievement and a relief. And surely a part of the technical production of that suspense, that uncertainty about these events, even for the re-reader who has long known the outcome, is the weight of Mrs. Jennings's pessimism, Mrs. Jennings who has nursed her husband in his last illness and perhaps has sat by many deathbeds. This pessimism adds substance to the undeniable drama of this episode, as the old lady's unwise communication to the maidservant is brought home to the waiting and exhausted Elinor through her second sleepless night: 'the servant [...] tortured her more, with hints of what her mistress had always thought' (III vii 353). On the last morning of suspense Mrs. Jennings herself can no longer resist confiding her belief that 'the severity and danger of this attack [was due] to the many previous weeks of indisposition' (III vii 355). Mrs. Jennings becomes explicit on what she takes to be Marianne's last day of life because she does not want to raise false hopes in Elinor, does not want to break *her* heart along with Marianne's.

And then there is Marianne's recovery, so hesitantly relayed—'About noon, however, [Elinor] began—but with a caution—a dread of disappointment [...] to fancy to hope she could perceive a slight amendment'—which enables the beautiful conclusion in which Mrs. Jennings, who like any elderly woman must have a great deal of store set by being right about illness, gives over that pleasure to share in Elinor's genuine relief at the recovery (III vii 355). There is no morbid or ghoulish tinge, and her presentation here is careful not to suggest any such thing; the maidservant may have been ghoulish, but Mrs. Jennings was not, nor is she stubborn: 'Mrs. Jennings [...] admitted with unfeigned joy, and soon with unequivocal cheerfulness, the probability of an entire recovery' (III vii 355–56).

The Vulgar Woman and the Lady: Two Matchmakers

So, having started with a comparison between Mrs. Jennings and Mrs. Bennet, I will close with a comparison between Mrs. Jennings and Emma, the vulgar woman and the born lady, both matchmakers. When Emma discusses her matchmaking proclivities with her father and Mr. Knightley, they both express horror at her choice of hobby, though for different reasons: Mr. Woodhouse seems—like Hamlet—to want 'no more marriages' ('"Pray do not make any more matches"') and laments her success with Miss Taylor and Mr. Weston, but Mr. Knightley feels that the activity is an improper one for a young unmarried woman—'"a worthy employment for a young lady's mind!"' (I i 10–11).

Discerning attachments between young people who have not announced their engagement is indeed allied, in Jane Austen's novels, with a certain coarseness of mind: Isabella in *Northanger Abbey* finding out flirtations, Mrs. Norris in *Mansfield Park* hinting about Julia and Mr. Crawford, Mrs. Clay in *Persuasion* and her insincere hints about Mr. Elliot and Elizabeth—and Mrs. Jennings, of course. One can prove her goodness without ever disproving her vulgarity. But her matchmaking is very different from Emma Woodhouse's, because it is founded in a realism about women's aspirations, their opportunities and expectations.

'"I never was very handsome [...] However I got a very good husband"', she declares cheerfully, and reminds her son-in-law Mr. Palmer, '"you have taken Charlotte off my hands, and cannot give her back again"' and discerns from Miss Steele that '"the Doctor is a single man"' (II iv 186; I xx 129; II x 247). The language, 'merry' like herself, nevertheless admits the hard necessities of life, its compromises and its constraints. Contrast this with Emma's hilariously misjudged comment to Harriet that she—Harriet, that simpleton—'"[understands] the force of influence pretty well"' (I iv 30) in marital matters, this being said while Emma herself, 'perverting the wit God gave her' as Mr. Knightley says, is industriously undermining every realistic possibility Harriet has for marriage, out of her own vanity and ignorance of the world.[5] Mr. Knightley's horror at her choice of matchmaking for a pastime deserves a second look: he realizes that there is something almost base about it, with its historic connection to pandering, and that in Emma's quixotic version it is as full of self-deceit and self-regard as Mrs. Elton's plans for Jane Fairfax's career; it comes from a mere wish to be doing something, like the Eltons. If, on the other hand, Mrs. Jennings's matchmaking is vulgar in the sense of 'common', it is also a reflection of her common sense.

The novel's end is in many ways nothing but a huge comic justification, a triumph, of Mrs. Jennings, for every girl (except poor Miss Steele) in whom she takes an interest, does marry. As she makes her Michaelmas visit to Delaford, Elinor has married the much-trailed 'Mr. F' and he is, not the curate, but the rector, of the parish, and the first marriage she planned in the novel, that of Marianne and Colonel Brandon, is well on its way to being achieved, since Marianne is married at nineteen, so within a year of that Michaelmas. Even Lucy Steele, for whom Mrs. Jennings wished a 'good husband', though she has now

---

5   Nora here creatively combines Mr. Knightley's words to Emma in Volume I: '"Upon my word, Emma, to hear you abusing the reason you have, is almost enough to make me think so too. Better be without sense, than misapply it as you do."' (I viii 67), and his words about Frank Churchill to her in Volume III: '"Mystery; Finesse —how they pervert the understanding! My Emma, does not every thing serve to prove more and more the beauty of truth and sincerity in all our dealings with each other?"' (III xv 486), along with Emma's estimate of herself in Volume III: 'She had herself been first with him for many years past. She had not deserved it; she had often been negligent or perverse, slighting his advice, or even wilfully opposing him, insensible of half his merits, and quarrelling with him because he would not acknowledge her false and insolent estimate of her own' (III xii 452).

been enlightened as to Lucy's real character and the qualities of her heart, even cold-hearted scheming Lucy Steele is well-married. Almost the last topic taken up by the novel is the promising future of Margaret Dashwood, as a girl for whom a good heart can wish a good husband, and we might linger over that Michaelmas visit for a second longer, for if Mrs. Jennings arrives a little earlier than the actual date of September 29, she will find that the old mulberry tree is still in season, and in a perfect orgy of wish-fulfilment, Mrs. Jennings can once again have the joy, along with the rewards of successful match-making, of 'stuffing' on the delicious fruit.[6]

---

6   Mrs. Jennings's memory of Delaford: '"Delaford is a nice place, I can tell you; exactly what I call a nice old fashioned place, full of comforts and conveniences; quite shut in with great garden walls that are covered with the best fruit-trees in the country: and such a mulberry tree in one corner! Lord! how Charlotte and I did stuff the only time we were there!"' (II viii 223).

5. Lady Susan

Lady Susan is about the adventures of a wicked aristocrat. That, even more than its epistolary form, makes it unique among Jane Austen's completed novels.[1] There are bad women in other novels—Lucy Steele in *Sense and Sensibility* is pretty bad, Mrs. Clay in *Persuasion* must be quite a schemer really, Mrs. Norris in *Mansfield Park* is one of the worst villains in fiction—but none of them are dastardly, in a James Bond villain way ('Ha! Ha! Now you are in my power!')—and no one else is an aristocrat. Lady Catherine de Bourgh, who, like Lady Susan, is the daughter of a nobleman, is a troublemaker rather than a villainess. As often noted, Jane Austen did not as a writer spend much time on, or give much attention to, the aristocracy.[2] She seems to share her heroine Anne Elliot's reluctance to follow in the train of aristocrats, preferring the gentry and the middle classes. Lady Susan, a character created probably in Jane Austen's late teens, looks back to the villainesses of eighteenth-century fiction, the wicked Lady Bellaston who tries to steal Tom Jones away from Sophia Western, Lady Booby who makes inappropriate advances to Joseph Andrews, and perhaps even to real-life scandalous aristocratic ladies like Georgiana, Duchess of Devonshire. Lady Susan can be compared, too, to the trouble-making aristocratic ladies featured in the novels of Austen's contemporaries such as Mrs. Radcliffe, Fanny

---

1   For a recent assessment of Lady Susan's force of personality, see William Galperin, '*Lady Susan*, Individualism and the (Dys)functional Family', *Persuasions*, 31 (2009), 47–58, http://jasna.org/publications/persuasions/no31/lady-susan-individualism-and-the-dysfunctional-family/

2   For Jane Austen's dismissive attitude to the aristocracy, see, for example, David Spring, 'Interpreters of Jane Austen's Social World', in *Jane Austen: New Perspectives*, ed. by Janet Todd (New York and London: Holmes and Meier, 1983), pp. 53–72: 'Her novels are [...] not much populated with aristocratic figures. Moreover, when they appear, they are almost invariably silly' (p. 59); for Austen as political radical, see Claudia L. Johnson, *Jane Austen: Women Politics, and the Novel* (Chicago and London: Chicago University Press, 1988).

       https://doi.org/10.11647/OBP.0216.05

Burney and Maria Edgeworth. But these writers use their wicked ladies as a foil to their more virtuous heroines, none places a wicked aristocratic woman at the centre of their novel, as the main character, the figure whose experiences we know the most about. That is the distinctiveness, and the strangeness, of *Lady Susan*.

And, of course, Lady Susan is an epistolary heroine, so that like Samuel Richardson's Pamela and Clarissa, her experiences are given to us in a steady stream of her own words.[3] At the time that Jane Austen was writing *Lady Susan*, probably the mid-1790s, it is possible that the early forms of *Sense and Sensibility* and *Pride and Prejudice* were still in epistolary form—there isn't any way, I think, of being certain about this—but what is certain is that, within a few years of writing *Lady Susan*, Jane Austen would abandon the fully epistolary style. *The Watsons*, which was written in 1804–05 about the time she was making a fair copy of *Lady Susan* and putting it away, has an omniscient narrator, the witty, but compassionate third-person narrator typical of the Austen novel. This would show readers a new way of getting to know a character by working its way unobtrusively into the character's thoughts, as well as by showing her speech and actions. I wonder whether in this process of changing methods *Lady Susan* may not have played a vital role. Jane Austen learned for good how confining novels-in-letters are, and I think it was *Lady Susan* which taught her that, because she learned in this little novel that, however much fun it is to create wicked and hypocritical characters, it is difficult to remain for long inside the head of such a central figure. I think she came gradually to find Lady Susan's machinations not amusing but repellent. And while this process gives us today's novel which is, I think, much more repellent than it is amusing, my guess is that it also gave her a shortcut realization to the way in which she really wanted to write character, and the nuanced, unexaggerated, complex characters which she would present to us, in the freer form of

---

3   For further discussion of *Lady Susan* as epistolary fiction, see Deborah Kaplan, 'Female Friendship and Epistolary Form: "Lady Susan" and the Development of Jane Austen's Fiction', *Criticism*, 29.2 (1987), 163–78; Patricia Spacks, 'Female Resources: Epistles, Plot and Power', *Persuasions*, 9 (1987), 88–98, http://www.jasna. org/persuasions/printed/number9/spacks.htm. For more general discussion of the genre, see Joe Bray, *The Epistolary Novel: Representations of Consciousness* (London: Routledge, 2003), https://doi.org/10.4324/9780203130575; Chapter five focuses on Jane Austen.

third-person indirect speech. So we can thank Lady Susan, that bad, bad mother, for being a kind of midwife at the birth of such rich characters as Elinor and Marianne Dashwood, Elizabeth and Jane Bennet.

Not that Lady Susan is not a rich and complex character. I will come on to that. First, I will just sketch a brief plot summary: recently widowed, as we meet her in Letter I, Lady Susan has found it suddenly necessary to invite herself to Churchill, the country house of her brother- and sister-in-law, the Vernons, who have a large family of young children. This is awkward—she tried to prevent the Vernons' marriage, and Mrs. Vernon knows it—but necessary, as she is in danger of being ejected from another country house nearer London, where she has flirted so openly with the gentleman of the house, Mr. Manwaring, that Mrs. Manwaring is after her blood. We learn this in her letters to her London friend, Mrs. Johnson, a woman of Lady Susan's age (thirty-five)—married to a rich and elderly man. At the Vernons, we learn from Mrs. Vernon's letters to her mother, that Lady Susan behaves with charm and decorum, and that quite unwillingly even resentful Mrs. Vernon is finding it difficult to dislike her quite as much as she wants to. Mr. Vernon is won over from the start, by Lady Susan's beauty, her apparent warmth, and—this is crucial—her charm.

Lady Susan has no fortune. This isn't said, but one imagines she was brought up among spendthrift aristocrats and that she encouraged her late husband to spend too freely, as they have had to sell their ancestral home, the Castle—perhaps, indeed, it was Lady Susan's ancestral home? She seems to have no hereditary nest egg, and—and this is something we should reflect on later—no family of her own to fall back on, no parents, sisters, brothers, cousins. She has a daughter, Frederica, whom she has neglected terribly, and who she wants to marry off to the rich but catastrophically stupid Sir James Martin, a young man who is actually in love with *her*, with Lady Susan, but whom she can manipulate into almost any action at all. Frederica does not want to marry Sir James, but she is terrified of her mother. Running away from school in an attempt to get right away from both of them, Frederica is caught and eventually brought to Churchill, the home of the Vernons, much to her mother's displeasure. For also there is Mrs. Vernon's younger brother, Reginald De Courcy, a young man who had heard so much ill of Lady Susan that he had to come and see her for himself and then found himself entrapped, as really in the novel every man must be—maybe every woman too—by Lady Susan's beauty and her charm. The elder De Courcys, his parents, and Mrs. Vernon, his sister, are appalled at the prospect of his being in love with a woman ten years his senior and of such a scandalous reputation. Everyone seems to know she cared nothing for her husband and flirted with every man in sight throughout her marriage. And everyone knows that she has been a cold and neglectful mother. But Lady Susan's marvellous talent for explaining things away keeps Reginald under her spell, even though sixteen-year-old Frederica falls in love with the handsome young man so quickly that she commits the unforgiveable sin—and we all know how terrible this is in the eighteenth century from our reading of the other novels—of writing a letter to a person of the opposite sex, and asking for his help in preventing her marriage to the booby Sir James.

That may be enough plot to be going on with, but, just to tie things up, Lady Susan's schemes to marry this very rich young man, whom she despises, are overturned when he learns, rather melodramatically, the extent of her flirtations with a married man. It's important that, once he learns the truth about Lady Susan, Reginald never sees her again; if he saw her, he would probably be bamboozled all over again. What is shown importantly throughout this little novel is that it is nigh on impossible to resist Lady Susan when you are in her company. This is one of the interests given to the novel by the epistolary form, as the letters which are not between Lady Susan and Mrs. Johnson (whether they are from Lady Susan's fans or her enemies) tend to reflect, and comment on, her spellbinding effects. 'I was certainly not disposed to admire her', admits her sister-in-law, 'but I cannot help feeling that she possesses an uncommon union of Symmetry, Brilliancy & Grace' (Letter VI 11). And Reginald De Courcy, who before he met her referred to her contemptuously as the 'most accomplished coquette in England' (Letter IV 8), is, a few weeks later, eating his words and telling his terrified parents, that 'the World has most grossly injured' Lady Susan, in supposing her motives to be anything but the purest and most disinterested (Letter XIV 25).

Jane Austen here must be exploring something like the effects she will work with in her early presentation of Wickham in *Pride and Prejudice*:

the total stunner, knocking them down like ninepins. We'll remember that an early title of *Pride and Prejudice* was *First Impressions*. Even on those determined to dislike her, Lady Susan's first impression is one of total enchantment. It is a rare moment anywhere in Jane Austen when we learn in detail what anyone looks like—Emma has 'the true hazel eye' (I v 39), Anne Elliot's and Elizabeth Bennet's eyes are dark, Marianne is tall, Mary Crawford tiny—but there is so much left to the imagination. However, in a letter to her brother, Mrs. Vernon has in all honesty to admit that her hated sister-in-law, an uninvited and unwelcome guest, whose star quality will obviously soak up all male attention wherever she goes, including at Mrs. Vernon's dinner table, 'is really excessively pretty [...] I have seldom seen so lovely a woman [...] She is delicately fair, with fine grey eyes & dark eyelashes [...] one would not suppose her more than five & twenty, tho' she must in fact be ten years older' (Letter VI 11). She may be ruefully thinking that, worn out as she must be by childbirth, no one would say that of her. And even more she confesses to Lady Susan's charm: 'her countenance is absolutely sweet, & her voice & manner winningly mild' (Letter VI 11). This is the effect she has in person, even on Mrs. Vernon's 'resentful heart' (Letter VI 12); her presence charms both men and women.

But *by letter*, she cannot charm anyone, unless, like her friend Mrs. Johnson, they are as unscrupulous as she is. And that is the fascination of the epistolary form as used here, where, in the letters *about* her, we see how she can dazzle, but in the main correspondence—of forty-one letters in all, seventeen are between Lady Susan and Mrs. Johnson, to whom she is wonderfully frank—there she shows us her heart. Although I hope to raise some sympathy for her later by talking about her situation, when she reveals her character in these letters we can only reel back in horror. My original exciting plan about this lecture was to give Lady Susan the famous 'psychopath test', which is always so worrying when you take it and turn out to be at least fifty percent psychopath, although you are given the reassuring coda that 'if you are worried by your results on this test, then you can't be a psychopath anyway, because a psychopath wouldn't worry'. Then in my researches I learned that someone had thought of this back in the 1980s, when scholarship on the minor works really took off and a 1989 essay proved Lady Susan to be a complete psychopath.[4] She has 'superficial charm, adequate intelligence, absence of anxiety, insincerity, lack of remorse or shame, antisocial behaviour, selfishness and egocentricity, lack of capacity for love, unemotional sexual behaviour, lack of long term life plans'. [5] This is all true. But I have decided not to use the categories that come from the *Diagnostic and Statistical Manual of Mental Disorders*, but some older categories, one used by Mr. Darcy when he has already begun, only half-consciously, to compare Elizabeth Bennet to Miss Bingley, and to the other accomplished young women of his acquaintance: 'Whatever bears affinity to cunning is despicable' (I viii 44).

Here is a passage from Lady Susan's first letter, to her brother-in-law, proposing a visit. The re-reader knows that she really, at this point, has nowhere else to go. Covering that up is just saving face, and is not a million miles away from Emma's stratagems for finding a place to dispose of Harriet after Mr. Knightley's proposal to *her*. We would never condemn a woman in the eighteenth century for trying to put the best possible gloss on her actions, or wanting to give a good 'first impression', would we? Here comes Lady Susan, that 'dangerous woman':

> My kind friends here are most affectionately urgent with me to prolong my stay, but their hospitable & chearful dispositions lead them too much into society for my present situation & state of mind; & I impatiently look forward to the hour when I shall be admitted into your delightful retirement. (Letter I 3)

Here is the de-sentimentalized version of her situation, which she gives to her friend Mrs. Johnson:

> I take Town in my way to that insupportable spot, a Country Village, for I am really going to Churchill.—Forgive me, my dear friend, it is my last resource. Were another place in England open to me, I would prefer it.—Charles Vernon is my aversion, & I am afraid of his wife. At Churchill, however I must remain until I have something better in view. (Letter II 5–6)

The two letters were probably written the same day.

---

4   Beatrice Anderson, 'The Unmasking of Lady Susan', in *Jane Austen's Beginnings: The Juvenilia and Lady Susan*, ed. by J. David Grey (Michigan: Ann Arbor, 1989), pp. 193–203.

5   Anderson, 'The Unmasking of Lady Susan', p. 194.

Much could be said about Mrs. Johnson, Lady Susan's friend and confidante. There are only a few letters from her, and I almost wish there were none, and we could intuit the other end of the correspondence from what Lady Susan deems it safe to say to her. From Mrs. Johnson's letters we learn that this young married woman can hardly wait for her husband to die, looks forward to his absences, is rather afraid of him, and has nothing but enthusiasm for her friend Lady Susan's plots and schemes. This must be the very young Jane Austen building up— out of books, as so many of her young writings did—a picture of the eighteenth-century *beau monde*, the '"thoughtless, gay set"' whom Mrs. Smith in *Persuasion* will ruefully describe, the group among whom for Mr. Elliot '"To do the best for himself passed as a duty"' (II ix 218).

Mrs. Johnson is thoughtless and perhaps heartless. Of a jilted young woman, she comments 'we both laughed heartily at her disappointment' (Letter IX 17–18), making the reader think of Mary Crawford's conniving in her brother's determination to make '"a small hole in Fanny Price's heart"' (II vi 267), and she encourages Lady Susan to marry Reginald for his money and to scandalize his stuffy relations. But whether because we see more of Lady Susan, with almost four times as many letters, her amorality has a hardened, polished, professional quality, while Mrs. Johnson is just a promising amateur. I want to look in detail at some of the later letters in the novel that convey this vitreous wickedness, but surely we are struck almost immediately by Lady Susan's coldness about her daughter:

> Frederica [...] was born to be the torment of my life [...] You are very good in taking notice of Frederica [...] but [...] I am far from exacting so heavy a sacrifice. She is a stupid girl, & has nothing to recommend her [...] I hope to see her the wife of Sir James within a twelvemonth. (Letters II 5; VII 13)

There is a way of responding to Lady Susan's character which marks quite a lot of critical discussion, including Margaret Drabble's introduction to the Penguin edition which is where I read the novel first, in which Lady Susan's 'vitality' is seen as rendering her attractive. As Drabble puts it, the 'opposition' to her badness, 'is dull'; so, bad as she is, 'she runs away with the novel'.[6] A panel of experts who discussed

---

6   Jane Austen, *Lady Susan, The Watsons, Sanditon*, ed. by Margaret Drabble (London: Penguin, 1974), p. 14.

the novel in the USA about twenty-five years ago took the line 'Go for it, Lady Susan!', largely because those characters who are ranged against her could be seen as being stuffy and insipid, merely embodying, as Lady Susan says witheringly, 'that great word, "Respectable"' (Letter II 5).[7] Now, I don't feel any sneaking sympathy for Lady Susan as a character, though I do sense along with these other readers that Lady Susan's voice is a remarkable one, and that the novel as a whole is, like a lot of the very early juvenilia, such as *Love and Freindship*, created with a vitality and energy and a commitment to what Jane Austen is doing as a very young, hugely gifted author. But the book about Lady Susan closes with a decisive slamming shut of the whole proceedings, such as does not happen in any other work, I think? Even the surviving heroine of *Love and Freindship*, Laura, that whirlwind of self-indulgent sensibility whom the young author has mocked for thirty eventful pages, retires to a Highland village and has a final letter full of contentedly melancholy news. But Lady Susan is silenced, as if Jane Austen did not want anything more to do with her wayward heroine. And yet it cannot mean nothing that around the same time as she was writing *The Watsons*, which in my view is much more in harmony with her later novels, in 1805 in a household in which paper was not squandered, she made a fair copy of *Lady Susan*. So she was not *ashamed* of it, she thought it worth preserving.

Before I say more about Lady Susan herself, I'd like to talk about that question Margaret Drabble raises, about what else there is in the novel to counter this—let's say 'impressive'—female character? And to that end I would like to look at the De Courcy family. Recall that Lady Susan took 'some pains' to prevent the marriage between her brother-in-law Charles Vernon and the young Catherine De Courcy, daughter of Sir Reginald De Courcy, baronet (Letter V 9). The whole family knows this, though we don't know (but can imagine!) what means Lady Susan must have employed. Catherine Vernon is probably around thirty, happily married, with an unstipulated, and, I would argue, a carefully unstipulated, number of children.[8] To a degree we see them through Lady Susan's

---

7   *Jane Austen's Beginnings*, ed. Grey, p. 228.

8   For the significance of casual enumeration of children in Jane Austen's fiction, see Christopher Ricks, 'Jane Austen and the Business of Mothering', in *Essays in Appreciation* (New York and Oxford: Oxford University Press, 1998), pp. 90–113, especially pp. 91, 110.

(perfunctory) attention: she knows all their names already, though does not repeat them, except for the youngest, who is named after her late husband, who 'I take on my lap & sigh over, for his dear Uncle's sake' (Letter V 10). The indefiniteness of the number demonstrates both Lady Susan's real indifference to them and, perhaps, the extent of Catherine Vernon's maternal commitments: they must all be under five, as she has been married less than six years.

Mrs. Vernon is the second-most prolific letter-writer in the novel, and her letters, to her mother, apart from one to her brother, are much longer and fuller of incident than Lady Susan's, and it is through her letters that we know most of what we know of the story, though after the action moves from Churchill, from the country village to London, there is only one more—one last, delighted—letter from her responding to the news that Lady Susan and her brother 'are really separated—& for ever' (Letter XLI 73).

Mrs. Vernon is clearly an affectionate wife, mother, daughter and sister, I don't think the reader of the novel could have any doubt of that; nor of her intelligence, and even quickness of observation, as she swiftly notes both Lady Susan's effect on her brother's heart, and her brother's effect on Frederica's: 'I so very often see her eyes fixed on his face with a remarkable expression of pensive admiration' (Letter XVIII 34). And she sees through Lady Susan pretty fast, while never ceasing to acknowledge her skill as a dissimulator: 'Here she pretended to cry.—I was out of patience with her' (Letter XXIV 52). Of course, as Lady Susan recognizes, Mrs. Vernon's ability to see through her flows out of her own jealousy: at this point in the novel the men at Churchill, Mrs. Vernon's husband and her brother, are both unable to see Lady Susan as anything but beautiful, intelligent, fascinating (true), as a delicate, drooping flower (false), and this must be galling; this must make it easier to penetrate Lady Susan's elegant veneer.

I cannot pretend that Catherine Vernon is a genuinely interesting character in her own right. I wonder if we might want to decide that the young Jane Austen has not yet learnt how to make characters both virtuous and interesting? Soon enough she will find this talent: Elinor Dashwood, Colonel Brandon, Jane Bennet—I could go on and on. However, in the juvenilia—and she was probably not yet twenty when she wrote *Lady Susan*—the morally upright characters are usually relegated to a minor role: Miss Lesley's confidante in *Lesley Castle*, whose letters are so exemplary and kind but not very memorable, or the mother in *Love and Freindship*, who is thoughtful and kind and wise, and quickly moved out of the limelight so that her daughter can learn from, and the reader can laugh at, the long, long tale of the absurd adventures of Laura and Philippa. What interests Jane Austen at this stage of her development is just that absurdity, hypocrisy, self-contradiction and self-seeking. Austen's juvenilia abound with vain, silly, ridiculous people and especially ridiculous women, young and old. Ridiculous and obnoxious, like Lady Greville in 'Letter From A young Lady in distress'd Circumstances to her freind' who tells the impoverished heroine that 'It is not my way to find fault with people because they are poor, for I always think that they are more to be despised and pitied than blamed for it, especially if they cannot help it' (*Juvenilia* 198), or the second Lady Lesley (also called Susan!) who tells her correspondent while on a visit to Scotland that 'I have been plagued ever since I came here with tiresome visits from a parcel of Scotch wretches [...] I hate everything Scotch' (*Juvenilia* 159). The few sensible, admirable people in these early works pale in comparison.

    This could be what happens in *Lady Susan*, but I don't think it is, quite. What we can't help noticing about Catherine Vernon is that, while lacking vivacity, she possesses a quality which her charming sister-in-law Lady Susan utterly lacks: she is genuinely interested in other people. It is not only respectability and a horror of scandal that distances her from Lady Susan: it is her real fear for what trouble that lady might bring on Catherine Vernon's brother, her parents and her whole family, whom she loves. And she has a very clear sense of the harm Susan already has done to her own daughter, to poor Frederica. Her mistrust of Susan's power is not just jealousy or envy, but is a just sense of what kind of havoc such a manipulative person might—no, has already wreaked—on her environment: 'I never saw any creature look so frightened in my life as Frederica when she entered the room [...] I am more angry with her than ever since I have seen her daughter.—The poor girl looks so unhappy that my heart aches for her' (Letter XVII 31–32). It won't have escaped your notice, of course, that nice, kind, well behaved Mrs. Vernon is as observant of Lady Susan's doings as if she were a policewoman staking out the house instead of its mistress, and I want to end by talking a little about Lady Susan's situation, as distinct from her character—her situation as the target of so much surveillance, as the main attraction.

But first let's look at the rest of the De Courcy family, and the flurry of letters that follows Catherine Vernon's warning to her mother that she thinks Reginald in danger from Lady Susan: 'I really grow quite uneasy my dearest Mother about Reginald [...] They are now [...] frequently engaged in long conversations together' (Letter XI 20). The contents of this letter are meant to be kept from the elderly and infirm Sir Reginald, the head of the family and young Reginald's father, but in a sudden lively outburst of plot, a cold keeps Lady De Courcy from being the first reader of the letter, and so Catherine Vernon's letter of guarded concern, Letter XI, is followed by Letter XII, from Sir Reginald to his son. This letter seems to me masterly on Jane Austen's part. We might want to remember here that she had been reading Dr. Johnson since childhood, and here she invokes his great combination of eloquence and simplicity of expression.[9] The letter wrings the reader's heart, because it is sorrowful and not angry, hurt but not threatening: this is not a stuffy man worried about the world's opinion of his son, this is a loving father fearful for his coming to harm:

> My Ability of distressing you during my Life, would be a species of revenge to which I should hardly stoop [...] I honestly tell you my Sentiments & Intentions. I do not wish to work on your Fears, but on your Sense & Affection.—It would destroy every comfort of my Life, to know that you were married to Lady Susan Vernon. (Letter XII 22)

What could be more naked and more pleading than this letter? It is followed by the mildly comic lament from Lady De Courcy about the cold which kept her from pre-empting all this by snatching her daughter's letter out of her husband's hands, and finally we have the letter from young Reginald, one of three altogether (the other two are his two-pronged goodbye to Lady Susan at the novel's end) from him which appear in the novel. All three letters mark him out as the sort of priggish young man whom a Lady Susan would really enjoy making

---

9   For Austen's assimilation of Dr. Johnson's style, see Cris Yelland, *Jane Austen: A Style in History* (London: Routledge, 2018), pp. 93–130, https://doi.org/10.4324/9780429486067

mincemeat of; it is only in his kindness to Frederica that Reginald is
appealing, I think, but he is very young, clever but inexperienced, and
in love, though he doesn't yet realize it: where the reader grasps it,
despite his quite honest assurances to his father that he 'can have no
view in remaining with Lady Susan than to enjoy for a short time [...]
the conversation of a Woman of high mental powers' (Letter XIV 25).
What the reader notes before his short letter closes is the way in which
he has picked up Lady Susan's tricks of speech, one of the surest signs of
infatuation, mocked by Jane Austen in the case of Miss Bingley echoing
Mr. Darcy and Isabella Thorpe repeating Captain Tilney's words. Lady
Susan, he tells his father, against all the evidence, is a truly affectionate
mother: 'but because she has not the blind & weak partiality of most
Mothers, she is accused of wanting Maternal Tenderness' (Letter XIV
26). Lady Susan's words exactly, and, what's more, her views; Reginald
concludes, unaware of the irony of his words, 'Every person of Sense,
however, will know how to value & commend her well directed affection'
(Letter XIV 26–27).

Luckily for his health, Sir Reginald, who has never heard Lady Susan's
voice and cannot recognize its rhythms in every phrase, is appeased by
this: but the reader—a person of sense—knows her well by now, knows
Lady Susan's scarily unshakeable plans for her daughter's marriage to
Sir James Martin, despite the misery she knows this will plunge the poor
child into. 'I hope to see her the wife of Sir James within a twelvemonth'
(Letter VII 13), she writes her friend, and this does not change, except
to be speeded up into a matter of weeks, or even days, even though
the mother knows that her daughter, as her quick perceptions where
her own interests are concerned soon reveal, is in love with Reginald
De Courcy. Nor does this knowledge stop this affectionate mother from
attempting to entrap Reginald into an engagement with herself.

Frederica's wretched letter to Reginald (Letter XXI) is completely
against the rules of conduct for young ladies. Widely-read courtesy
books such as *The Lady's Preceptor* held as their first rule for young ladies
as letter writers, 'Never unless upon some singular Emergency which
may warrant it, to write to anyone but of your own Sex [...] nor to anyone
whatsoever without the Permission of those under whose Jurisdiction
you may be'.[10] This transgressive letter comes at the midpoint of the

---

10 Abbé d'Ancourt, *The Lady's Preceptor or A Letter to a Lady of Distinction* (London: J.
Watts, 1743), p. 63.

novel, and is its turning point, for though Lady Susan's machinations and her magic bewitch Reginald all over again, there is something heartfelt and sincere in the letter:

> I am very miserable about Sir James Martin [...] if you do not take my part [...] I shall be half-distracted [...] I would rather work for my bread than marry him.—I do not know how to apologise enough for this Letter, I know it is taking so great a liberty, I am aware how dreadfully angry it will make Mama, but I must run the risk. (Letter XXI 41–42)

Its misery has stirred something more tender and more noble in Reginald than his erotically charged submission to Lady Susan.

Frederica's heartrending cascade of commas—'I do not know [...], I know [...], I know'—is followed in the novel by Lady Susan's fury: she had 'actually written to him' (Letter XXII 44). We'll return to this fury, and its exact cause, but let's jump ahead to the next letter, in which Catherine Vernon whoops with joy at what seems an irreparable rift between her brother and Lady Susan: 'The affair which has given us so much anxiety is drawing to a happy conclusion' (Letter XXIII 45). What is important in the letter, though, is less the sister's premature triumph than the brother's suddenly unpriggish, unaffected kindness to the poor young girl, whom he has belatedly realized is the most vulnerable person in the house, and in the novel: 'remember what I tell you of Frederica,' he tells his sister; 'you must make it your business to see justice done her' (Letter XXIII 46). Suddenly here, among all these middle-aged jealousies and anxieties, are the young hearts crying who will become so central to Jane Austen's later work.

But neither of these decent, moral, possibly a little unexciting, siblings reckons here on the powers which Lady Susan can still unleash. Once she has reeled Reginald back in with one of her explanations, in which her sexual magnetism must play a very large part, she sits writing to Mrs. Johnson, and plotting her revenge on them all:

> I cannot forgive him [Reginald] such an instance of Pride; & am doubtful whether I ought not to punish him, by dismissing him at once [...] or by marrying & teizing him for ever [...] I have many things to compass. I must punish Frederica, & pretty severely too, for her application to Reginald;—I must punish him for receiving it so favourably, & for the rest of his conduct. I must torment my Sister-in-law for the insolent triumph of her Look & Manner. (Letter XXV 57)

What I think we want to notice here is the almost universal hatred by which Lady Susan lives: everyone is her rival or her enemy, actual or potential, unless they are her dupe. Where she does not hate, it is only because she feels too much contempt for hatred to come into play. This is terribly ugly to watch, and it is hard not to think that Jane Austen herself, clever and cool as she was, from, as E. M. Forster says, 'a hard humorous family', grew horrified at what she had made when she made Lady Susan.[11] Why else would she race her, as she does, to her conclusion, the two and a half pages of omniscient narration in which she ties things up, and ties the knot between Lady Susan and that despised booby, her intended son-in-law, Sir James Martin? It is the kind of metafictional last hurdle which she also jumps in *Northanger Abbey*, where she wittily notices that the reader will 'see, in the tell-tale compression of the pages before them, that we are all hastening together to perfect felicity' (II xvi 259)—well, not quite to 'perfect felicity', in this case. The reader of *Lady Susan* is left to wonder 'Whether Lady Susan was, or was not happy in her second Choice [...] for who would take her assurance of it, on either side of the question?' (Conclusion 77). This finally relegates her to the fate of all liars, not, finally, to be believed. Even by the reader.

I don't want to leave her just there, though. As with many great novels—and this, too, though small and horrible, is touched with Jane Austen's greatness—the character at the heart seems to have the kind of kicking life that will not allow her to be forgotten. Whatever the novel tells us at the end, I don't think Lady Susan thinks of herself as a liar. No, she thinks of herself as eloquent. 'If I am vain of any thing, it is of my eloquence', she says to Mrs. Johnson (Letter XVI 30). There is a strange naivete in this self-belief. When, she thinks aloud to her friend that she 'shall be able to make [her] story as good as [Frederica's]' (Letter XVI 30), it gives her not a moment's anxiety that the difference in their 'stories' is that Frederica's is *true* and hers is not. So used is she to performing emotions that it does not occur to her that others' displays of emotion might be based on real feeling, or, if it does occur, it is as a cause of contempt. Of Frederica's feeling for Reginald, she writes, 'Her feelings are tolerably lively, & she is so charmingly artless in their display, as to

---

11   E. M. Forster, *Abinger Harvest and England's Green and Pleasant Land* (London: Andre Deutsch, 1996), p. 156.

afford the most reasonable hope of her being ridiculed & despised by every Man who sees her' (Letter XIX 36).

This is what it is like inside Lady Susan's head, where there is no place for trust, or truth, or tenderness. But what is in a way tragic is that this woman is far, far from stupid. Like Emma Woodhouse, who at ten could answer questions which puzzled her sister at sixteen, she runs rings round those she lives among, not only by her sex appeal but by her wit. It is her intelligence which is universally recognized: Reginald is spellbound by her talk as well as by her beauty; even Mrs. Vernon is frequently dazzled by her words. But what Lady Susan has is a raw, almost animal kind of intelligence, which is conspicuously unschooled. Over and over she laments her lack of a proper education, even of the vapid sort she wishes Frederica to attain:

> I want her to play & sing with some portion of Taste [...] I was so much indulged in my infant years that I was never obliged to attend to anything, & consequently am without those accomplishments which are necessary to finish a pretty Woman. (Letter VII 13)

That is what she thinks is missing in her: her education having been so lacking that she does not have the least sense of what it is she truly lacks, the affectionate disposition and strong feelings which Jane Austen would give to Elinor Dashwood, a heroine first imagined only a little while after Lady Susan. Elinor, we are told, knows how to control her feelings; Lady Susan knows how to manipulate the feelings of others, and how to trample over them.

But somewhere in those indulgent early years Lady Susan gained a terrifyingly acute sense of how dangerous the world is for unprotected women and how they must take care, whatever their real wishes and real actions, to maintain some semblance of outward respectability, some appearance of self-control. What enrages her about Frederica's behaviour with Reginald is not that it is *wrong* in any serious way, but that it is unconventional. Behaving herself with no regard for the deeper connections of blood or family, Susan Vernon is horrified by her daughter's really quite courageous flouting of convention. This indulged, spoiled, highborn child who has grown into a cold and unloving mother has missed not only the lessons in music and languages that 'are necessary to finish a pretty Woman', but the education of the heart that is always Jane Austen's real subject. What has happened to

Lady Susan, alone among Jane Austen's unprotected women struggling to make a place for themselves in a dangerous world, is that she herself has mutated into one of the dangers.

6. In Sickness and in Health: Courting and Nursing in Some Jane Austen Novels

I'm going to be talking about the role of illness in Jane Austen's novels, but I want to begin with her own last illness: not so much the controversy about what exactly the illness was (though I will touch on that) as what her experience of illness, and its treatment, was. Her letters rarely complain about her symptoms, more often joking than complaining about what sound like alarming experiences, but they do describe them, and it is possible to use stray remarks in her letters to build up a picture of what the last year and a half of her life, the part really marked by illness, was like.

To give those last years a context: as many of you may know, Jane Austen was born in the rectory of Steventon, Hampshire, in 1775 and was one of seven children. Her brothers, except for one brother who was mentally and physically disabled, all married, but she and her sister Cassandra did not. In a phrase that is perhaps no longer in use they 'remained at home', though home moved several times, not always to their liking. She wrote three novels in her twenties which were not published until she was over thirty, and three further novels in the years leading up to her death, by which time she was living with her mother, who was a lifelong hypochondriac, and sister in another Hampshire village, Chawton. The novels were published anonymously ('By a Lady') but by 1816, when she had turned forty, a number of people were in on the secret of their authorship.

© Nora Bartlett, CC BY 4.0   https://doi.org/10.11647/OBP.0216.06

Her biographer Claire Tomalin says that 'Early in this difficult year Jane began to feel unwell in some unspecified way'.[1] Her letters, and other family papers, mention backache, abdominal pain, gastric upsets, lack of appetite, headache, sudden rises and drops of temperature. She herself comments on a blotchy complexion; 'black and white', she calls it in one letter, trying to make light of it but obviously in distress.[2] As a young girl she had been feted for her complexion, and she minded this change in her appearance. She was dead within four months.

In 1964 the eminent medical historian, Sir Zachary Cope, suggested that her illness had been Addison's disease, a tuberculosis of the adrenal glands.[3] Another famous sufferer was John F. Kennedy, a man who otherwise seems to have had little in common with Jane Austen, and who, living a century and a half later, was treated with cortisone. Addison's disease would explain the blotchy complexion, the diarrhoea and some of the other symptoms. But more recently there have been suggestions that an earlier, mild illness mentioned in her letters was actually the onset of a cancer that eventually produced these Addison's-type effects. In either case, she was suffering from an illness that the medicine of her time was unable to cure.

Unable to cure—but not unable to treat. Those of us who are familiar with Jane Austen's novels will remember that dependence on medical advice, fussing about one's own health or that of others, is frequently made fun of. We'll be looking at this attitude in more detail later but here it is enough to remember that she often found humour, not in illness, but in those who fancy themselves ill. In her letters she poked gentle fun at her mother's hypochondria, which was of that sort familiar to most of us, which stops sufferers doing what they don't want to do, while permitting them a wide range of activities they enjoy. It has been suggested by some biographers that her impatience with her mother's malingering was sometimes less than gentle, and that that is one of the reasons why her relatives destroyed so many of her letters. We do know that, when she was genuinely ill, indeed dying, Jane Austen spent

---

1   Claire Tomalin, *Jane Austen. A Life* (London: Penguin, 1998; repr. 2000), p. 259.
2   'I [...] am considerably better now, & recovering my Looks a little, which have been bad enough, black & white & every wrong colour' (*Letters*, p. 335).
3   Zachary Cope, 'Jane Austen's Last Illness', *British Medical Journal*, 2 (1964), 182–83, https://doi.org/10.1136/bmj.2.5402.182

her days on an arrangement of 'two or three chairs' ('I think she had a pillow, but it never looked comfortable', one of her nieces remembered), while her mother, who lived to be almost ninety and survived Jane by ten years, hogged the sofa.[4] There is more than one way of reading this apparently ghastly situation, however, and we'll come back to this picture of the three women in their living room later.

We can imagine that Jane Austen, who enjoyed activity and disliked pity, hated being ill. But as her symptoms worsened, as she grew weaker, she turned more and more to the local medical man nearest to Chawton, and in 1817 that gentleman, Mr. Curtis, suggested she needed more specialist advice. A trip to London to a physician was mooted, then discarded—it was very much against Jane Austen's wishes— and what was decided upon was seeking the advice of Mr. Lyford, a surgeon at the county hospital at Winchester, sixteen miles away. This gentleman was able to put a stop to the dreadful diarrhoea—she calls it a 'Discharge'—that was weakening and shaming her, but he wanted to see what a few weeks under his care could do for her other symptoms.[5] Towards the end of May she was conveyed by carriage to Winchester. She never returned. According to family tradition, the surgeon, whose uncle had been an apothecary who treated the Austens during Jane's childhood, knew she was dying the first time he looked at her, but hoped to alleviate her suffering. She did not attend his surgeries at the hospital but was treated in her lodgings as a private patient; she was accompanied by her sister Cassandra, who nursed her day and night. For a time, a professional nurse, a local woman, was hired to watch her in Cassandra's absences, but this was found to be unsatisfactory and a sister-in-law—alas, a much-disliked one—came to share the nursing. Jane died in Cassandra's arms during the night of July 17. Earlier that day she had taken leave of her medical man, Mr. Lyford, and 'almost her last voluntary utterance' was to thank him for his care.[6]

---

4   J. E. Austen Leigh, *A Memoir of Jane Austen by her Nephew* (London: Folio, 1989), p. 147; Deirdre Le Faye, *Jane Austen. A Family Record*, 2nd edn. (Cambridge: Cambridge University Press, 2004), p. 239.
5   *Letters*, p. 340.
6   Henry Austen, 'Biographical Notice of the Author': 'Her last voluntary speech conveyed thanks to her medical attendant; and to the final question asked of her, purporting to know her wants, she replied, "I want nothing but death"'. Reprinted in *Jane Austen: Critical Assessments*, ed. by Ian Littlewood, 4 vols (Mountfield: Helm, 1998), I, p. 38.

I stress this, and I name the otherwise little-known practitioners, because as well as giving poignant details of the passing of a brilliant woman who was also part of a loving family, this incident provides a tiny window through which we see the medical professions at work in the English provinces near the close of what historians call 'the long eighteenth century'. The local man, probably an apothecary, so on a lower tier of the accredited medical professions but licensed, a member of the Society of Apothecaries, a man who has served a long apprenticeship and who probably called in frequently to such a well-connected family as the Austens, has much experience, nevertheless feels himself unequal to the situation.[7] He suggests, first, the visit to a London physician, who will probably be a university graduate and a member of the Royal College of Physicians, the top tier in the hierarchy of the medical professions. But what is decided upon is a visit from a surgeon, a compromise, and a welcome one for a woman who does not want to spend her last days in London. By 1817, most cities the size of Winchester had hospitals, and some were training centres. Surgeons had, of course, only been technically sundered from their association with barbers for a little over sixty years, but their seven-year apprenticeship was, for some, a rigorous training, and the diaries of university-trained physicians from this period reveal that some of them stood in awe of their surgeon-colleagues as practitioners. So the Austen family, who would be paying large fees for Mr. Lyford's private visits and for the rooms they rented for the last months of her illness, were not taking the low road.

For a time, let's not forget, they also paid for a nurse, but she was found—no explanation provided, no name given—wanting. A family member, also female, was substituted. And this fills out the picture, for although, as this story shows, the middle classes consulted a variety of medical men and also paid for nursing care—watching the sick was a recognized profession—in the main it was the family who provided assistance to the ill. In Jane Austen's life this was provided by female family members, though the coach that took her to Winchester had three outriders, two of her brothers and a nephew, to be there in the case of any sudden emergency. In the novels, too, we will see that though the

---

7   The social status of the apothecary is discussed in Roger Sales, *Jane Austen and Representations of Regency Society* (London: Routledge, 1994; repr. 1996), pp. 147–55.

heroine of *Persuasion* says explicitly that 'Nursing does not belong to a man, it is not his province', some kinds of nursing, as well as a great deal of accident and emergency activity, fall to men (I vii 61).

Jane Austen's novels famously pay little attention to politics and warfare, and some readers (erroneously, of course) have found them wanting in action and event.[8] I will be talking in detail about only four of the six novels, but if I could start with just a quick run-through of the events in the novels that might be thought to call for medical intervention: of the three written when Jane Austen was young and in full health, in *Sense and Sensibility* there are two deaths, a sprained ankle, four fainting fits and five fits of hysterics, a nervous breakdown, a case of questionable anorexia, and a putrid fever; in *Pride and Prejudice* there is a feverish cold requiring bed-rest, a twenty-year bout of nerves, a pregnancy and a case of permanent invalidism in a very young woman, plus a few fainting and hysterical fits; in *Northanger Abbey* there is a female complaint of an undisclosed nature which ends in a mysterious death; among the later novels, *Mansfield Park* has alcoholism, chronic fatigue, depression, a fall which brings on a near-fatal fever, and two deaths among the clergy, one from over-eating; *Emma* has hypochondria, throat infections, a turned ankle, another pregnancy, more mysterious feminine complaints, and toothache; *Persuasion* has a death at sea, depression again, chronic indisposition/hypochondria, gout, rheumatism, and a couple of life-endangering falls. Is it any wonder that one critic asks, 'Why is it that this most traditional English family—whose Englishness is alluded to more than once—is so accident prone?'[9]

To move in closer: *Sense and Sensibility* was not the first novel Jane Austen wrote—that was a version of what later became *Pride and Prejudice*—but it was the first published, coming out in 1811. It is the story of two sisters, Elinor and Marianne, whose father's early death has left them in genteel poverty, and who are both in love with young men

---

8   For discussion of Austen's attention to politics and warfare, see Marilyn Butler, *Jane Austen and the War of Ideas* (Oxford: Clarendon Press, 1975; repr. 1989); Claudia L. Johnson, *Jane Austen: Women Politics, and the Novel* (Chicago and London: Chicago University Press, 1988); Brian Southam, *Jane Austen and the Navy* (London: Hambledon and London, 2000); Jocelyn Harris, *A Revolution Almost beyond Expression: Jane Austen's Persuasion* (Detroit: University of Delaware Press, 2007).

9   Julia Prewitt Brown, 'Private and Public in *Persuasion*', *Persuasions*, 15 (1993), 131–38 (p. 135), http://www.jasna.org/persuasions/printed/number15/brown.htm?

who are, or seem to be, out of their reach. When I listed the medically relevant events in *Sense and Sensibility*, I neglected to say that most of them happen to one person: Marianne, the sister who represents 'sensibility' or feeling, or excessive feeling. Marianne, at sixteen, believes in true love, but unfortunately falls in love with someone who is untrue, one of Jane Austen's attractive rascals, Willoughby.

But before she falls in love, she falls: down a hill, twisting her ankle, and making it necessary for Willoughby, at this point a complete stranger, to touch her, to pick her up and carry her, displaying not only his strength but his presence of mind, as well as his total ignorance of proper accident and emergency procedures, as of course we all know he ought not to move her before seeking medical advice! We will see this again, I am sorry to say, but here I would just like to point out a few things about this scene. The girls are running down the hill toward their house to get away from a sudden rain:

> Marianne had [...] the advantage, but a false step brought her suddenly to the ground [...] A gentleman carrying a gun [...] was passing up the hill [...] when her accident happened. He put down his gun and ran to her assistance. She had raised herself from the ground, but her foot had been twisted in the fall, and she was scarcely able to stand. The gentleman offered his services, and perceiving that her modesty declined what her situation rendered necessary, took her up in his arms without farther delay, and carried her down the hill [...] he bore her directly into the house [...] and quitted not his hold till he had seated her in a chair in the parlour. (I ix 50)

Jane Austen's novels are very often treated as though they were written by a brainy middle-aged spinster who was not much interested in bodies.[10] This novel was written, of course, by a young woman who had every reason to look forward to marriage, but even her later novels, as we'll see, concern themselves with the workings of the body—sick or well. Here we see Willoughby carefully putting down his gun before he runs to the young lady's side; right now he doesn't want to kill her, though later he nearly will. He lifts her without hesitating ('without farther delay'), despite her maidenly protests, and 'doesn't let go' until he sees her safe. Here he shows a readiness to touch, to act, both strength and

---

10 For a full-length study devoted to countering to this view, see John Wiltshire, *Jane Austen and the Body* (Cambridge: Cambridge University Press, 1992; repr. 2004).

tenderness. He is going to turn out to be a cad in Volume II, but before we are distracted by that, we ought to note how much male nursing he seems capable of giving. The key seems to be the capacity for gentle, but unhesitating, action. And this is, of course, before the two young people have been formally introduced. Next day he comes to visit her where she is resting on the sofa. The family have not sought other medical help, the experience and knowledge of mother and sister, and the visits of Willoughby, are rightly deemed to be enough. It is only when Marianne is languishing on the sofa that her appearance is actually described for the reader for the first time: it is Chapter x, but we are only just now seeing (along with Willoughby) that she is 'a beautiful girl', as if the attitude of patient were a particularly flattering one (I x 55).

A good thing, too, if it is; for Marianne, after only five chapters of extravagant courtship from Willoughby, is deserted by him, and begins a slow decline into first, psychosomatic, then real organic illness, after months of unhappiness and a couple of evening walks in wet grass. And wet feet were taken seriously in this period; one physician writes in 1807, 'Many evils befall the sex from cold feet'; and not only the fair sex, for at least one of George III's physicians attributed his famous malady to wet feet.[11] Marianne's 'two delightful twilight walks' in wet grass and sitting in wet shoes and stockings give her fever: 'a pain in her limbs, a cough, and a sore throat' (III vi 346). Home remedies are tried, but two racking nights watching Marianne by herself, since their mother is absent, lead her sister Elinor—the girl who represents sense, and who is managing her own broken heart more quietly—to send for the apothecary.

An entire chapter is devoted to the nursing of the acutely ill Marianne by Elinor, along with another friend who has much experience of nursing, some unnamed servants, and the apothecary. Mr. Harris comes every morning, and even though at first he regards it as not a very serious case, 'allowing the word "infection" to pass his lips' results in the owners of the house where the girls are staying immediately decamping with their young baby (III vii 347). Marianne was abandoned by Willoughby in

---

11 'The lady of weak health, who may wish to display a fine ancle, should be very guarded how she throws off her warm socks. Many evils befall the sex from cold feet', from Thomas Trotter, *A View of the Nervous Temperament* (Newcastle: Longman, Hurst, Rees, Orme, 1807), https://archive.org/stream/viewofnervoustem00trot?ref=ol, p. 79.

Volume I, Chapter xv and this is almost thirty chapters later. For a very long time she has pined in the romantic fashion which she approves, eating next to nothing, sleeping little, avoiding company. When infection comes, the fever nearly overwhelms her weakened body, and Elinor, who has sometimes tried to reason Marianne out of the nervous, the emotional part of her affliction, now that it has become a physical illness, is a devoted nurse, scarcely leaving her sister for a moment, giving her the apothecary's cordials, taking her pulse, watching her even while she sleeps, in the hope that sleep will refresh her. But sleep only brings delirium. In one particularly harrowing instance, the poor young girl, only sixteen, after all, starts up from her pillow and begins looking everywhere for her absent mother. Elinor, only nineteen herself, is terrified. Marianne is delirious for a long time. Even if she lives, will she ever come back to her right mind?

In these events, the apothecary is a shadowy figure, coming and going; his only quoted word the frightening 'infection'. Elinor seems almost impatient with him, though the careful reader can note that his morning visits occur around 5 a.m., followed by another less than twelve hours later:

> Mr. Harris was punctual in his second visit;—but he came to be disappointed in his hopes of what the last would produce. His medicines had failed;—the fever was unabated; and Marianne only more quiet—not more herself—remained in an heavy stupor. Elinor, catching all, and more than all, his fear in a moment, proposed to call in farther advice. But he judged it unnecessary; he had still something more to try, some fresh application, of whose success he was almost as confident as the last, and his visit concluded with encouraging assurances which reached the ear, but could not enter the heart, of Miss Dashwood [Elinor]. (III vii 354)

Despite Elinor's doubts, the 'fresh applications'—or something—bring about the hoped-for change in Marianne, and within a few hours the apothecary and the nurses are congratulating each other: 'he declared her entirely out of danger' (III vii 355). Elinor, relieved but still worried, continues to watch over her—now naturally sleeping—sister until her mother finally does arrive. Aside from a 'putrid tendency' (III vii 347), the category of Marianne's illness is not named, and the reader sees the illness entirely through Elinor's, through the nurse's, experience of it. Here Jane Austen is not interested in a set of symptoms, but in a situation, in the emotional and physical tenderness between people who share an experience. The two sisters have become for a time nurse and patient, and we see the patient through the nurse.

Pride and Prejudice, the next novel to be published, again, a novel written by a woman in her twenties, though revised by the same woman ten years later, presents the same situation. Early in the novel, Elizabeth, the heroine, is moved by sisterly devotion—though it is a much less serious illness, a sore throat and headache suffered by her sister Jane— to walk three miles on a wet day, in order to watch at Jane's bedside. (By doing so she gets her stockings dirty, earning the scorn of the Bingley sisters; though not that of Mr. Darcy.):

> When breakfast was over, they were joined by the sisters; and Elizabeth began to like them herself, when she saw how much affection and solicitude they shewed for Jane. The apothecary came, and [...] said as might be expected, that she had caught a violent cold [...] advised her to return to bed, and promised her some draughts. The advice was followed readily, for the feverish symptoms increased, and her head ached acutely. Elizabeth did not quit her room for a moment, nor were the other ladies often absent; the gentlemen being out, they had in fact nothing to do elsewhere. (I vii 37)

The last line points out with characteristic tartness the distinction between genuine and affected solicitude, between Elizabeth and the Bingley sisters. Though, as I have said, we probably all know the plot, readers may have forgotten that this illness of Jane's, as well as being much milder than Marianne's, is much more nakedly a plot device: Jane is ill enough to desire Elizabeth's nursing, so much more genuine than that of the cold-hearted Bingley girls or the servants or even that of Mr. Jones the apothecary, so Elizabeth stays in the Bingley house for a week and is thrown together with Mr. Darcy in the evenings. It is during these evenings at Netherfield that Mr. Darcy falls in love with Elizabeth.

At the novel's end, happily talking to and teasing Mr. Darcy, she asks him what made him fall in love with her, and he reminds her of the time he spent watching her nurse her sister through that bout of illness; it was not only her lively mind which drew him, he tells her, but the 'affectionate behaviour' he saw in her then (III xviii 422). Nursing here is read as a visible sign of goodness, of being—that very important quality in Jane Austen—'good-natured'. In the recognized rituals of courtship—dancing, flirting, conversing—one might hide as well as show one's real nature. In illness one cannot hide it, and perhaps the care of the sick is as revealing as illness itself?

Before we leave *Pride and Prejudice* I would like to consider an illness that we might as readers, forget, and one which we are surely encouraged to make light of, and that is Mrs. Bennet's 'nerves'. Here Mrs. Bennet, the mother of five unmarried daughters, castigates her husband's refusal to show enthusiasm for her campaign to find them husbands:

> 'Mr. Bennet, how can you abuse your own children in such a way? You take delight in vexing me. You have no compassion on my poor nerves.'
>
> 'You mistake me, my dear. I have a high respect for your nerves. They are my old friends. I have heard you mention them with consideration these twenty years at least.'
>
> 'Ah! You do not know what I suffer.' (I i 5)

Mr. Bennet may have compassion on his wife's nerves—though I see little sign of it—but the reader has been guided, from the very beginning of the novel, not to. In the famous catalogue of abuse that closes the first chapter, 'She was a woman of mean understanding, little information, and uncertain temper. When she was discontented she fancied herself nervous' (I i 5).

There we are then, instructed *not* to trouble ourselves over her nerves. The twenty-year duration is interesting: her 'nerves' date from some time after the birth of Jane and Elizabeth, the beautiful, talented, rational first children, presumably born and passing their early childhood in the honeymoon period when sexual attraction to the young Mrs. Bennet blinded her husband to her grosser faults of intellect and temperament; the nerves seem to start around the birth of Mary, the girl whose plainness and pedantry is treated so comically, and continues, understandably, through the births and childhoods of the two noisy hoydens, Kitty and Lydia.

Now, when Mrs. Bennet is attributing her frustration at the circumstances of her life to 'nerves', to an illness, she is not only joining the ranks of Jane Austen's hypochondriacs, she is using a fashionable term. 'It was in fact only in the eighteenth century', writes the medical historian W. F. Bynum, 'that it became possible to suffer from the "nerves"'. [12] Fibres and tendons in human and animal bodies that had been poked and prodded in experiments to discover the nature of physical feeling in the first part of the century had come, by the end of the century, to be connected with the language of feeling in another sense, a sense that is referred to in the *Oxford English Dictionary* as 'non-scientific' and by Dr. Johnson as 'medical cant'.[13] I take this to be analogous with the way in which in our lifetime the word 'trauma', which once had a distinct medical meaning, is now on everyone's lips to describe the effects of a lost wallet or a bad party. The term 'nerves' by the close of the eighteenth century was used in England to refer to feelings or to spirits, usually, though not always, to afflicted ones. It is taken by at least one writer to be characteristically English; the title of one popular eighteenth-century treatise on nervous disorders is *The English Malady*.[14] Whether that is true or not, the term, interestingly, has stood the test of time: 'Nerves of steel' is a phrase from a nineteenth-century poet; 'My nerves are bad tonight' is a phrase from a twentieth-century one.[15] And it is still possible to buy nerve tonics on the Internet.

Mrs. Bennet was in good, or at least high-class, company in having nerves she liked to talk about. George III, not himself believing that wet feet were the cause of his sufferings, said in 1788, very movingly, 'I am nervous. I am not ill, but I am nervous: if you would know what is the matter with me, I am nervous'.[16] The symptoms of the King, unlike those of Mrs. Bennet, received a great deal of attention at the time and still do. His, of course, seem to have proceeded from an organic cause, whereas hers—certainly as we are encouraged to read them—are so variable and so dependent on circumstances and mood, as to arise, we decide, purely from the desire for attention that is one of the characteristics of the hysterical personality. And, though they erode her husband's and

---

12 W. F. Bynum, Roy Porter and Michael Shepherd (eds.), *Anatomy of Madness: Essays in the History of Psychiatry*, 3 vols (London and New York: Tavistock, 1985), I, p. 91.
13 Ibid.
14 George Cheyne, *The English Malady or, a Treatise of Nervous Diseases of all Kinds; as Spleen, Vapours, Lowness of Spirits, Hypochondriacal, and Hysterical Distempers, Etc.* (London: Strahan, 1733), https://archive.org/stream/englishmaladyort00cheyuof t?ref=ol
15 Henry Howard Brownell, 'The Artisan', line 19; T. S Eliot, 'A Game of Chess', line 36.
16 Entry from Fanny Burney's diary November 5–6, 1788; *Diary and Letters of Madame D'Arblay*, 7 vols (London: H. Colburn, 1854), IV, p. 239, https://babel.hathitrust. org/cgi/pt?id=uva.x000618206&view=1up&seq=7

her children's respect for her, they do the job: when, in one of the novel's major plot events, her sixteen-year-old daughter Lydia elopes with the wastrel Wickham, Mrs. Bennet moves, not to assist or advise, but to claim all the attention that she can. Jane, her chief carer, tells Elizabeth that, on receiving the terrible news, '"My mother was in hysterics, and though I endeavoured to give her every assistance in my power, I am afraid I did not do so much as I might have done! but the horror of what might possibly happen, almost took from me my faculties."' (III v 322).

During the anxious days in which they await news of the scapegrace couple, Mrs. Bennet takes to her bed and remains there, claiming the constant attendance of Jane, or the housekeeper, or another nurse-attendant of some kind.

> Mrs. Bennet [...] received them exactly as might be expected; with tears and lamentations of regret, invectives against the villainous conduct of Wickham, and complaints of her own sufferings and ill-usage; blaming everybody but the person to whose ill judging indulgence the errors of her daughter must be principally owing [...]
>
> 'Tell [Mr. Bennet] what a dreadful state I am in,—that I am frightened out of my wits; and have such tremblings, such flutterings, all over me, such spasms in my side, and pains in my head, and such beatings at heart, that I can get no rest by night nor by day.' (III v 316–18)

The symptoms in this are 'all over' her body; as one nerve specialist of the time commented, thinking perhaps of the potential range of his practice, 'the nerves go everywhere'![17] The list is designed precisely *not* to elicit the reader's sympathy. We don't see it through a tender nurse's eye but through a cold authorial one that enjoys producing the diffuse litanies of self-contradiction that characterize Mrs. Bennet's speech: she interrupts this medical report to speculate about what Lydia will wear to a wedding that may never happen.

And if she has little hope of appealing to the reader's sympathies, she is *really* wasting her breath where Mr. Bennet is concerned. As he watches Jane bearing a heavy-laden tray of tea things up to her mother's room, he gloomily considers the state of the marriage and family life he shares with this demanding weakling: '"This is a parade," cried he,

---

17   Thomas Trotter, cited by W. F. Bynum et al. in the *Anatomy of Madness*, I, p. 94: 'Trotter's nervous patient might suffer from almost any organ of the body because the nerves go everywhere'.

"which does one good; it gives such an elegance to misfortune! Another day I will do the same; I will sit in my library, in my nightcap and powdering gown, and give as much trouble as I can"' (III vi 330). Like Mr. Bennet, the novel seems unable to forgive Mrs. Bennet for anything: but her constitution is forgiving. When catastrophe is averted and Lydia is married to Wickham, Mrs. Bennet's recovery is instantaneous—she leaps out of bed, with not a thought for her poor nerves, or for her daughter's real disgrace in having lived with a man outside marriage, and, though she has spent two weeks in bed being waited on, she joins her family at dinner again in—the phrase is memorably acid—'in spirits oppressively high' (III viii 342). In low or high spirits, Mrs. Bennet isn't given a chance to appeal to the reader. In a move that seems characteristic of the discussion in the period about nervous complaints, her faults are seen as moral and not physical, and so her nerves, which in other fictional females are proof of sensitivity and sensibility, are merely mocked.

Also mocked, though perhaps more subtly, in the much later novel *Persuasion*, are the illnesses of the young housewife Mary Musgrove, one of the great comic hypochondriacs. *Persuasion* follows the progress of Anne Elliot, at twenty-seven Jane Austen's oldest heroine, who has years before been persuaded to break an engagement to the love of her life, the sailor Captain Wentworth, who meets him again and after a series of accidents—and I mean accidents; this is the novel in which the two life-endangering falls occur—is reunited with him. At the novel's outset Anne is presented to the reader as having recognized her mistake, and suffering as a consequence from 'early loss of bloom and spirits', a kind of gentle depression (I iv 30). She often sighs; she is often agitated. But there is no talk of nerves and, indeed, though she has much to complain of, since she is unloved and unrecognized in her family and exploited by everyone, there is little complaint of any kind. Any complaint from Anne would go unheard, anyway, in the general clamour that surrounds her. The novel's early chapters take her on a visit to her sister Mary. Mary is ill. Mary is often ill.[18]

---

18 See Jan Fergus, '"My Sore Throats, You Know, Are Always Worse than Anybody's": Mary Musgrove and Jane Austen's Art of Whining', *Persuasions*, 15 (1993), 139–47, http://www.jasna.org/persuasions/printed/number15/fergus.htm?

> While well, and happy, and properly attended to, she had great good humour and excellent spirits; but any indisposition sunk her completely [...] She was now lying on the faded sofa [...] and, on Anne's appearing, greeted her with,
>
>   'So, you are come at last! I began to think I should never see you. I am so ill I can hardly speak. I have not seen a creature the whole morning!'
>
>   'I am sorry to find you unwell,' replied Anne. 'You sent me such a good account of yourself on Thursday!'
>
>   'Yes, I made the best of it; I always do; but I was very far from well at the time; and I do not think I ever was so ill in my life as I have been all this morning—very unfit to be left alone, I am sure. Suppose I were to be seized all of a sudden in some dreadful way, and not able to ring the bell! [...]'
>
>   'Well, you will soon be better now,' replied Anne, cheerfully. 'You know I always cure you when I come.' (I v 39–40)

Anne's hopes are not misplaced. Within minutes Mary is up scoffing cold meat and making plans for an afternoon walk. Part of what she needs is—like Mrs. Bennet—simply company, someone to listen to her complaints, to 'attend' to them. The word 'attend' appears over and over in Jane Austen, with regard to the real (Marianne's fever) and the imaginary complaint: Mrs. Bennet, Mary. Some characters, mostly, but not always, women, have the capacity to supply this kind of attendance.

Though Anne spends much of her time coping with Mary's phantom illnesses ('"my sore-throats, you know, are always worse than anybody's"' (I vii 178)), on two occasions she has the opportunity to attend to the needs of someone who is really ill. In both these cases we see her sterling qualities—she is tender, resolute, clear-thinking as well as quick-thinking—and it is not only the reader who sees this, but Captain Wentworth, once her fiancé, now returned, wealthy, successful, still eligible, but determined to ignore the woman who spurned him. He flirts with other young women and scarcely acknowledges Anne's existence. But on one signal occasion, after a fall, one of Anne's little nephews, one of Mary's two badly-brought-up little boys, is confined to bed with a broken collarbone. Anne offers to nurse him, much to Mary's relief, and on this occasion Captain Wentworth, Anne and the little invalid are left alone together; Anne is kneeling at the little boy's side, Captain Wentworth is pretending to read a newspaper and wondering how he can get away without being rude; a tense silence ensues, broken only by the entrance of the younger child, who begins bullying and pestering his long-suffering aunt:

> [...] as his aunt would not let him teaze his sick brother, he began to fasten himself upon her, as she knelt, in such a way that [...] she could not shake him off [...] 'Walter,' said she, 'get down this moment.' [...] But not a bit did Walter stir.
>
> In another moment, however, she found herself in the state of being released from him; some one was taking him from her, though he had bent her head so much, that his little sturdy hands were unfastened from around her neck, and he was resolutely borne away, before she knew that Captain Wentworth had done it. (I ix 86–87)

This is the beginning of the transformation in their relationship: the man who has never stopped loving her—but does not know himself well enough to know that—cannot bear to see her made physically uncomfortable, in particular while she is wholly absorbed in the sort of physical care for others that is characteristic of her. His tenderness approves and supports and joins with hers there. It is a kind of silent duet enmeshed in care for others. She nurses one child, while he plays with the other. They might already be married; though it takes many chapters, and one more accident, before they are.

The second and more famous fall in *Persuasion* is, of course, the fall at Lyme, when Louisa Musgrove, the young woman with whom Captain Wentworth has been flirting, insists on being jumped down the steps of the famous Cobb:

> to shew her enjoyment, [she] ran up the steps to be jumped down again. He advised her against it [...] but no, he reasoned and talked in vain; she smiled and said, 'I am determined I will:' He put out his hands; she was too precipitate by half a second, she fell on the pavement on the Lower Cobb, and was taken up lifeless! (I xii 118)

In case anyone here hasn't read *Persuasion*, Louisa is not dead; despite her propensity for writing about falls, Jane Austen never kills anyone that way. But she is badly hurt: concussed, certainly, and seems to remain unconscious for a worryingly long time. Worrying, too, to modern readers, is the way in which the injured girl is hoisted about and flung from person to person before she has been examined by a surgeon and declared to have no broken limbs or injury to the spine.

What this incident does, aside from putting Louisa out of action, is to show very completely the wonderful competence of Anne. There are two other ladies present, Mary, and Louisa's sister Henrietta, but they succumb, respectively, to hysterics and a dead faint. It is Anne who has smelling salts to revive those who have fainted, Anne who thinks of the surgeon and of sending someone for him who knows the town, Anne who organizes the party that carries Louisa from the scene. She rallies Captain Wentworth, and they manage *together* to get Louisa indoors, where she can be examined, and where the nursing can begin. Anne, too, though she has every reason to resent Louisa as a rival, is willing to remain in Lyme and help nurse her: 'she would have attended on Louisa with a zeal above the common claims of regard, for his sake' (I xii 125). But she is prevented, predictably, by Mary, who cannot bear to lose such an opportunity for attention. Anne returns home against her will, and goes unwillingly to Bath—like Lyme a resort famous for invalids and medical treatments. The novel's action follows her there, and we never really see Louisa again; we learn of her recovery, but also that the effects of her accident will be lifelong: she will marry someone she meets in the house where she is being nursed, a young sailor who has helped to 'attend' to her, and she will be turned, through the accident and its effects, from a bright and breezy young woman to one who '"starts and wriggles like a young dab chick"' at any sudden noise (II x 237).

The noise that is referred to, here, is a slammed door, and readers of Austen's *Emma* will recall that much effort is expended throughout that novel to shut doors and to shut them properly. Maids are praised for knowing just how to do this, eligible young men are frowned on for not knowing, or not caring. All of this watchfulness about doors is part of the symphony of care that surrounds Mr. Woodhouse, Emma's father, Jane Austen's most celebrated hypochondriac. Like Mrs. Bennet, Mr. Woodhouse is nervous, 'a nervous man', whose 'spirits required support', but unlike her he is very rich, so his wobbly spirits are supported by almost everyone with whom he comes in contact; an army of servants; his neighbours; the apothecary, Mr. Perry; and most of all Emma, his devoted daughter. Mr. Woodhouse is distressed not only by slamming doors but by draughty passages, sudden snowstorms, late nights, loud voices, strangers, travel, heat, cold, rich food, whether eaten by him or by others, and any change at all in his routine. But against all of these, perceived by him not as dangers to his equanimity but to his health, he is protected.

Early on, the reader realizes Emma and Mr. Knightley are made for each other as they co-manage her father's nervous symptoms. Mr. Woodhouse is not really ill, but it is everyone's job to prevent his ever becoming ill, or even feeling more than momentarily uncomfortable. This is Emma's life. On the night after Miss Taylor's wedding, she is gloomily surveying her prospects for the coming winter; her father has, as is typical, fallen asleep after dinner. The pace of their life is torpid, their social circle very confined, but with Miss Taylor's company this was tolerable. What will it be like without her? she is wondering, and as if in answer, in walks Mr. Knightley. He knows they will be missing their companion and refers delicately to the wedding. Mr. Woodhouse wakes up long enough to reply: "'Ah! Poor Miss Taylor! 'tis a sad business'" (I i 8). A glass half-full person himself, Mr. Knightley comments that now Mrs. Weston—he firmly uses her married name—will "'have only one to please, than two'"; Emma takes up the baton:

> 'Especially when *one* of those two is such a fanciful, troublesome creature!' said Emma playfully. 'That, is [...] what you would certainly say if my father were not by.'
>
> 'I believe it is very true, my dear, indeed,' said Mr. Woodhouse with a sigh. 'I am afraid I am sometimes very fanciful and troublesome.'
>
> 'My dearest papa! You do not think I could mean *you*, or suppose Mr. Knightley to mean *you*. What a horrible idea! Oh, no! I meant only myself. Mr. Knightley loves to find fault with me you know [...] We always say what we like to one another.' [...]
>
> 'Emma knows I never flatter her,' said Mr. Knightley, 'but I meant no reflection on any body.' (I i 9)

He says this drolly and the situation is, between Mr. Knightley and Emma, rescued, like many other situations in the novel. No one can say 'what they like' *to* Mr. Woodhouse, but these two can say what they like *near* him, around him, in a sort of continual flow of tactfulness. There are half a dozen scenes like this, presented in a comic-opera style in which Emma soothes her father from one side while Mr. Knightley distracts him from the other.

This is the sort of attendance Mr. Woodhouse's unhysterical (unless threatened) and uncomplaining (unless dissatisfied) hypochondria requires from the laity: a constant, quiet attention to his state of mind that takes the form of almost ritually dull conversation—pleasant for Mr. Woodhouse, exhausting, I should think, for others, often hilarious for the reader. These rituals, sometimes expanded to include board games, are all that he requires in terms of family care. For Mr. Woodhouse, unlike other Austen characters, whether ill, or imagining themselves ill, has constant professional attendance in the shape of the apothecary, Mr. Perry. We remember that Jane Austen, when genuinely ill, moved from apothecary to surgeon, from small village to major town. Mr. Woodhouse, 'a nervous man, easily depressed', and a rich man, well-protected, needn't do this (I i 6). He has Mr. Perry at his right hand. Mr. Perry never actually speaks in the novel. He doesn't need to, as other characters are continually quoting him, or seeing him, or mentioning him in their letters. Unlike Emma, the great Miss Woodhouse, whose status in the village is so high, and sense of her position so acute, that she can't enter certain houses without mulling over the consequences, Mr. Perry is comfortable everywhere. He goes to the houses of the poor, where, it is intimated, he does not charge, but then perhaps he doesn't need to, as he sees Mr. Woodhouse, presumably for a fat fee, every day.

One person who does not consult Mr. Perry on her own behalf is Emma. Emma is '"the complete picture of grown-up health"', as her former governess tells Mr. Knightley (I iv 39). But she is almost alone among Highbury's female population in being so. Harriet, her weak-headed friend, has, in the course of the novel, a septic throat, a turned ankle, several headaches and a toothache which finally causes her to exit from its pages. Jane Fairfax, a young woman who is exactly Emma's age, and who, like her, is beautiful and intelligent but who, unlike her, is poor, and is enduring the strain of a secret engagement, suffers from a number of complaints including headache, lack of appetite, 'deranged' health, and a cold that lasts from November into June (III ix 424). Jane Fairfax sees plenty of Mr. Perry. But it is not Mr. Perry who cures her. In the novel's last quarter Jane's prospects change, and her health changes with them, as Frank Churchill is suddenly free to marry her and their scandalous secret engagement can be openly acknowledged. The pale, drawn young woman whose family feared she might be consumptive has a full recovery; even that nagging cold seems to be gone. The new situation, intriguingly, is due to the sudden death of Frank's aunt, Mrs. Churchill, another chronic invalid, who enters the novel only by reputation, as someone who suffers (like Jane) from a 'nervous disorder', but dies of something else altogether, a mysterious 'sudden seizure of a different nature from any thing foreboded by her general state' (III ix 421). Mr. Woodhouse, who has the professional invalid's generous interest in others' ills, is filled with sympathy, but he is in a minority, as her death is so convenient. In Jane Austen, some illnesses are more equal than others.

To conclude, Jane Austen is, as I have said, a novelist of courtship, but in *Emma* there is very little in the way of courting. Emma thinks she is being courted by Frank Churchill, but isn't; she drives away the decent man who wants to court Harriet, and points her in the direction of two men who don't want to court her. When she finally comes to terms with Mr. Knightley, there is no courtship; only love—a love that has grown up between them while they attended together to her father's imaginary illness. In the other novels I've discussed, too, there is less conventional courtship than might be supposed from the book jacket blurbs. And more illness, real and imagined. I'd like to end where we began with Jane Austen's yielding of the sofa to her mother: 'I live upstairs however for the present & am coddled [...] but a weak Body must excuse weak Nerves. My Mother has borne this forgetfulness of *her* extremely well;—her expectations for herself were never beyond the extreme of moderation'.[19] There is more going on here, I'd suggest, than simply the older woman's selfishness, the younger's disdain. More reticence. More love. And we should not forget her courtly thanking of her physician, either, almost her last words. Jane Austen was certainly a novelist of passion, but she was also a novelist of tenderness, and an observer of self-delusion: for her there is as much loving-kindness, and as much foolishness, between the sick and the well, as there is between men and women in love.

---

19   *Letters*, p. 338.

7. Food in Jane Austen's Fiction

All of Jane Austen's novels end with weddings, sometimes with multiple weddings. Each of her heroines becomes, in the end, a bride. The road that leads to marriage is always so full of suspense that even when we are reading for the tenth time we reach the denouement with relief: she has landed him at last. What we never see is the bride becoming, as all will have to, the mistress of her husband's household. '"Catherine would make a sad, heedless young housekeeper, to be sure"', worries her mother, in *Northanger Abbey*, about her eighteen-year-old daughter's approaching nuptials (II xvi 258). But we never see Catherine burning the toast, nor her young husband Henry good naturedly feeding it to the dog. However, this reticence contrasts with the amount of detail we are given, in all of the novels, of the domestic lives of the other characters, of the heroines' parents and sisters and friends—and enemies. If we hardly ever see any of the heroines bending over anything more demanding than a tea table or a coffee pot, we see others, usually but not always women, involved in providing more substantial meals, occupied in trying to make people eat, occasionally trying to keep them from eating. Food, in the world of these novels, is not only for sustaining people in health and comfort. It has other purpose as well, other meanings.[1]

These six great novels full of wit and romance and class conflict, are also full of food, of people eating and refusing to eat. Along with the dance floor, and those morning visits which took up so much of her characters' time, the dinner table is the place where Jane Austen's men

---

1 For previous articles on this topic, see Juliet McMaster, 'Hospitality', *Persuasions*, 14 (1992), 26–33; Eileen Sutherland, 'Dining at the Great House: Food and Drink in the Times of Jane Austen', *Persuasions*, 12 (1990), 88–98, http://www.jasna.org/persuasions/printed/number12/sutherland2.htm; Michele Roberts, 'When Jane Austen Describes Meals, They Are Never Innocent', *New Statesman*, 132 (July 21, 2003), 56. See also Amanda Vickery, *The Gentleman's Daughter: Women's Lives in Georgian England* (New Haven and London: Yale University Press, 1998).

   https://doi.org/10.11647/OBP.0216.07

and women meet, talk, look at each other, and listen; and, of course, where they eat.

In *Pride and Prejudice*, Jane Austen's most popular novel, the early meeting which takes place between the Bennet family, with their five daughters who are so in need of husbands, and the well-off Bingley party that will provide husbands for two of them, is soon followed by a raft of morning calls, evening card parties and dinners. Within two weeks of the first meeting, Elizabeth, the heroine, can remark to her friend Charlotte Lucas, that her sister Jane, who has already fallen in love with nice Mr. Bingley, '"has dined in company with him four times"' (I vi 25). The Hertfordshire neighbourhood the Bingleys have moved to is a sociable one. Elizabeth's mother, of whom more later, boasts that '"we dine with four and twenty families"', meaning not that her table has room for fifty, but that there are twenty-four families living nearby whose social rank makes them suitable dinner companions for the Bennets (I ix 48). The Bingleys, who have a house in London and who, as the novel progresses, we see doing practically nothing but dining out, are not impressed: their own social connections are presumably too many to count.

Early in the novel we see Elizabeth as a guest at the dinner table in the Bingleys' rented country house, failing a social test. She has been seated next to Mr. Hurst, the husband of one of the Bingley sisters, 'a man of more fashion than fortune [...] who lived only to eat, drink, and play at cards [...] when he found her prefer a plain dish to a ragout, he had nothing to say to her' (I iv 17; I viii 38) When I read the last sentence as a child, I was puzzled by it, and for many years after: what was a 'plain dish', what was a 'ragout', why did it matter? I could, however, tell that it did matter, and that I was meant, I think, to approve Elizabeth's taste and to despise Mr. Hurst's. The novel was describing one sort of social distinction, observed by Mr. Hurst, while endorsing another, embodied in Elizabeth. Without knowing quite what is happening, we are led, as readers, to side, in that little exchange of values, with Elizabeth; we, too, reject the ragout.

And something more than that is happening, too, I think, and I want to look at one of Jane Austen's other novels to help us see it better. We'll come back to that ragout, and despicable Mr. Hurst, later; I want to move to *Sense and Sensibility*, an earlier and slightly less popular novel, in which two sisters, Elinor and Marianne Dashwood, also, like the Bennet girls, in need of a husband, move from Sussex to Devonshire, and are introduced to a lively social circle which includes a fat, jolly, gossipy, vulgar (but also very decent, very good-hearted) elderly woman called Mrs. Jennings. Food has provided Mrs. Jennings with much enjoyment—"'how [we] did stuff'", she chortles, describing a day spent picking luscious mulberries on another character's estate (II viii 223)—and when Mrs. Jennings manages to persuade the two Dashwood sisters to accompany her to her London house, she also tries to feed them up. On the journey, Mrs. Jennings was 'only disturbed that she could not make them choose their own dinners at the inn, nor extort a confession of their preferring salmon to cod, or boiled fowls to veal cutlets' (II iv 182). Later, when Marianne has a broken heart, Mrs. Jennings hopes that some sweetmeats and olives, or dried cherries, or a glass of especially good fortified wine, will cheer her up (II viii 220; II viii 224). Again here, though this time the character is far from dislikeable, there is the contrast between the hearty eater who is seen as slightly comic, and the heroine, presumably not comic, shaking her head and, if not exactly refusing to eat, refusing to take any positive pleasure in eating. The girls won't say whether they like salmon better than cod. Why not? It seems almost rude.

I could multiply examples of this lack of appetite among Jane Austen's heroines, and I want just to think about it a little with you. Throughout the novels, though occasionally the heroines get hungry, they never say so, and though they do eat, to be polite, they are never shown having any relish for food. The characters who are shown taking an interest in eating are always comic, often vulgar, and sometimes, like Mr. Hurst, positively beastly. I find this fascinating. Jane Austen's satirical eye is attracted by any exaggeration, so her heroines usually avoid extremes of any kind, and are lampooned when they do not avoid them: Catherine's reading of Gothic novels in *Northanger Abbey*, Emma's snobbery, Marianne's "'passion for dead leaves'" in *Sense and Sensibility*, are all treated as jokes (I xvi 101). So, perhaps, their very moderate appetites for food, displaying no exaggeration of any kind, are simply a form of admirable self-control? Perhaps.

This might be the moment to talk about what is called conduct literature or courtesy literature, handbooks of advice on topics from dress to marriage choices that were written for young people, especially women, and read by them, for centuries, from ancient times. Those self-help articles published in the twenty-first century on 'how to walk in high heels' and 'why French women don't get fat' are contemporary examples—it's still going strong. In the eighteenth century, with the rise of circulating libraries and the growth of a literate middle-class reading public which included many women, these books of advice to the children, especially the daughters, of upwardly mobile families were widely disseminated. In 1788, when Jane Austen was thirteen years old, the Reverend John Trusler, a London clergyman, published a famous work, *The Honours of the Table*, 'for the use of young people', a book about table manners.[2] In it, among suggestions that it was not a good idea to sit too near or too far from the table, eat greedily, lean elbows on the table, pick one's teeth before dishes are removed, scratch, spit or blow your nose at the table, and that one should refrain from 'smelling the meat whilst on the fork before you put it into your mouth';[3] more particularly, he remarks that 'eating a great deal is deemed indelicate in a lady; (for her character should be rather divine than sensual)'.[4] The advice not to spit was aimed at both sexes, the advice not to eat heartily aimed only at 'ladies'. We do not know whether the Austen family owned a copy of the Reverend Trusler's book, but we do know that Jane Austen had read some of this conduct literature, and we can also be sure she found some of what she read in it funny. We can make that assumption because the little fragments of writing that she produced as a child and as a teenager and read aloud to her family, all of which are satires of the books she had read, contain some satirical allusions to the high-flown feminine behaviour advocated by those courtesy books.

One of these fragments in particular, *Lesley Castle* of 1792, satirizes feminine attitudes to food. Like *Sense and Sensibility*, *Lesley Castle* has two heroines. One of them, Charlotte, is the only one of Jane Austen's heroines who actually does any cooking. Indeed, she is obsessed with cooking, and with food. *Lesley Castle* contains a much cruder version of the opposition in *Sense and Sensibility* between 'sensible' Elinor and

---

2   John Trusler, *The Honours of the Table or, Rules for Behaviour during Meals with the Whole Art of Carving* (London: Literary-Press, 1788), https://wellcomecollection. org/works/qszhwdv8/items?canvas=1&langCode=eng&sierraId=b21526199

3   Ibid., p. 17.

4   Ibid., p. 7.

'sensitive' Marianne. Charlotte, the cook, is the sensible, practical one, contrasted with her romantic sister Eloisa. Eloisa is in love, about to be married, but her fiancé is melodramatically thrown from his horse on the eve of the wedding. Eloisa's shock turns her face, the food-obsessed Charlotte remarks, 'as White as a Whipt syllabub'; but Charlotte is distressed not by Eloisa's suffering but because all the cooking she has been doing for the wedding feast will now go to waste. '"Good God [...] what in the name of Heaven will become of all the Victuals?"', she exclaims as her sister sobs and faints (Letter II 146). And Charlotte and her mother agree

> that the best thing we could do was to begin eating them immediately, and accordingly we ordered up the cold Ham and Fowls, and instantly began our Devouring Plan on them with great Alacrity. We would have persuaded Eloisa to have taken a Wing of Chicken, but she would not be persuaded. (Letter II 147)

Eloisa continues true to the memory of her lost fiancé, and to the norms of feminine sensibility. Weeks later, she is still pale and silent, still unable to eat, too sad to consume 'even a pidgeon-pye' (Letter VII 165). With the juxtaposition of the two sisters here, Jane Austen is laughing, heartless though it may seem, at both, and at the distinction, implicit in the conduct books and other literature of sensibility, between people feeding themselves and *feeling*. Here, as in those 'how to be a lady' books, those who eat cannot feel, those who feel cannot eat. In *Lesley Castle* it is a romp, a burlesque, not to be taken seriously, the work of a teenager who finds most adult behaviour screamingly funny, and lampoons it beautifully.

But in the later novels, too, heroines who are struggling with feelings, especially feelings they cannot express, secret feelings, starve themselves: Marianne in *Sense and Sensibility*, Jane Fairfax in *Emma*, Fanny in *Mansfield Park*, Anne Elliot in *Persuasion*, all weep secretly and grow thin. This romantic opposition between emotion and appetite, particularly among women, continues into literature of the later nineteenth century. The Brontë sisters' heroines starve themselves, too, to dramatize their unhappiness. If they cannot have what they want, these heroines refuse to want anything else, especially food. In *Wuthering Heights*, Catherine Earnshaw starves herself to *death*, and when her creator Emily Brontë, herself died at thirty, her coffin was said to be the narrowest the local carpenter had even made, 'narrower than a child's'.[5]

But Jane Austen, though closer, I think, to the Romantic movement than is often recognized, was not a romantic, and did not identify with her characters' passions as Emily Brontë did. For her, both sense and sensibility, both reason and emotion, matter, and when her heroine Marianne recovers her health and her senses, she blames herself for her weeks of self-starvation: '"Had I died,—it would have been self-destruction"', she tells her sister, very soberly, after her recovery (III x 391). Elinor, her sister, who has been nearly as wretched as Marianne throughout most of the novel, does not allow herself the luxury of such showy acts of self-harm. She always politely clears her plate, and on one occasion she philosophically downs the fine old wine that is meant to alleviate Marianne's heartache, reflecting that she, too, has a broken heart, and might as well try it as a cure.

This motif, in which the romantic heroine is someone who does not have an appetite, is further complicated when we read Jane Austen's letters, which often display her own straightforward pleasure in food. 'You know how interesting the purchase of a sponge-cake is to me,' she writes to her sister, and to her brother at sea she writes, 'Rostock Market makes one's mouth water, our cheapest Butcher's meat is double the price of theirs'.[6] She grew up in a country parsonage full of children, her siblings and the young boys whom her father taught, and it seems reasonable to imagine lively and talkative and satisfactory mealtimes. In her city life, in the unsettled years in which she lived with her family in lodgings in Bath and Southampton, she welcomes a snack of toasted cheese, and looks forward to being able to 'drink as much wine as I like'.[7] When she and her mother and sister, and the female cousin who lived with them, settled in the cottage in Chawton which would be her final home, Jane Austen was in charge of providing the breakfast. Not, I emphasize, of cooking it—do not imagine her with spatula in hand. Like her heroines, she prepared, it is thought, nothing but coffee and tea, just possibly toast, but she was responsible for making sure breakfast was on the table, and for the small, all-female, family's supplies of tea, coffee

---

5   Winifred Gerin, *Emily Bronte. A Life* (Oxford: Oxford University Press, 1971), p. 259.
6   *Letters*, pp. 128; 229.
7   *Letters*, pp. 110; 251.

and sugar—all expensive, imported commodities. Her own relationship to food seems to have been fairly enthusiastic, so it is interesting that her heroines are so very refined in their appetites.

One thought I have had about this is that perhaps the mature novels are not so different from the juvenile works as we often think, and that, as in *Lesley Castle*, both the heroine figure and the housekeeper figure, both the Biblical Mary and the Biblical Martha, as it were, are being satirized, in the later novels as well. Perhaps when Elinor swallows Mrs. Jennings's fine old Constantia, the novel is showing her to be more truly sensible, and more courteous, than when she and Marianne are conducting themselves in the ultrafeminine, unsensual style recommended by the courtesy books, and refusing to give the kind-hearted old lady the satisfaction of knowing whether or not they like the salmon she's bought them!

There is no doubt, though, that the 'housekeepers', those who provide the food, are very often the target of Jane Austen's satire, as in the case of Mrs. Jennings's housekeeping. We should remember that all these fictional women are well off enough to employ servant housekeepers to whom they give the orders for meals, though the Austens themselves, in the country parsonage in Steventon in which Jane Austen passed her happy childhood, did not employ such a person and Mrs. Austen must have spent much of her time in and around the parsonage kitchen. Mrs. Jennings's housekeeping displays generosity, and hospitality, and genuine care for others, but it has a somewhat limiting effect on her imagination. Here is her description of Delaford, the hero, Colonel Brandon's, well-endowed country estate, where eventually both sisters will find their happiness: "'Delaford is a nice place [...] a nice old fashioned place [...] with the best fruit-trees in the country and such a mulberry tree in one corner! [...] Then, there is a dove-cote, some delightful stewponds [...] A butcher hard by in the village'" (II viii 223). It is hard to miss that almost all the amenities she admires are not to do with architecture or the beauty of the countryside, but with food. The dovecote is there to provide the household with the pigeon pie a sensitive heroine shouldn't eat, and the stewponds are to ensure a regular supply of fresh fish at a time when fish transported from the sea were liable to arrive stinking and uneatable.

Mrs. Jennings's warm-hearted doings can be compared with those of other busy housekeepers, and one interesting contrast is with *Pride and Prejudice*'s Lady Catherine de Bourgh, in her own way much more vulgar than Mrs. Jennings despite her noble birth.[8] Lady Catherine is shown inquiring after Charlotte's chickens and her pigs, and on the occasions when she 'condescends' to take any refreshment in the parsonage 'does so only for the sake of finding out that Charlotte's joints of meat were too big for her family'.[9] An interest in food this minute is seen as intrinsically ridiculous, and Lady Catherine, *grande dame* though she is, is a fool. But such obsessive, absurd interests in domestic minutiae, in food, clothing, shelter or health, these preoccupations always struck Jane Austen as funny, and she found myriad ways in which to present them. We see obsession with food in particular in two vastly different characters, Mrs. Norris in *Mansfield Park* and Mr. Woodhouse in Emma. In both novels the obsession renders them comic, in utterly contrasted ways.

Mr. Woodhouse, the heroine's father in *Emma*, is a man older than his years, a hypochondriac, with what the eighteenth century called nervous complaints. He lives a mild, regimented life ruled by 'habits of gentle selfishness' (I i 6) which include regular tea drinking with a group of old ladies of his acquaintance, but though he is hospitable, and generous, continually sending gifts of food to his poorer neighbours, food is a problem for him, indeed a danger:

> He loved to have the cloth laid [...] but his conviction of suppers being very unwholesome made him rather sorry to see anything put on it [...] 'Mrs. Bates, let me propose your venturing on one of these eggs. An egg boiled very soft is not unwholesome, [...] you need not be afraid—they are very small, you see—one of our small eggs will not hurt you. Miss Bates, let Emma help you to a *little* bit of tart—a *very* little bit. Ours are all apple-tarts. You need not be afraid of unwholesome preserves here. I do not advise the custard. Mrs. Goddard, what say you to *half* a glass of wine? A *small* half glass—put into a tumbler of water?' (I iii 23–24)

<p>8   'Mr. Darcy looked a little ashamed of his aunt's ill breeding' (II viii 195) when she tells Elizabeth that she is welcome to play the piano in the servants' quarters.</p>

<p>9   'Now and then, they were honoured with a call from her Ladyship, and nothing escaped her observation that was passing in the room during these visits [...] if she accepted any refreshment, seemed to do it only for the sake of finding out that Mrs. Collins's joints of meat were too large for her family' (II vii 190).</p>

The reader is relieved to know that 'Emma allowed her father to talk—but supplied her visitors in a much more satisfactory style' (I iii 24).

Mansfield Park, written just before *Emma*, presents us with Mrs. Norris, who is both one of the great villains of literature and a finely tuned comic figure. A parson's widow, she has finagled her way into a dominant role at her sister's home, Mansfield Park. Mrs. Norris enjoys penny-pinching, others' pennies as well as her own. More than once we catch her shooing the poor and hungry away from the door of Mansfield Park, and she is driven almost insane by the thought of the good living which is going on in the parsonage which was once her domain but is now occupied by the gourmand Dr. Grant and his easy-tempered, high-spending wife. But the real outlet for her passion for economy is shown in her talent for scavenging. She has a genius for accumulating free gifts. After the Mansfield Park family makes a visit to a much grander household at Sotherton Manor, Mrs. Norris is described in the carriage that takes them home with her lap '"full of good things"': a small heather plant, a large cream cheese, pheasants' eggs (I x 123). '"What else have you been spunging?"', her niece teases her, and Mrs. Norris begins one of her hypocritical parades: '"it is a cream cheese, just like the excellent one we had at dinner. Nothing would satisfy that good old Mrs. Whitaker [the housekeeper], but my taking one of the cheeses. I stood out as long as I could, till the tears almost came into her eyes, and I knew it was just the sort that my sister would be delighted with"' (I x 123). The reader sees through this, and knows that no one but Mrs. Norris will ever see any of that cream cheese, and here we witness an intriguing variant of the delicate relationship between women and food—Mrs. Norris is never greedy or demanding for *herself*, oh no, but for *others*...

Mansfield Park is the only one of the novels in which eating is shown in anything but genteel circumstances. Fanny, the young heroine, has been sent away to Mansfield Park as a child from her large, indigent family in Portsmouth, and when she returns to Portsmouth as a young woman she is shocked by the squalor with which she was once, presumably, at home; shocked also to find herself disgusted at her family's food, and their table manners:

> Betsey's eating at table without restraint, and pulling every thing about as she chose [...] (III x 472)

> [Fanny's] eyes could only wander from the walls marked by her father's head, to the table cut and knotched by her brothers, where stood the tea-board never thoroughly cleaned, the cup and saucers wiped in streaks [...] (III xv 508)
>
> the half-cleaned plates, and not half-cleaned knives and forks, [...] After being nursed up at Mansfield, it was too late in the day to be hardened at Portsmouth. (III xi 479)

Anyone who has read *Mansfield Park* and recalls how badly Fanny is treated *there* will be offered food for reflection: conditions at Portsmouth must be truly dreadful. In the eighteenth century, food in urban areas, for the lower middle classes to whom Fanny's family belongs, was uneven in quality, often spoilt before it was sold, and often adulterated with products that included white lead, sulphuric acid and the ash of human bones. City milk was legendarily bad, brought up from the country and sold by milkmaids from open pails in the dirty street, or, later, the product of badly housed and badly fed urban cows who lived in conditions similar to our battery hens. At Portsmouth, the milk we see Fanny struggling to drink is 'a mixture of motes floating in thin blue' (III xv 508).

Food habits in *Mansfield Park* are so harshly depicted as to be almost beyond comedy. In the other novels, housekeepers who are better off and more competent than Fanny's mother are satirized because all they are interested in is opulence and display. Mrs. Bennet, in *Pride and Prejudice*, assumes the world will overlook her drawbacks as a mother and a wife because she can offer 'two full courses' at a family dinner, and because her daughters are brought up fashionably, without being taught to cook (I xxi 135). She sneers because their neighbours, the Lucas girls, might be 'wanted about the mince pies' (I ix 48). But surely the lack of housewifery in the Bennet girls' education is a metaphor for the other, more serious lacks, for the younger girls' bad manners, and most importantly, for fifteen-year-old Lydia's never having been taught that safe sex, in Georgian England, comes after marriage and not before.

Another housekeeper much given to display is the new bride, Mrs. Elton, in *Emma*, whose life in Bath and Bristol had led her to think herself a fashion leader. She boasts that the everyday fare provided by her housekeeper is always good enough for her guests, and she offers catering advice to all and sundry, even to the formidable Mr. Knightley. Barging in on his plans for a strawberry picnic, she preens, 'by the bye, can I or my housekeeper be of any use to you with our opinion?—Pray be sincere, Knightley. If you wish me to [...] inspect anything—' 'I have not the least wish for it, I thank you,' is his dry answer.[10] (III vi 386)

But nothing can stop Mrs. Elton:

'Well—but if any difficulties should arise, my housekeeper is extremely clever.' 'I will answer for it, that mine thinks herself full as clever, and would spurn any body's assistance.' (III vi 386)

Not only revealing of the two characters through dialogue, this little passage suggests the intimacy of the relationship between the proprietor of the household and the paid servant housekeeper. Mr. Knightley, that defender of women, is here defending his housekeeper's independence as much as his own.

Scattered throughout the novels are warmer kinds of comedy which deal with food, and chime better with the wholehearted attitudes in the letters. The Christmas scene in *Persuasion*, where the picture of 'tressels and trays, bending under the weight of brawn and cold pies, where riotous boys were holding high revel, the whole completed by a roaring Christmas fire' (II ii 145) is almost Dickensian, and in the same novel there is the astonishing hospitality of the poor sailor family, the Harvilles, who want not only to feed but to house huge numbers of complete strangers in their tiny lodgings: 'They were only concerned that the house could accommodate no more; and yet perhaps by "putting the children away in the maids' room, or swinging a cot somewhere," they could [...] [find] room for two or three besides' (I xii 122). These scenes of family warmth and hospitality are deepened for the reader because we see them through the wistful eyes of Anne Elliot, whose own family life has been so cold and loveless. This sort of framing is characteristic of Jane Austen: the reader watches every scene, participates in it, through one of the heroines.

I would like to take you through a day of eating with Jane Austen. Georgian mealtimes, and indeed Georgian meals, were different from ours, and a partial source of my own interest in this topic was my

---

10 The long dash at the end of Mrs. Elton's last comment is often placed by Murray's editorial team to indicate an interruption, suggesting that Knightley comes as close as a gentleman could to cutting her off.

confusion when I was first reading Jane Austen at what seemed to be the strange hours at which, in the different novels, meals were taken. Though Jane Austen famously took as her topic '3 or 4 Families in a Country Village', it seemed to be the case that, for each different village, often for each family, meals were on a different schedule.[11] Looking at these differences helps us to appreciate that Jane Austen's world is a bigger one than is sometimes thought.

You will not be surprised to learn that, even in the late-eighteenth and early-nineteenth centuries, fashionable life went with late hours. When Elizabeth Bennet leaves her own completed breakfast, about 9 o'clock of a September morning, the three-mile walk to Netherfield finds the Bingley party, and Mr. Darcy, the high-fashion set, still at breakfast. Elizabeth is a fast walker, but this has to take an hour, so the Bingleys must breakfast at 10 at the earliest. As does Mary Musgrove, the young mother with aristocratic aspirations in *Persuasion*, and the Londoners, Henry and Mary Crawford, in *Mansfield Park*. Country people like Mr. Knightley in *Emma*, and probably Emma and her father too, little influenced by city life, kept rather early hours, at least in summer. But in all of Jane Austen's mature novels the main action starts in the autumn and, almost always, is completed over the course of a year. What we need to remember is that, as autumn and winter came on, almost every household would want to spare expense on candles. Large country households probably kept bees, as Cassandra Austen did, to provide wax as well as honey, but few households could keep enough bees to provide all the candles needed through a long winter. In the winter of 1810, wax candles cost one shilling and a penny per pound in London, and an urban working family might go through more than that in a week—how many more must have been consumed at a great country house like Mansfield Park! Therefore, unless absolutely necessary, breakfast would wait, at that time of the year, until full daylight eliminated the need for candles, rarely occurring before 9 o'clock and often delayed until 10. People often rose earlier and accomplished what work they could, probably using lanterns outside and tallow candles indoors. At Chawton, Jane Austen practised the piano for two hours before breakfasting with her family, and in London she sometimes shopped before breakfast.

---

11   *Letters*, p. 275.

Georgian breakfasts were light for the most part, tea and coffee and chocolate to drink, sweet and plain cakes and toast to eat (continental visitors were delighted by British toasted bread, which apparently was not eaten much abroad). But the early (9:30) breakfast which follows the ball at Mansfield Park, and sends two strong young men off to London, and the boastful breakfasts of General Tilney in *Northanger Abbey* probably both echoed the plenty of an earlier era and prefigured, in their variety, the heartier breakfast of the Victorian period. The *Northanger Abbey* meal is early, too, because they are travelling from Bath down to the country, but General Tilney worries his timid teenage guest, Catherine, half to death, by his predatory fussing: 'his continual solicitations that she would eat, and his often-expressed fears of her seeing nothing to her taste—though never in her life before had she beheld half such variety on a breakfast-table—made it impossible for her to forget for a moment that she was a visitor' (II v 157). This is a lovely play on the General's inability to make anyone feel 'at home' and an indicator that there was more on that table than toast.

With breakfast the 'morning' began, as for most of us, but with the difference that the morning did not end, as it does for us, with lunch, but with dinner, and dinner, which had once, in the mid-eighteenth century, taken place about the middle of the day or even earlier, by its end took place at a time which could vary, and does in Jane Austen's novels, between 3 p.m. and 7 p.m. Not until later in the nineteenth century did lunch come into fashion. The word 'luncheon' occurs once in these novels, and once also occurs its variant 'nuncheon', and both times refers to a catch-as-catch-can meal taken at an inn. In the increasing gap between breakfast and dinner there would be either, and this most often seems to be the case, nothing at all (don't feel too sorry for them, wait until you see what they ate for dinner) or what the food historian Maggie Lane calls 'the meal with no name' a meal we see several times in Jane Austen's novels, once when Mary Musgrove snacks on a little cold meat, once at Mr. Knightley's on the strawberry picking day, but most grandly at Pemberley, Mr. Darcy's elegant country house in *Pride and Prejudice*, when the social chill between the warring Bingley and Bennet ladies is thawed a little by food:

The next variation which their visit afforded was produced by the entrance of servants with cold meat, cake, and a variety of all the finest fruits in season [...]. There was now employment for the whole party; for though they could not all talk, they could all eat; and the beautiful pyramids of grapes, nectarines, and peaches, soon collected them round the table. (III iii 296)[12]

Eating, here, is a welcome distraction; conversation was running out. The combination of meat, cake and fruit is something which may strike us as odd, but which is the staple of this odd snack: meat, in particular, as the well-off ate much more meat than bread or vegetables, and the acidity of fruit was believed, in eighteenth-century medical theory, to counteract the 'alkaline' character of meat. Everyone who could afford it, in this period, ate vast quantities of meat. When the diarist James Woodforde, 'Parson Woodforde', totted up his yearly expenses, the bill for meat was something like forty times the bill for flour, and even when allowances are made for the difference in price per pound of meat and grain, the proportion does not greatly change.[13] It is no wonder than so many wealthy Georgians flocked to spas seeking a cure for gout.

We have seen people socializing over breakfast and over this nameless meal, but there is no doubt that the social meal of the day, then as now, was dinner. Dinner takes place, in Jane Austen, any time between the early hour preferred by Emma and her father, about 3 p.m., and the fashionable 6:30 p.m. favoured by the Bingley sisters in *Pride and Prejudice*. The ideal dinner Mrs. Bennet schemes for Mr. Bingley must have 'two full courses'. Courses succeeded each other, as they do today, but in eighteenth- and early-nineteenth-century England, in what was called the 'French style' of dining, the first course, consisting of large and small dishes carefully spread on a substantial, probably oval or circular, cloth-covered table, was visible to diners as they entered the dining room. Part of the splendour, the meaning, of any formal dinner, was in

---

12 Maggie Lane, *Jane Austen and Food* (London: The Hambledon Press, 1995), p. 35: 'During Jane Austen's lifetime, in a domestic context, refreshments would be offered without giving them any name [...] As the meal had no name, it is not surprising that it had no fixed hour but was offered whenever guests appeared'.

13 John Beresford, ed., *The Diary of a Country Parson: The Reverend James Woodforde*, 5 vols (London: Oxford University Press, 1924–31). Woodforde kept regular accounts for all items of household expenditure and Lane mentions him as a rich source of information on food and housekeeping (Lane, *Jane Austen and Food*, p. 9).

the careful arrangement of dishes. Mrs. Frazer's *The Practice of Cookery* (1791) contains a diagram of the layout of the table form.

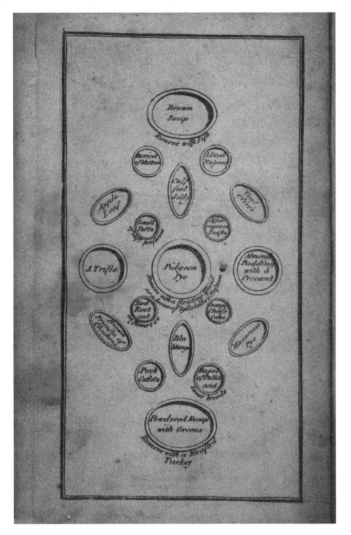

Fig. 1 Frontispiece from Mrs. Frazer, *The Practice of Cookery, Pickling, Preserving* (Dublin: Cross, Burnet, Wogan, Moore, Jones, Rice and McAllister, 1791), Public Domain, https://hdl.handle.net/2027/nyp.33433057527347?urlappend=%3Bseq=8

Note the prevalence of meat dishes, though sweet dishes often appeared also. Dinner would typically begin with a soup, served out by the host. Soup was eaten, and dishes removed, before the guests proceeded with the rest of their eating. This could take a long time; I'll say a little more about that in a moment. The second course, if it is like the dinners Parson Woodforde ate with his friends, might consist of slightly 'lighter' food: fish cakes, pasties, macaroni, and perhaps some sweet tarts and milk puddings. Though not necessarily: sometimes the *pièce de résistance* was saved for a second course—a swan once, for Parson Woodforde, a swan that had been killed three weeks before it was eaten. When the cloth was removed after the second course, the table, often bare now so that the gleaming mahogany could be seen, was laid with 'dessert', finger food, including fruit and nuts and dried fruit.

You may be interested to know that, aside from the host and hostess, who sat at the head and foot of the table as often still today, and sometimes a strategically placed 'principal guest' who would be seated by the hostess, the Georgians practised what was called 'promiscuous seating', that is, a scramble for places. That is why Frank Churchill, in *Emma*, finds himself so often next to her, because he's grabbed the seat he wants. That is probably why poor Jane Fairfax, his secret love, gets icier and icier to Emma, and has less and less appetite for her own dinner. And your dinner partner, if you were a lady, was important, because ladies, even if they were not themselves of the 'divine type' who preferred not to eat, did not, conventionally, help themselves to dishes but were helped by the gentleman next to them, or by the hostess if you could catch her eye—we remember Emma side-stepping her papa and helping her guests to the fish and the chicken. This, of course, is the context in which Mr. Hurst lost interest in Elizabeth. Hoping to help her to a ragout, and perhaps slosh a little extra onto his own plate as he did so, he found she only wanted the 'plain dish'. The ragout, like the Italian or French dishes of the same name is a highly seasoned dish. The 'plain dish' might have been undressed meat, indeed probably was. That prissy little Miss Elizabeth Bennet has spoilt her partner's chance to have an extra helping, as well as, probably, her own. One imagines him devoting himself to his plate, watching for other opportunities to swoop, while Elizabeth slices her 'plain dish' into smaller and smaller pieces in order to look occupied. There are only six people around this dinner table; that two of them do not talk and one does not eat must be hard to avoid noticing.

The first course would be eaten, or grow cold, and was then taken away by servants, and a new cloth laid for the second course. In *Emma* we see a dinner party at the home of the nouveaux riches Coles, who are not used to giving dinner parties to the gentry, and Emma's and Frank's lively conversation is disrupted by 'the awkwardness of a rather long interval between the courses' (II viii 235). The pair are unable to resume gossiping until 'every corner dish was placed exactly right' (II viii 236). No doubt Emma's servants, and even Mrs. Bennet's servants in *Pride and Prejudice*, are more used to handling the shift of courses. It is not only parsimony that stops the snobbish Elizabeth Elliot from inviting her sister's family to dinner in Bath, but an unwillingness to have even a sister see the way in which her reduced establishment there would manage such details as the change of course.

In *Pride and Prejudice*, dinner is usually a lively affair, too lively, as Elizabeth is more than once forced to watch her family's embarrassing misbehaviour and its effect on Mr. Darcy and the Bingleys. But dinners in the other novels are often long and dreary. Frequently, the period before the drinking started for the men, and the ladies escaped to the drawing room to wait for tea, could be longer than two hours, and when we know this we see how ghastly some of the duller dinners must have been. In *Sense and Sensibility*, 'though not much in the habit of giving any thing' (II xii 262), the rich and selfish young Mr. and Mrs. John Dashwood do give a dinner to the equally chilly Lady Middleton: 'The dinner was a grand one, the servants were numerous, and everything bespoke the Mistress's inclination for shew, and the Master's ability to support it. [...] no poverty of any kind, except of conversation, appeared—but there, the deficiency was considerable' (II xii 265–66).

We see equally lifeless family dinners in Mansfield Park where the adult children of the household sit sullenly, awed by their elders' formidable silences: as Fanny explains it, '"There was never much laughing in his presence [...] I cannot recollect that our evenings formerly were ever merry, except when my uncle was in town"' (II iii 230). Sir Thomas is solemn but well meaning. General Tilney, in Northanger Abbey, is a bully whose mere presence spoils every mealtime. Here, we see him at home in the Abbey: 'General Tilney was pacing the drawing-room, his watch in his hand, and having, on the very instant of their entering, pulled the bell with violence, ordered "Dinner to be on table directly!"' (II vi 169). From these grim meals it is a relief to turn even to Mrs. Bennet's gabbling or to the dinner at Lady Catherine de Bourgh's where we see Mr. Collins take 'his seat at the bottom of the table, [...] and looked as if he felt that life could furnish nothing greater' (II vi 184).

Dinner, of course, was not the end. There was tea to follow, and tea, taking place less than two hours after the completion of the two-hour dinner, often involved cakes and sweetmeats. And if the evening was long enough, tea could be followed by supper. In the opening chapter of *Emma*, Mr. Woodhouse, having slept since dinner, wakes for tea. That evening, with only Emma and her father and Mr. Knightley, there is perhaps no supper, and supper does not figure at the Bingley house either, as they dine so late, nor do the mean Elliots seem to feature suppers at their elegant lodgings in Bath. Nor does Lady Catherine, nor the Bennets at home, nor others who aspire to fashion. Dinner is getting later, supper, an eighteenth-century staple, is going out of fashion in the early years of the nineteenth century. But Mr. Woodhouse, who would have in his youth eaten dinner even earlier, 'loved to have the cloth laid [for supper], because it had been the fashion of his youth' (I iii 23–24), and Emma is, as always, happy to see her father happy (one of her most endearing characteristics). So she serves suppers, especially when friends come to play cards: in the scene we have looked at, when Mr. Woodhouse and his daughter struggle over whether or not their guests should be endangered by eggs and apple-tarts, and in the scene with which I would like to close, which is the lovely Christmas reunion of Emma, her sister and the Knightley brothers, the evening when we see Mr. Woodhouse indulging in his favourite pastime of eating gruel.

For anyone who, like me, grew up on Dickens and the Brontës, gruel has had a rather bad press as a means of starving paupers to death. Growing up in America, indeed, I had no idea what gruel might even be made of, and thought of it as a thin soup, possibly with a few weevils floating in it for protein. But, as I am sure you know, gruel is a very thin oatmeal porridge, consisting of oatmeal, water, milk and salt. This is the 'discourse in praise of gruel' by Mr. Woodhouse and his equally hypochondriac elder daughter, observed with affectionate amusement by the Knightley brothers and Emma—and by us, the readers:

> The gruel came and supplied a great deal to be said—much praise and many comments—undoubting decision of its wholesomeness for every constitution, and pretty severe Philippics upon the many houses where it was never met with tolerably. (I xii 108; I xii 112)

Those of you who know the novel well, know that the gruel, in this instance, leads to a family argument, but I am sure that in most cases it leads to good digestion and a pleasant night's sleep.

8. Emma and Harriet: Walking Companions

The aspect of *Emma* which has always disturbed me, and made me keep company with those readers whom Jane Austen imagined would not like a heroine whom she herself liked very much, is Emma's friendship with Harriet, which involves her from the start in unwarranted intrusion into the life of another woman, and an assumption of her right to launch such an invasion that I have always found shocking and almost frightening. But Mark Twain, who did not, of course, like Jane Austen, tells us that if we're afraid of something the best thing is to take a good hard look at it[1]—and that is what I have tried to do in preparing for this talk, which will examine the way the novel presents Emma and Harriet's relationship, the way it treats Emma's notions of friendship, and in particular the way it looks at the usefulness of friends as 'walking companions' (I iv 25). Emma, I don't need to remind you, has begun the novel by losing her oldest, dearest friend, Miss Taylor, to marriage. At the novel's opening she is contemplating a humdrum existence in a small Surrey village, with, at age twenty, her adoring but unstimulating father as more or less her only companion. Emma is bored and—we'll look at this in a moment—lonely.

---

1   See, for example, 'Jane is entirely impossible. It seems a great pity to me that they allowed her to die a natural death!' (from a letter dated January 18, 1909 to W. D. Howells; reprinted in *Jane Austen: Critical Assessments*, ed. by Ian Littlewood, 4 vols (Mountfield: Helm, 1998), I, p. 435. Twain's advice about the value of keen scrutiny does not seem to appear verbatim as above, but might be a memory of the episode in which Tom Sawyer and Huck Finn find reasons to delay entering the haunted house and then eventually enter, 'ready for instant retreat [...] In a little while familiarity modified their fears and they gave the place a critical and interested examination', *The Adventures of Tom Sawyer*, ed. Peter Stoneley (Oxford: Oxford University Press, 2007), p. 148.

    https://doi.org/10.11647/OBP.0216.08

But in this fast-moving novel, Emma meets a new friend, Harriet Smith, in another moment we will look at later, in Chapter iii, and as Chapter iv opens, Emma's 'Quick and decided' ways have insured that the 'intimacy' between the two girls is becoming 'a settled thing'; there we learn that:

> As a walking companion, Emma had very early foreseen how useful she might find [Harriet]. In that respect Mrs. Weston's loss had been important [...] since Mrs. Weston's marriage her exercise had been too much confined. She had ventured once alone to Randalls, but it was not pleasant; and a Harriet Smith, therefore, one whom she could summon at any time to a walk, would be a valuable addition to her privileges. (I iv 25)

The late-eighteenth and early-nineteenth centuries had reconfigured walking from a mode of transport for those who could afford no other, to a leisure pastime, and in a way that looks forward to the country and sports supply stores of our own time, had invented knapsacks, walking boots, customized walking coats with side pockets and pocket books of poetry and fiction to be carried in them.[2] We see much walking in Jane Austen's other novels. You'll recall that, after some struggle, *Northanger Abbey's* Catherine Morland manages a country walk with the Tilneys, where they discuss up-to-the-minute topics such as politics and the Picturesque, as well as Gothic fiction, and that in *Pride and Prejudice,* Miss Bingley winds up an attack on Elizabeth Bennet with the sneer that '"She has nothing, in short, to recommend her, but being an excellent walker!"' (I viii 39). Mary Musgrove, in *Persuasion,* resents 'not being supposed a good walker' (I x 89) and, of course, it is a last walk to the Cobb at Lyme Regis which proves to be that novel's turning point.

But I think in *Emma,* walking is particularly highlighted by the village setting, and the small distances which this very confined, almost claustrophobic, novel allows its characters to travel. Hartfield, Emma's home, is on the edge of the village of Highbury, its grounds are 'a sort of notch in the Donwell Abbey estate' owned by Mr. Knightley; it is a half-mile from Randalls where Miss Taylor/Mrs. Weston has gone (I xvi

---

2   See Donna Landry, *The Invention of the Countryside: Hunting, Walking, and Ecology in English Literature, 1671–1831* (Basingstoke: Palgrave Macmillan 2001). See also Olivia Murphy, 'Jane Austen's "Excellent Walker": Pride, Prejudice, and Pedestrianism', *Eighteenth Century Fiction,* 26.1 (2013), 121–42, https://doi.org/10.3138/ecf.26.1.121

147). All of these are within walking distance, though not, or at least not very willingly, within the reach of a solo female walker, even an energetic and healthy young one like Emma, something which we will think about soon. But first let us glance at the busy walkers of Highbury: it might be possible to map the area as a kind of walking course, to track the walkers we see and hear about. Leaving Emma and Harriet for later, we see first of all Mr. Knightley, who walks over to Hartfield, with '"Not a speck"' on his shoes at the end of Chapter i (I i 8). Mr. Knightley is later applauded by Emma for *not* walking to the Coles's dinner party, but using his carriage but this reflects how often, with much to do and lots of vigour and energy (and a lot on his mind, as we later learn) he walks—'keeping no horses, having little spare money and a great deal of health, activity, and independence, was too apt, in Emma's opinion, to get about as he could, and not use his carriage so often as became the owner of Donwell Abbey' (II viii 230). Mr. Knightley's tenant, Robert Martin, as we'll see in a moment, similarly active and independent— and lovelorn—frequently gets from place to place by walking, too. And Mr. Perry, who sometimes rides, and is having a carriage pressed on him by his anxious wife, also frequently walks. Like Mr. Knightley and Robert Martin he walks to and from his work. Emma, lingering outside Ford's shop while Harriet dithers within, sees 'Mr. Perry walking hastily by' (I ix 251).

But most of the walking we see in *Emma* is what might justly be called leisure walking, or even pleasure walking, a pastime. When Emma and Harriet out walking meet Robert Martin, it is an interesting example, almost Wordsworthian, of leisure walkers meeting someone who is walking for transport. Robert Martin, moving purposefully back and forth to his work on the farm, may not be trying for an elegance of appearance on this accidental meeting with the most consequential young woman of the neighbourhood and her new friend. At one he looks 'very respectfully', at the other—poor love struck man! 'with most unfeigned satisfaction' (I iv 31). As always for Emma the wish is mother to the thought so although, when she first sees Martin, her actual observation is that 'His appearance was very neat, and he looked like a sensible man' (I iv 31), she forsakes the truth, for a crushing dismissal of their fellow pedestrian (and a man Harriet has known and liked for a long time), and declares him '"remarkably plain [...] very clownish [...] totally without air"' (I iv 32). Harriet is 'mortified', but does not attempt to defend her old friend against her new one, and as they walk on, Emma begins her campaign of using Mr. Elton 'for driving the young farmer out of Harriet's head' (I iv 32; 34).

Emma wants to transplant Harriet from the environment where she has found her to one which is defined in the novel precisely *by* its habits of leisured walking: 'Her father never went beyond the shrubbery, where two divisions of the grounds sufficed him for his long walk, or his short' (I iv 25); Mrs. Weston and her stepson, Frank Churchill, strolling from Randalls to Highbury, Hartfield as their avowed goal (at least as far as deceived Mrs. Weston knows) and the Bates's house, and Jane, as their real one; perhaps most tellingly, Mr. Elton, turning from his purposeful walk to work, of visiting the poor, turning at the very door of the poor parishioners' cottage, where those within are hungry and sick, to join the young ladies in their *amble*. Walking thus becomes a kind of quiet metaphoric powerhouse for the novel, an emblem of its confinement to one place, its deliberate repetitiveness, and its mode of presenting character through comparison and contrast.[3] Walking in *Emma* is almost as revealing as speech. We will see how this operates even in the last walk we see Emma take, but first let us look at some other modes of walking, other motives.

A notion had arisen, in the eighteenth century, that an important part of life for those who did not do physical labour for a living, was exercise. George Cheyne, the influential eighteenth-century physician, born in Scotland, but practising in Bath, that hive of hypochondria, attributed both 'the English malady' of nerves, and the obesity from which he himself suffered, in part to lack of exercise.[4] On meeting Emma, Frank has inquired whether she is a rider or not. Now, though Jane Austen rode when she had the opportunity, and though several of her heroines, including timid Fanny Price, are equestriennes, one surmises that Mr. Woodhouse's anxieties for both his daughter and his horses would

---

3   For recent discussion of this topic, see Susan Morgan, 'Adoring the Girl Next Door: Geography in Austen's Novels', *Persuasions On-line*, 21.1 (2000), http://www.jasna. org/persuasions/on-line/vol21no1/morgan.html

4   George Cheyne, *The English Malady or, a Treatise of Nervous Diseases of all Kinds; as Spleen, Vapours, Lowness of Spirits, Hypochondriacal, and Hysterical Distempers, Etc.* (London: Strahan, 1733), https://archive.org/stream/englishmaladyort00cheyuof t?ref=ol, pp. 120–21.

prevent their indulging in that dangerous exercise, so walking—given her few opportunities to dance—is Emma's only physical outlet, her only exercise. We see vigorous Mr. John Knightley out exercising his little boys during a spring visit to Hartfield and, on that outing, they meet Jane Fairfax walking alone to the Post Office; the re-reader knows why, and if any first-time reader is fooled by Emma's fantastic notions about Jane's adulterous passion for Mr. Dixon, a clandestine motive can be supplied by that; but what Jane *says,* in the protracted defence of her solitary walking that she is obliged to mount against the whole assembled company while in the drawing room at Hartfield in Chapter xxxiv, is to bring up health and exercise: '"I am advised to be out of doors as much as I can"' (II xvi 319). Presumably the advice is from fellow-pedestrian Mr. Perry, who, as really a very subtle man, knows how hard it must be for a sensitive young girl to be cooped up all day long in a single parlour with a deaf grandmother and an endlessly talking aunt. Later we see Jane setting out on a solo walk home from Donwell to Highbury, though Emma attempts to prevent her—it's a hot day!—and Frank Churchill, we learn later, tries to accompany her, with nearly disastrous consequences; and later still, Jane is 'seen wandering about the meadows, at some distance from Highbury' and this is reported, in this highly surveillant neighbourhood, to Emma, who is mortified, since Jane has on the same day refused an outing with *her.* In Highbury, even those who walk alone are not really by themselves (III ix 426). But Jane tries. Late in the novel, we learn along with Emma, and perhaps a little ahead of Emma, that Jane has spent a great deal of the novel hating Emma, who spends much of the novel disliking her. But Jane does make one straightforward admission to Emma, even during this period of mutual antagonism—it 'seemed to burst from an overcharged heart': '"Oh! Miss Woodhouse, the comfort of being sometimes alone!"' (III vi 394).

So, walking alone, nearly impossible though it may be to avoid observation even if you avoid company, is not a positive error of conduct in Highbury in 1813–14, as, say, being seen walking side by side with Frank Churchill would have been. Why then can't Emma do it? Why can't she walk alone? Randalls is, once again, a half-mile away. We never see Emma walk there unaccompanied. And when we do finally see her take a few walks alone—I will save one for last, but we can take a second to glance at her walk to Highbury to atone to Miss Bates for her rudeness on Box Hill—this solitary endeavour is unquestionably a moment of high moral victory for her, of real self-conquest and accomplishment: she 'went early, that nothing might prevent her' (III vii 410). The visit, coinciding with Jane's momentous decision to change one nightmarish situation for another, does not go terribly well, but Emma has shown her contrition and her good will, and returns, again walking alone, and pensively meditating, to find that her unaccompanied expedition has raised her in the estimation of the waiting Mr. Knightley.

But that is, I think, the first time we see her venture alone beyond the shrubbery. Emma, with all her resources, and her scorn for Mrs. Elton's passion for company, is not shown, herself, bearing solitude very well. We will turn to our first view of Harriet in a moment; let's pause to turn right back to page 1 and our first look at Emma. When we meet Emma, the heroine who of all Jane Austen's heroines, puts herself forward for our notice from the very beginning, she is dejected, genuinely bereft after Miss Taylor's departure from Hartfield into her new life as Mrs. Weston of Randalls, and it is important for the reader's very complicated connection with Emma, I think, that we meet her on this first occasion of her experiencing 'mournful thought of any continuance' (I i 4). Very soon we will be hearing Emma boast of her '"active, busy mind, with a great many independent resources"', and her music and drawing, but on this afternoon of 'melancholy change' none of that manifests itself (I x 92; I ii 5). In a mood of post-wedding let-down, 'she had then only to sit and think of what she had lost', and this grief over the marriage she believes she has engineered, this 'black morning's work', takes us into Emma's thoughts for six paragraphs, until her father awakens and echoes those thoughts back to her word-perfectly (I i 4). Never one himself to boast of his activity or resources, Mr. Woodhouse says with wonderful simplicity just what Emma is thinking: '"I wish she were here again"' (I i 6).

Emma has to fight off tears until, of course, Mr. Knightley walks in. But before we leave this chapter and move a couple of chapters on to the one which will introduce Emma to her new friend, to her walking companion Harriet Smith, just note one aspect of Emma's existence that is seldom discussed by critics, never referred to by Mr. Woodhouse, Miss Taylor or Emma herself, but only, and only once, by Mr. Knightley, which is the loss of her mother, mentioned in an almost cavalier fashion as having happened 'too long ago [for Emma] to have more than an indistinct remembrance of her caresses' (I i 3). Emma was five when her mother died and was replaced by Miss Taylor; five-year-olds talk, and feel, and remember, though perhaps not very clearly. Mr. Knightley, who would have been twenty-one at the time of this event, obviously has memories which are not so indistinct, and later tells Mrs. Weston, '"In her mother she lost the only person able to cope with her. She inherits her mother's talents"' (I v 37–38).

The loss of a mother, in those days of multiple childbirths and primitive medical care, was a much less rare event in childhood than now. It happened to several of Jane Austen's own nephews and nieces, and to three of her heroines, if we include Eleanor Tilney. But I have always thought of it as more a part of Emma's life, and felt as such by Jane Austen, than might seem at first obvious. Emma's brittleness and her fantasies of self-sufficiency and omnipotence seem plausible effects of being early deprived of a mother, as might also Harriet's 'habits of dependence and imitation', Frank Churchill's tricks and mischief and Jane Fairfax's seeming reserve (I x 94). Each member of this whole strange foursome, for which some country dance involving three women and one man ought to be invented, has lost one or both parents in infancy: Jane Fairfax is utterly parentless, Harriet virtually so, and Frank and Emma, who perceive '"a little likeness"' in each other—a like littleness?—have lost mothers (III xviii 522). Whether losing Miss Taylor does or does not revive the death of Emma's mother, it is in itself a real loss, of a friendship described in thoughtful, unexaggerated language that nevertheless displays honest warmth and tenderness: 'a friend and companion such as few possessed, intelligent, well-informed, useful, gentle [...] one to whom she could speak every thought as it arose' (I i 4–5). Hold onto those words when we look at the dawning friendship with Harriet.

Female friendship, in its many aspects, is always to Jane Austen an interesting topic. She found unintended comedy in the romantic notions of eternal friendship at work in sentimental novels such as Richardson's *Sir Charles Grandison*, in which every girl who falls in love with the eponymous hero tries to step aside to give place to someone worthier, or Maria Edgeworth's *Belinda* where female friendships shift like musical chairs. These exaggerations of feeling were burlesqued by the Irish writer Eaton Barrett in his 1813 novel *The Heroine,* which Jane Austen admired, but she had already done a very good job herself while still in her teens, in her tiny epistolary novel *Love and Freindship.* Most of the letters in that are written by Laura, sentimental (and selfish) heroine who rejects one candidate for friendship because the young lady 'neither in the Course of her Visit [half an hour], confided to me any of her Secret thoughts, nor requested me to confide in her, any of Mine' but a few hours later, having been, as she tells her correspondent 'deprived during the course of 3 weeks of a real friend', Laura comes across a perfect candidate, Sophia, and on first meeting each other they 'flew into each others arms and after having exchanged vows of mutual Freindship for the rest of our Lives, instantly unfolded to each other the most inward Secrets of our Hearts' (Letters VII 112; VIII 113–14). Again, let's keep that in mind, deliberately silly as it is: friendship at first sight, like love at first sight (we might recall that love at first sight does not usually work out in Jane Austen) and the sharing of confidences.

Here comes confiding little Harriet Smith, seventeen years old to Emma's twenty, from the parlour of Mrs. Goddard's school, into Emma's world:

> She was a very pretty girl, and her beauty happened to be of a sort which Emma particularly admired [...] She was not struck by any thing remarkably clever in Miss Smith's conversation, but she found her altogether engaging—not inconveniently shy, not unwilling to talk [...] shewing so proper and becoming a deference, seeming so pleasantly grateful for being admitted to Hartfield [...] that she must have good sense and deserve encouragement. Encouragement should be given [...] *She* would notice her; she would improve her [...] she would inform her opinions and her manners. It would be an interesting, and certainly a very kind undertaking; highly becoming her own situation in life, her leisure, and powers. (I iii 22–23)

Even on a first reading one is aware of the satiric voice at work in this passage, as Emma's thoughts are exposed in a way that raises doubts about her *judgment* as it shows her flattering herself about her *intentions.* We have already been told of her 'disposition to think a little too well of herself' (I I 3). But what is also worth noticing here is that Harriet's development as a character, such as it is, her very existence as a figure in the novel, is from the start coolly and deliberately placed *inside*

Emma's imaginings and scheming. We are told almost nothing about Harriet that does not come to us through Emma. We do sometimes hear others talking about her, memorably Mr. Knightley and Mrs. Weston, and occasionally Frank Churchill—and of course, Mr. Elton has remarks about Harriet dragged out of him by Emma—but it is all really as an accessory to Emma, in the context of her effect on Emma's life, that Harriet exists, as if she were a character in a fiction not by Jane Austen but by Emma, or as if she were a doll. Let us pause to think about this a little: Emma herself recognizes from the outset that Harriet will not be the sort of friend she had in Miss Taylor, but that's fine:

> Such a friend as Mrs. Weston was out of the question [...] Two such she did not want. It was quite a different sort of thing—a sentiment distinct and independent. Mrs. Weston was the object of a regard, which had its basis in gratitude and esteem. Harriet would be loved as one to whom she could be useful. (I iv 25–26)

We can only shudder at the ways in which Emma turns out to be 'useful' to Harriet. 'Useful' is not always a bad word in Jane Austen, it does not mean what we might mean by 'using' people; Miss Taylor, too, was a 'useful' friend. But when applied to Emma's incursions into Harriet's existence as an autonomous being, her meddling, the word becomes almost savagely ironic. Harriet, scarcely an entity in the novel outside Emma's thoughts, provides an outlet for her imagination. Her illegitimate origins do not, for Emma the imaginist, signify shame as they do for realistic Mr. Knightley. Though we scarcely ever see Emma reading anything (I'll say a little more about that), she must have read novels such as Henry Fielding's *Tom Jones* or Fanny Burney's *Evelina,* in which a young person's obscure origins eventually reveal their fathers to be a squire or even a baronet, a grand marriage following as a matter of course. This is the type of story she invents for her little friend, Harriet Smith.

The introduction of Harriet into the text ('she was the natural daughter of somebody', later expanded by Mr. Knightley into '"the natural daughter of nobody knows whom"' (I ii 22; I viii 64)) are almost the only words attached to Harriet until much later in the novel that are not located inside Emma's thoughts. When Emma stops thinking about Harriet, as once the first infatuation is passed, she does for quite long periods, it is almost as if Harriet ceases to be. The story of Emma and

Harriet is really located in Volume I (though it threatens to come back with a bang in Volume III) while Volume II is given to Emma and Frank Churchill, and Volume III to a wider set of relationships, among which Jane Fairfax moves into greater prominence. The stories of Frank and Jane are, like the story of Harriet, versions of fairy tales about foundlings and orphans. But these stories occupy a place, in the novel, much more independently of Emma than does that of poor Harriet. Frank's story appears first, in Chapter ii, as part of his father's, Mr. Weston's, but is also added to in several later instalments before he appears. We learn of the death of Mr. Weston's first wife, and Frank's mother, the grand Miss Churchill of Enscombe, and of how that was soon followed by the little boy's adoption by his proud, snobbish uncle and aunt, who 'having no children of their own [...] offered to take the whole charge of the little Frank [...] the child was given up to the care and the wealth of the Churchills [...] it had become so avowed an adoption as to have him assume the name of Churchill on coming of age' (I ii 14–15).

Later we hear of '"the letter [...] the very handsome letter"' Frank writes his stepmother on her marriage (I ii 16). We never see that letter, nor, in this novel, any other letter until Frank's long last self-exonerating letter to Mrs. Weston near the end of the novel, although in another way the novel is full of letters, letters talked about and letters not talked about until much later. Frank, 'one of the boasts of Highbury [...] [though] he had never been there in his life' (I ii 16), is woven into the texture of the novel and into the thoughts both of Mr. Knightley, so comically and touchingly prejudiced against this unknown young man, and of Emma, who

> in spite of [her] resolution of never marrying [... found] something in the name, in the idea of Mr. Frank Churchill, which always interested her. She had frequently thought [...] that if she *were* to marry, he was the very person to suit her in age, character and condition. (I xiv 128)

And is not what attracts Emma exactly what alarms and even threatens Mr. Knightley?—the air of romance attaching itself to the never-seen, youthful Frank, the foundling story which plays such a role in sentimental and Gothic eighteenth-century fictions and which is ubiquitous in this novel. In their different ways, both Emma and Mr. Knightley are paying their respects to this literary tradition in their response to Frank, but, unlike the romance Emma invents for Harriet's origins, the romance of Frank's story is alive in other minds than Emma's.

Jane Fairfax is also known, like Frank Churchill, by her letters and, just as Mr. Knightley will later exclaim about Frank, '"His letters disgust me"', Emma will express her own exasperation with Jane's epistolary traces: '"Every letter from her is read forty times over [...] I wish Jane Fairfax very well; but she tires me to death"' (I xviii 260; I x 92). Her hostility to Jane is a double of Mr. Knightley's to Frank, and, like his, has a strongly comic side. In Chapter xix Emma, visiting the Bateses under the illusion that there will not be a letter from Jane to be read, fairly sprints from the house on finding to her horror that there is. But the chapter that follows Emma's lucky escape takes the same format in telling Jane's story from the beginning as is used for Frank's birth: loss of *both* parents, early childhood in Highbury, and her adoption by the well-off Campbells. But it is clear that in her case there is no pending inheritance except work: 'she should be brought up for educating others [...] To provide for her otherwise was out of Colonel Campbell's power [...] his fortune was moderate and must be all his daughter's [...] Such was Jane Fairfax's history' (II ii 175). And how neatly Jane's history slots into Frank's, matching in so many respects, and contrasting only in the matter of fortune—enough to make a Cinderella conclusion for these two so very appropriate. And Emma, as we have seen and will see, has a taste for fairy tale endings, but she wants to control to which cases they apply. She has always been drawn to Frank as a fantasy figure, and when she meets him, the reality seems to match up but, whether in reality or fantasy, she has always been repelled by Jane's reserve: 'she could never get acquainted with her' (II ii 178).

Instead, it is Harriet with whom she chooses to become acquainted. We have examined the heartfelt language of female friendship which Emma attached to her feeling for Mrs. Weston—'"I certainly do forget to think of *her* [...] as having been anything but my friend and my dearest friend"' (II vi 216), she declares, in one of the warmest and most sincere statements she makes anywhere in the novel—and we have glanced at her lack of enthusiasm for Jane Fairfax's virtues. This might be the moment to examine the language that grows up around her attachment to Harriet. We will see quite quickly, I think, that though Mr. Knightley terms her feeling an '"infatuation"', there is a sense in which, almost throughout the novel, Emma is aware of nothing so much about Harriet as her limitations: as a friend; as a fellow creature; as anything at all (I viii 64).

Certainly as an intellect. In Chapter iii and again in Chapter iv we are told, and this is the judgment of Emma Woodhouse, whose cleverness is declared in the first sentence of the novel, 'Harriet certainly was not clever' (I iv 25). This chapter, detailing the early stages of their intimacy, establishes that Emma is not seeking any sort of equality in this friendship she has taken up: 'Harriet [...] only desiring to be guided by any one she looked up to [...] exactly the something which her home required' (I iv 25). Again, the language displays Emma's vanity in a manner at once unflinching, and, as many critics have noted, rather forgiving.[5] The tone of the narrative, as Emma's mode of being useful to Harriet ranges from the mildly absurd to the nearly catastrophic, retains a comedy to which the much-repeated word 'blunder' gives the clue. Emma is being foolish, is deluded. The potential which this meddling holds for real damage and real wrongdoing is kept out of sight for many chapters, for she is *aiming* at improvements—the girls are 'meaning to [...] read together' (I v 37)—but, as Mr. Knightley foresees, this does not happen, and throughout this first part of the novel Emma and Harriet really do little but stroll from place to place idly chattering. And as winter sets in and the weather grows cold for walking, the girls are shown preoccupied, not with even the first chapters of books which they once managed, but with Harriet's riddle collection, a perfect occasion for showcasing Emma's cleverness, Harriet's stupidity, and the banal emptiness of their joint object, Mr. Elton. Scarcely pausing to glance at Harriet as she sits puzzling over his courtship riddle 'in all the confusion of hope and dullness', Emma romps through it with the ease of a born cryptic crossword-solver (I ix 76). Even in the moment, Emma is given pause by the thought that Mr. Elton's charade attributes to her friend a 'ready wit', or any wit at all. '"Humph! [...] A man must be very much in love indeed, to find her so"' (I ix 76). Later, as her confidence that Mr. Elton is in love with Harriet begins to wane in view of his marked attentions to *her*, she still clings to the hope that a man who 'can see

---

5   See, for example, Tony Tanner, *Jane Austen* (Houndmills: Macmillan 1986) and Janet Todd, *The Cambridge Introduction to Jane Austen* (Cambridge: Cambridge University Press, 2006), https://doi.org/10.1017/cbo9780511607325

ready wit in Harriet' may still prove to be stupid enough to marry her (I xiii 119).

In the chapters after she realizes her blunder over Mr. Elton, she often wearies of Harriet's droning on about him, and finds that Mr. Martin is sometimes 'useful as a check' to Mr. Elton (II iv 198). And it is always clear to the reader that Harriet's devotion to 'dear Miss Woodhouse'— what Mr. Knightley calls her unconscious flattery—operates as a kind of imitation, flattery's sincerest form: her words often echo Emma's, if in a muddled fashion. There is comedy in this, as when in their talk about Jane Fairfax's superb musicality, the discussion of taste and execution, in which Emma ruefully admits that Jane Fairfax has both, Harriet's reply is the clueless, '"I saw she had execution, but I did not know she had any taste. Nobody talked about it"' (II ix 250) Emma, so aware of tone, and taste, and vocabulary—how she will despise Mrs. Elton '"with her Mr. E., and her *cara sposo*"' must notice Harriet's feeble grasp of anything resembling an idea (II xiv 301). She shows, indeed, that she does, in Chapter xxi, when she discounts Harriet's quite moving account of her meeting with the Martin family with the inward shrug of 'and besides, what was the value of Harriet's description?—so easily pleased—so little discerning;—what signified her praise?' (II iii 192). This is phrasing that the reader sees, though Emma does not yet, that is incompatible with real friendship. In a terrible, unmissable contrast to the language of friendship attached to Mrs. Weston, the language of Emma's affection for Harriet combines patronization with dismissiveness and almost with contempt.

In the course of the novel we see Emma make up stories about Frank Churchill: he is in love with her; and she with him; all poppycock. And about Jane Fairfax: she is in love with Mr. Dixon; also utterly untrue. But the story she is busiest at, and most dangerous, to herself and to others, her most active foolishness, which amounts, from its first effects, to real harm, is the story of Harriet Smith, whose illegitimacy and obscurity *must*—because Emma Woodhouse wills it—be a cloak for high birth and no impediment to a grand marriage. The friendship with Harriet ('"You have been no friend to Harriet Smith"', Mr. Knightley tells her early on, and he is more right than he knows (I viii 66)) is no more than a story she tells herself '"one idle day"' (I i 11)—one idle season, perhaps—a sort of daydream, such as a very little girl might have about her doll.

Ferociously young for her age, Emma treats Harriet as a plaything: her fancies about Harriet imagine no independent action on Harriet's part at all. And this is what gives the moment late in the novel, when, as it were, Harriet the doll, the walking doll, comes to life, and begins talking back, a quality almost of horror. It is of course set on a sunny morning at Hartfield; *Emma* must be, in setting, the least Gothic of Jane Austen's novels. But the moment when Harriet stops behaving as if Emma had made her up, dressed her, taken her from one suitor and handed her to another, stifled her schoolgirl giggle and given her, as Mr. Elton stupidly but prophetically says, '"So much superadded decision of character! "', when Harriet decides, for herself, that she is going to marry Mr. Knightley, this moment has a distinctly chilly, Gothic feel (I vi 44).

It is Chapter xlvii, and it is—almost—the last in a veritable cascade of revelations: Mrs. Weston has astonished Emma with the news that Frank Churchill is in love with Jane Fairfax, and she with him; they are engaged and have been for nine months; Emma has relieved Mrs. Weston with the news that she is not in love with Frank Churchill herself; and now Harriet's being mildly surprised but not really interested in the news, has amazed Emma further. But there is much more to be revealed: as Harriet shrugs off Frank Churchill, Emma

> could not speak another word.—Her voice was lost; and she sat down, waiting in great terror till Harriet should answer [...]
> 'Are you speaking of—Mr. Knightley?'
> 'To be sure I am.' (III xi 441–42)

If Emma has lost her voice, Harriet has found hers. It is the only chapter in which Harriet's words outnumber Emma's, for some of the exchange she is turned away from Emma (also rare) but she talks in great, long paragraphs, fifteen, sixteen lines at a time, and even her single lines signal a new independence. '"Oh! Miss Woodhouse, how you do forget!"' (III xi 442) is something the Harriet of Volume I would never have been able to say. As Harriet's words roll on, more than once, 'Emma could not speak' (II xi 443). It is an intensely dramatized, stage-worthy but never stagey, scene, Harriet at the window, Emma clinging to her seat: so, Emma is looking up at her as she asks 'in consternation, "Have you any idea of Mr. Knightley's returning your affection?"' and Harriet is looking down at her as she replies 'not fearfully'—'"Yes [...] I must say that I have"' (III xi 444). The momentary reversal of the usual power relation between the two young women is sudden and absolute: if Harriet has been something of an automaton, she now partakes of the horror-effect of the automaton who comes to life.

And the trappings of courtesy which conceal the workings of the marriage market are stripped away to reveal the skeleton beneath, of sheer head-to-head rivalry over scarce resources; the two friends are really only rivals. But, of course, Harriet is, even here, very 'useful' to Emma, is she not? For what else would have revealed to this young woman, so clever but so lacking in instinct, what else would have made her 'understand, thoroughly understand her own heart'? (III xi 449). The revelation which follows on Harriet's wish to marry Mr. Knightley is that 'Mr. Knightley must marry no one but herself' (III xi 444). And no one does. For this chapter, with its hundreds of Harriet's words, is also the last chapter in which she speaks. Emma, entirely understandably, suggests by note that they not meet just then. The novel, perhaps less sympathetically, removes Harriet, once Mr. Knightley is out of her reach, to London and the dentist in 1814, the year before Jane Austen's nieces visit a London dentist and end up having a number of surprise extractions, and a few years before the composition of *Sanditon*, with its dental horrors. It might seem that Harriet is well punished for those less-than-deferential speeches to Miss Woodhouse. We never hear Harriet speak again, and we never again see her walking with Emma.

Instead, we see a sad, suffering Emma, have at least one sleepless night to mull over her 'blunders' of the past few months, now given the stronger and more accurate name of 'blindness' (III xi 448). Sad Emma reflects rightly on her 'insufferable vanity [...] her arrogance [...] mischief [...] evil [...] a folly which no tongue could express' (III xi 449–50). Just as the novel's opening established a forgiving tone toward Emma's 'disposition to think a little too well of herself', this crashing recognition of that propensity, so fully and almost humbly shared with the reader, disarms much of the desire which may have grown up in the reader over the novel's 400 or so pages, to see Emma humbled. We realize we don't really want that to happen: or we don't want it to be the last thing that happens, don't want this black day to be 'but the beginning of wretchedness' (III xi 448). So sorrowing, self-accusing Emma takes a walk, alone with her very uncomfortable thoughts, but she is joined on the walk, and by Mr. Knightley. They take one turn around the shrubbery, as though they were embarking on Emma's father's winter walk, and reach almost total misunderstanding on the way. All is lost. But it is not winter but summer: they take another turn, and this final, shared walk, is the occasion for Mr. Knightley to produce one further, greatest of all, revelations: he loves her, and for Emma, full of the deliriously happy, if also shockingly egotistical, recognition that 'Harriet was nothing […] she was every thing herself'—for Emma to offer one more revelation, the novel's final one: that Emma and Mr. Knightley, are meant to be, and always will be, the perfect walking companions (III xiii 469).

9. Emma in the Snow

Those who wrongly categorize Jane Austen as a writer with a narrow compass—'3 or 4 Families in a Country Village', as she teasingly said of herself—must have failed to notice the significance in her novels of the global phenomenon that is the weather.[1] What reader has not shuddered over the prospect of a 'wet Sunday evening' at Mansfield Park, like the one evoked in Chapter xlvii, even more perhaps than at the confession to Fanny that takes place that night, of the details of Edmund's final sad interview with Mary Crawford?[2] And all of Elizabeth Bennet's many admirers will have delighted in her 'crossing field after field at a quick pace, jumping over stiles and springing over puddles' to arrive at Netherfield, '"her petticoat, six inches deep in mud"' (I vii 36; I viii 39), on her errand of mercy to sister Jane.

But it is in *Emma* that the weather is allowed to make the most difference to people's behaviour: consider the hot day at Donwell in Chapter xlii which renders Mrs. Elton speechless and brings out Frank Churchill's wicked temper, or the following day at Box Hill where perfect weather wreaks almost universal wretchedness and havoc. And is it not just hearing about the high wind at a water party at Weymouth that starts that 'very dear part of Emma, her fancy' (II viii 232) speculating on Jane Fairfax's relationship with Mr. Dixon—while in fact it may have been that same 'sudden whirling round of something or other among the sails' (II I 171) that originally directed the wayward eye of Frank Churchill toward the lowly Miss Fairfax?

Like most of Jane Austen's novels, *Emma* has a central action which unfolds over about a year, and therefore takes its characters through a

---

1   *Letters*, p. 275.
2   Austen characterizes the wet Sunday as: 'the very time of all others when if a friend is at hand the heart must be opened and every thing told' (III xvi 524).

    https://doi.org/10.11647/OBP.0216.09

winter: *Northanger Abbey*'s action is the most compressed, and nearly misses winter out, beginning after the Christmas holidays which introduced James Morland to the Thorpes, but in *Pride and Prejudice*, *Sense and Sensibility*, *Emma* and *Persuasion* the action begins in the autumn and covers much of the ensuing year; *Mansfield Park*'s main action begins with the summer arrival of the Crawfords at Mansfield Parsonage, but continues for almost a year, including of course the Christmas when Edmund is ordained. So, all the novels have some winter chapters.

But only *Emma* has a snowfall. In *Mansfield Park* a little snow on the ground prompts Sir Thomas to ask why Fanny does not have a fire in the East room and snow features in Aunt Norris's account of the trouble she took to shepherd the household to Sotherton.[3] Jane Austen's letters mention snow from time to time, usually unenthusiastically: but that may be because she seems often to be in a city when it is snowing, so that by snow she must most often mean slush. But perhaps she just did not like it—the combination of impassable roads and impractical garments—think how often a moment in one of her novels turns on who has the thickest boots, or whether the ground is unsuitable for ladies' shoes.

But as a snow-loving North American deprived of my birthright by living in Britain, where it really does not snow nearly enough, I have always treasured the snowfall in Chapter xv of *Emma*, which endangers no one's safety, despite Mr. Woodhouse's fears, but threatens everyone's equanimity: at the news that snow has fallen while the party from Hartfield is having an unwonted evening out at Randalls, 'every body [...] had something to say'—most of it absurd (I xv 136).

We should not forget, though, that this tense chapter in which snow falls, threatening to overturn carriages, and keep Mr. Woodhouse from his dish of gruel and his elder daughter from her children, this chilly chapter begins and ends with the heat emanating from the amorous Mr. Elton. His overindulgence in Mr. Weston's good wine first '[elevates] his spirits' (I xv 141) so that his attentions to Emma—attentions the reader has understood, while Emma has refused to recognize them—these

---

3   'what with frost and snow upon beds of stones, it was worse than anything you can imagine, I was quite in an agony about him [the senior coachman]. And then the poor horses too!— To see them straining away! You know how I always feel for the horses' (II i 222).

attentions breathily, vinously increase, prompting 'surprize' in Mrs. Weston and offending Emma even before the announcement of snow produces a general atmosphere of alarm (I xv 135).[4] His over-indulgence, once the carriages are in motion and he is alone with Emma, will lead Mr. Elton as the chapter moves to a climax, to seize her hand, demand her attention and then to be 'actually making violent love to her' (I xv 140); though her contemptuous rejection sobers him up fast, so that the last image we have of this ill-starred pair is of them sitting in the burning silence of 'mutually deep mortification' as the carriage inches its way toward Hartfield through the snow (I xv 143). So the snow panic, my main interest here, is bookended by segments of one of the great drunk scenes in literature—again, this is an experiment Jane Austen does not attempt again in her mature fiction. What *is* it about Chapter xv?

The main action is set, as is that of the preceding chapter, at Randalls, the Westons' house, and focuses less on Mr. Elton than on the young Knightleys, on Mr. Woodhouse and his daughter—and on Mr. Knightley. John Knightley, the younger brother, the London lawyer, cool, clever, not-entirely-amiable and distinctly unsociable, is spending an evening out under duress, a constraint which affects most of the Hartfield family: Isabella, John's sweet-natured wife, is never very willing to be separated from her children; Mr. Woodhouse prefers to have no break or variation in his routine. This party, an opportunity for the newlywed Westons to offer hospitality at Christmastime to their oldest and dearest friends, has been achieved by Mr. Weston's sociability working alongside Emma's gift for events management.

As the chapter opens it is getting late, and Mr. Woodhouse, whose postprandial tendency is to withdraw along with the ladies rather than to remain at table with the gentlemen, is already 'quite ready to go home' (I xv 134) when Mr. John Knightley floors the assembly 'with the information of the ground being covered with snow, and of its still snowing fast, with a strong drifting wind' (I xv 136). We have already learned that when he loses patience with his father-in-law's anxieties, John Knightley expresses that impatience with sarcasm: '"I dare say we shall all be safe at Hartfield before midnight"' (I xv 136). He 'pursues

---

4   The 'breathy' attentions of Mr. Eliot might recall Austen's portrait of the 'broad-faced, stuffy uncle Phillips, breathing port wine, who followed them into the room' in *Pride and Prejudice* (I xvi 85).

this', as the narrative puts it 'rather unfeelingly': he is not at all a heartless man, as we learn from his kindness to Jane Fairfax later in the novel, but John Knightley can be rendered almost savage by his father-in-law's dithering—probably because he cannot help but recognize that Mr. Woodhouse's great virtue, his gentleness, is one he himself lacks.

But the snow in *Emma* is one of those events which provides everyone present with the opportunity to act intensely in character: as John Knightley waxes ever more sardonic, and his wife more passionately and absurdly maternal—'The horror of being blocked up at Randalls, while her children were [a half-mile away] at Hartfield was full in her imagination'—Mr. Weston becomes ever more affable and convivial, Mrs. Weston more comforting and kind, Mr. Woodhouse more anxious and nervous, and more dependent on Emma: '"What is to be done, my dear Emma?—what is to be done?"' (I xv 137).

But it is the elder Mr. Knightley, who is like his younger brother in 'penetration' (I xvi 146), but unlike him in forbearance with others' weakness, whose sterling characteristics jump to life here, as he behaves quickly and calmly—and kindly: and it is so low-key as to be almost invisible. Having 'left the room immediately after his brother's first report of the snow,' while the others were fretting and fussing and worrying each other, he has walked out by himself along the Highbury Road—and, in his report back, the rumoured snow, with all its terrors, becomes the real snow, 'nowhere above half an inch deep' (I xv 138). He has spoken to the coachmen, which no one else has thought of doing, despite the fact that this is the single Jane Austen novel in which a coachman (James) attains something like the status of a character. And the two experienced servants have told him that there is 'nothing to apprehend'—and, of course, where Mr. Woodhouse is concerned, apprehensiveness is all (I xv 138).

But Mr. Knightley's quiet heroism here should not blind us to Emma's equally strong-minded behaviour: both of them act fast, and they act fast together:

> Mr Knightley and Emma settled it in a few brief sentences: thus—
>   'Your father will not be easy; why do not you go?'
>   'I am ready, if the others are.'
>   'Shall I ring the bell?'
>   'Yes, do.'
> And the bell was rung, and the carriages spoken for. (I xv 138–39)

A frank, intelligent, mutually confiding, mutually reliant exchange: no 'he said ... she said' on the author's part, no demurring and no hesitation on the characters'—here, these two are calmly decisive amidst all the confusion; they are co-operating, they are equal. They are both forceful, and tactful—tactfulness, whatever the weather, being the single most important requirement for survival in Highbury.

Are they not made for each other? Though it will take them more than 300 pages, and well into a very hot summer, before they both know it.

Some reflections: much writing about Jane Austen emphasizes, indeed, presumes, that she rarely if ever uses literary techniques that could be described as symbolism. I think her treatment of weather contradicts this truism, and here, where the snow is at once a metaphor for the cut-off, snow-globe quality of life in Highbury, and a meteorological phenomenon with its origins in a cyclone of the North Pole as it dissipates itself across the North Atlantic to arrive as a light fall of snow in Surrey, we see the way in which, like her contemporary Wordsworth, she weaves together the realistic and the symbolic. The weather is a symbol of the enclosed and circumscribed world in which Emma has grown up, but it is also a part of the endangering real world which threatens and beckons to the inhabitants of this English village. It is like the war in Europe that has been going on for decades—it was 'the chances of his military life', after all, that introduced Captain Weston to Miss Churchill and produced Frank (I ii 13). Not fully understood by these inhabitants of a slowly changing rural England, or by anyone who lives through them, and rarely discussed in any depth, both 'the weather [... and] the war' (the phrase is from 'As the Team's Head-Brass' by Edward Thomas, who was writing about rural England 100 years later during another war) have deep consequences for Austen's characters.

10. What's Wrong with *Mansfield Park*

I have been thinking about this moment with trepidation ever since it became apparent that I was not going to be allowed to get away with just talking to you about *Pride and Prejudice*. I find *Mansfield Park* the most troubling, the most complicated of Jane Austen's novels, and I am not alone. R. W. Chapman, the great modern editor of her works, calls it 'the most difficult' and acknowledges that it divides readers, not least on the subject of its heroine, Fanny Price.[1] As we'll see, it divided Jane Austen's own family. It is, along with *Northanger Abbey,* the least re-read. Often, when I mentioned I was writing about it, I was told, 'oh, I haven't read it for years', or 'I haven't read it since I was in school and they made us read it'. It's the one I usually re-read only every few years, as, if I am honest, I feel it to cause a kind of darkening of mood I am not always willing to undergo.

I feel as though I need to approach it as Henry Crawford approaches the task of improving Sotherton, from more than one direction, though I hope with more sincerity. Last year I did a workshop on *Mansfield Park* whose title was 'what's the matter with Fanny Price?' I don't want to forget that important question, but I want to approach it from a new direction, so this talk will be in, I think, three parts: my first part examines the question, 'what's the matter with Mansfield Park?' meaning the estate, not the novel; in the second I am going to look at Fanny by examining the novel's presentation of her in a series of settings; and in the last part I want to interweave some questions about Fanny and the

---

1   'Many readers, I suspect, like myself, have found *Mansfield Park* the most difficult of the works, in the sense that it is there hardest to be sure of the writer's general intention.' R. W. Chapman, *Jane Austen: Facts and Problems* (Oxford: Clarendon Press, 1948; repr. 1949), p. 194.

   https://doi.org/10.11647/OBP.0216.10

men in her life: Fanny and William, Fanny and Henry Crawford, Fanny and Edmund; the first two love affairs can't happen, the first because it's against the law of God and man, the second for reasons I want to investigate. The third does happen, but it doesn't make us happy the way that, say, Elizabeth and Darcy, Anne and the Captain, Emma and Mr. Knightley, do.

I am going to read from the novel's opening:

> About thirty years ago Miss Maria Ward, of Huntingdon, with only seven thousand pounds, had the good luck to captivate Sir Thomas Bertram, of Mansfield Park, in the county of Northampton, and to be thereby raised to the rank of a baronet's lady, with all the comforts and consequences of an handsome house and large income. [...] She had two sisters to be benefited by her elevation; and such of their acquaintance as thought Miss Ward and Miss Frances quite as handsome as Miss Maria, did not scruple to predict their marrying with almost equal advantage. But there certainly are not so many men of large fortune in the world as there are pretty women to deserve them. Miss Ward, at the end of half a dozen years, found herself obliged to be attached to the Rev. Mr. Norris, a friend of her brother-in-law, with scarcely any private fortune, and Miss Frances fared yet worse. Miss Ward's match, indeed, when it came to the point, was not contemptible: Sir Thomas being happily able to give his friend an income in the living of Mansfield; and Mr. and Mrs. Norris began their career of conjugal felicity with very little less than a thousand a year. But Miss Frances married, in the common phrase, to disoblige her family, and by fixing on a Lieutenant of Marines, without education, fortune, or connections, did it very thoroughly. She could hardly have made a more untoward choice. (I i 2–4)

The novelist Karen Joy Fowler, in *The Jane Austen Book Club*, remarks that the opening of *Mansfield Park* resembles the story of '[T]he Three Little Pigs'.[2] Frances Ward has married a man of straw, and like that other runaway, Lydia Bennet, will never have a substantial or settled home. Miss Maria Ward—Lady Bertram when we meet her—very much does have a substantial home. Indeed, she hardly ever leaves it, hardly ever goes farther than the shrubbery (and there only in fine weather, I vi 65). The house could almost be said to be a kind of confinement for her, an enclosure, an imprisonment. I want to explore her situation further, but

---

2   Karen Joy Fowler, *The Jane Austen Book Club* (London: Penguin, 2005), p. 94.

first just to note in passing that this beginning 'about thirty years ago' is unique in Jane Austen. Contrast it with other openings:

> It is a truth universally acknowledged...[3]
> No one who had ever seen Catherine Morland...[4]
> Sir Walter Elliot, of Kellynch-hall...[5]
> Emma Woodhouse, handsome, clever and rich...[6]

Closest to it is *Sense and Sensibility*, which takes us through ten years of Dashwood family history before introducing us to the heroines. *Mansfield Park*'s opening, with its thirty-year retrospective, has, has it not, a Victorian feel to it? Even the title might make us think of *Wuthering Heights* or *Bleak House*.

Quite late in the novel, Henry and Mary Crawford will be worried about the air of Portsmouth, about whether confinement there is good or safe for Fanny.[7] No one ever seems to worry about the air of Mansfield Park. But let's look for a moment about what it does to people, especially to women: 'Lady Bertram [...] was a woman of very tranquil feelings, and a temper remarkably easy and indolent' (I i 4). Now I do not dislike Lady Bertram as much as some of her critics do, but something about her life, either as beautiful Miss Maria Ward or as the mistress (nominal) of Mansfield Park, has robbed her of vitality, has made her a moral and intellectual cipher, and a complete nonentity as a parent in a way that makes Mrs. Bennet, in *Pride and Prejudice*, by contrast, seem a woman of uprightness and energy. Mrs. Bennet does, at least, *stand* upright most of the time.

The woman who is contrasted with Lady Bertram in the novel, of course, is not a parent at all. It is her childless sister, Aunt Norris, who

---

3   *Pride and Prejudice.*
4   *Northanger Abbey.*
5   *Persuasion.*
6   *Emma.*
7   When he visits Fanny in Portsmouth, Henry is 'convinced that her present residence could not be comfortable, and, therefore, could not be salutary for her' (III xi 475); he tells her sister, '"I am considering your sister's health [...] which I think the confinement of Portsmouth unfavourable to. She requires constant air and exercise. When you know her as well as I do, I am sure you will agree that she does, and that she ought never to be long banished from the free air, and liberty of the country"' (III xi 476). Mary Crawford writes to Fanny, 'My dear little creature, do not stay at Portsmouth to lose your pretty looks. Those vile sea-breezes are the ruin of beauty and health' (III xii 483).

is a bundle of energy and determination but also a moral cipher, indeed worse than that, a vicious hypocrite. Is this not interesting? That at Mansfield Park there is either too much or too little vitality among the older women, and no morality? And if we look down the family tree at the younger Bertram ladies, plenty of vitality, but no moral life at all, no family affection. They very nearly hate their father, who loves them but does not know them, and, almost worse than no love, there is no fun. Until the Crawfords come, Julia and Maria ride and dance and dress and lord it over Fanny, but the 'winter [...] gaieties' (I iv 39) promoted for them by their busy aunt in Chapter iv seem strangely glacial:

> The Miss Bertrams were now fully established among the belles of the neighbourhood; and as they joined to beauty and brilliant acquirements a manner naturally easy, and carefully formed to general civility and obligingness, they possessed its favour as well as its admiration. Their vanity was in such good order, that they seemed to be quite free from it, and gave themselves no airs; while the praises attending such behaviour, secured, and brought round by their aunt, served to strengthen them in believing they had no faults. (I iv 40)

The arrival of the Crawfords changes this in many ways, bringing lively walks and rides, impromptu dances, theatricals! This all changes the environment of Mansfield Park in a way that cannot be reversed by their departure.

To be sure, the house can grow quiet again, as it was before. There is a brief exchange of views on this in Chapter xxi between Fanny and Edmund, in which, for the first time, she corrects his picture of things: '"it does not appear to me [Fanny tells Edmund] that we are more serious than we used to be; I mean before my uncle went abroad. As well as I can recollect, it was always much the same. There was never much laughing in his presence"' (II iii 230). And Edmund is forced to concede that she is right; what has altered things for him is his passion for Mary Crawford, which robs him, and Fanny, of some of their peace. But Maria has lost all of hers in her passion for Henry: 'She was less and less able to endure the restraint which her father imposed [...] being prepared for matrimony by an hatred of home, restraint, and tranquillity' (II iii 236). Since marriage in the nineteenth century involves all of those things for women, Maria's state of mind, from the moment she refuses to accept her father's offer to help her escape from it, is truly harrowing to contemplate.

But let other pens dwell on guilt and misery. I want to put that off a little—we will find plenty of both, I think, in our consideration of Fanny—and look at one of Mansfield Park's livelier moments, when, later in the novel, Mr. Crawford, somewhat valiantly, one feels, tries to teach the unwilling Fanny and the unable, practically moronic, Lady Bertram, the game of Speculation:

> In the evening it was found, according to the predetermination of Mrs. Grant and her sister, that after making up the Whist table there would remain sufficient for a round game, and every body being as perfectly complying and without a choice as on such occasions they always are, Speculation was decided on almost as soon as Whist; and Lady Bertram soon found herself in the critical situation of being applied to for her own choice between the games, and being required either to draw a card for Whist or not. She hesitated. Luckily Sir Thomas was at hand.
> 'What shall I do, Sir Thomas?—Whist and Speculation; which will amuse me most?'
> Sir Thomas, after a moment's thought, recommended Speculation. He was a Whist player himself, and perhaps might feel that it would not much amuse him to have her for a partner.
> 'Very well,' was her ladyship's contented answer—'then Speculation, if you please, Mrs. Grant. I know nothing about it, but Fanny must teach me.'

The game of Speculation, like the game of Lottery Tickets in *Pride and Prejudice*, is packed with meaning.[8] Here, again, as in *Pride and Prejudice*, an ambiguous male is seated between two women of unequal abilities; even the name of the game is significant, for Henry Crawford is speculating as to his intentions toward Fanny, just as in *Pride and Prejudice* Wickham was after a prize and Lydia was being lined up to pay a forfeit.

Speculation was played by the Austens, and introduced by Jane Austen to enliven the evening entertainments at her wealthy brother Edward Austen Knight's house. So, unlike Fanny and Lady Bertram, she knew the rules, had played it, had, like Henry Crawford, taught others to play it! Like Lottery Tickets, it's a 'round game' with an unfixed number

---

8   For discussion of the Lottery Tickets game in *Pride and Prejudice*, see Chapter 1.

of players, and a noisy game; here it is contrasted with the stately silence which prevails at the Whist table. But might it be the case that such noisy, lively round games were not played at Mansfield Park, even though with four children and an aunt there would have been enough people to play? I want to suggest that the Mansfield Park party's ignorance of the game is symbolic of the strange, solemn, vitiated quality of life among the family there. When the sons, who have other influences, good and bad, in their lives, are excepted, there is Sir Thomas, whose company his daughters find insupportable, Lady Bertram, who does not enliven, does not talk, barely thinks, and Aunt Norris, who provides a kind of fidgety parody of activity, but who is really a life-sucking parasite.

It seems significant that Fanny picks up the rules of the game in three minutes: Fanny is clever and quick. In a family situation, indeed in two family situations, in which the prevailing ethos does not observe or value those abilities, she has nevertheless continued to develop her intelligence, and we'll look at how in a moment. What is more curious, is that in family situations which seem to offer no opportunity for moral development, she should have developed such a deep (and deepening, as the novel progresses) moral being. I want to make some suggestions about that, and about why I think Fanny's moral life remains a problem, at least for me, a little later. What I would like to point out here is that one disappointment for the lover of Jane Austen's other novels, is that we miss that wonderful cross-fertilization between different social strata and contrasting personality types that crowns the liveliest of them: Elizabeth and Darcy, Wentworth and Anne Elliot, Catherine and Henry, all so unlikely at the start, all so perfect in the end. We feel that nothing like that happens here: Fanny marries someone she meets in the first chapter, and with whom she grows up. No surprises, no influx of energy.

What I would like to suggest is that the surprise, and the influx of energy—the cross-fertilization we think is denied—does happen, but it happens in Chapter i, when Fanny comes to live at Mansfield Park. She is the stranger who changes Mansfield Park, who grows in such a way as to give this vacuum a moral centre, and the novel is an examination of what it costs her. In this sense, I think *Mansfield Park* is, like *Emma*, not a romance but a psychological study. *Emma* is, crudely speaking, an experimental novel about how to live, as a woman, with too much ego; *Mansfield Park* is about what can be accomplished with too little.

There is a famous essay by Kingsley Amis called, 'What Became of Jane Austen?' in which he makes the unforgettable remark, 'To invite Mr. and Mrs. Edmund Bertram round for the evening would not be lightly undertaken'.[9] This remark combines the true and the unfair pretty much as Kingsley Amis's always do, but I think it does show us something about Fanny and why so many people find her hard to like: she is the most hidden and unsocial of Jane Austen's heroines, and unlike say Anne and Elinor who have no equal to speak to but who seem to turn to us, Fanny does not *seem* to need us, either. I emphasize 'seem' there because I think she does reach out to the reader, but in the most hesitant, almost reluctant fashion. We see in Anne Elliot someone whom time has subdued, and in Elinor someone whom circumstances have required to be discreet, but in Fanny we see someone who has been made, throughout a childhood that we see—at greater length than that of any other Austen heroine—to feel small, to feel almost invisible. The brilliance with which this is rendered almost outdoes itself in succeeding in making her invisible to us.

But not quite. We need to try a little of the patience and sensitivity that enable Edmund, even when a boy, to find her worth talking to, but we also have to look for her, as he does when he finds her on the stairs, in unexpected places. Because she is, in a way none of the other heroines are, elusive. Just a quick run-through, though, of the whole gang of seven, will show up a lot more shyness than we expect: Elizabeth doesn't speak until Chapter ii, Elinor, Marianne and Anne until Chapter iii. It is only Emma and Catherine who appear on the first pages of their novels, and only Emma who speaks in Chapter i. Fanny is a Chapter ii speaker. This is the timid conversation that begins on the attic stairs with Edmund that wins a little girl's heart, fixes her affections on her kind cousin for life. I want to look at that lovely moment:

> The grandeur of the house astonished, but could not console her. The rooms were too large for her to move in with ease; whatever she touched she expected to injure, and she crept about in constant terror of something or other; often retreating towards her own chamber to cry; and the little girl who was spoken of in the drawing-room when she left it at night as seeming so desirably sensible of her peculiar good fortune, ended every

---

9   From *Spectator*, 199 (1957), 339–40; repr. in *Jane Austen: Critical Assessments*, ed. by Ian Littlewood, 4 vols (Mountfield: Helm, 1998), IV, pp. 74–77 (p. 75).

day's sorrows by sobbing herself to sleep. A week had passed in this way, and no suspicion of it conveyed by her quiet passive manner, when she was found one morning by her cousin Edmund, the youngest of the sons, sitting crying on the attic stairs.

'My dear little cousin,' said he, with all the gentleness of an excellent nature, 'what can be the matter?' And sitting down by her, he was at great pains to overcome her shame in being so surprised, and persuade her to speak openly. [...] For a long while no answer could be obtained beyond a 'no, no—not at all—no, thank you;' but he still persevered, and no sooner had he begun to revert to her own home, than her increased sobs explained to him where the grievance lay. He tried to console her.

'You are sorry to leave Mamma, my dear little Fanny,' said he, 'which shows you to be a very good girl; but you must remember that you are with relations and friends, who all love you, and wish to make you happy. Let us walk out in the park, and you shall tell me all about your brothers and sisters.' [...] He talked to her more, and from all that she said, was convinced of her having an affectionate heart, and a strong desire of doing right; and he could perceive her to be farther entitled to attention, by great sensibility of her situation, and great timidity. [...] From this day Fanny grew more comfortable. She felt that she had a friend. (I ii 16–19)

Even the most heartless reader—even Kingsley Amis—must be moved by that picture, and what it tells us about the nature of Fanny's heart. Her 'attachments', to use a frequent Jane Austen phrase, are strong. Edmund notices that and admires it. I want us to note that capacity for strong attachments, because I think it is, for Jane Austen, one of the foundations of moral life.

But I would like to note also that Edmund, often described from later events as a bit of a stick himself, is here quick-witted and active. He goes swiftly through all the things that might upset any little girl, then reminds himself that *this* little girl has been separated from her family. He finds out quickly which people matter, finds out about her beloved brother William, and he also swiftly finds something for them to do—to write a letter to William—and does it with dispatch. His invitation, 'Then let it be done now. Come with me into the breakfast-room', makes him hero material (I ii 18). How many other busy young boys would have suggested doing it tomorrow, and then forgotten? Edmund does not forget, and Fanny does not forget *that*. This is quiet, unemphatic information about him, about both of them. Just as, tucked way back at the beginning of the passage, Fanny's not being wooed by the grandeur of the house, her family and home and those she loves mattering more, opens her up to us a little; again, a foundation of moral life suggested here, in being attached not to things but to persons. And we see also here a thing we will see over and over again in Fanny: her sense of her own smallness and insignificance: 'The rooms were too large for her to move in with ease.' And—the plot thickens—a curious sense of guilt or shame: 'whatever she touched she expected to injure, and she crept about in constant terror of something or other'.

Fanny is, of course, *the child who could be spared*; the child who, we learn here, required an adored brother (who is an adored son) to be her 'advocate' with her mother, a mother we will later see outrageously favouring her sons over her daughters (I ii 17). Fanny is not the favourite of either parent, and she has come to a new environment where not much favouritism will fall her way, either. In each environment she finds a brother or brother-substitute to be a sort of advocate, and she locks herself into a connection with that brother which prevails over other attachments, even, I think, that attachment with the *reader* which Jane Austen's other heroines encourage us to form. What is distinctive about the presentation of Fanny is that despite this tender introduction and our natural interest in the lonely child, the little girl orphan of much great fiction, for, though of course Fanny has two parents, they just don't need her to be around, Fanny remains for the early chapters of the book comparatively hidden and distanced from the reader.

There are a number of reasons for this. One of these is the relative rarity of her speech, and I want to talk about that in a minute in greater detail, but another is that the action of the opening chapters is not given us through her eyes as happens in the other novels. The omniscient narrator stays much more active and remains aware of things and events that Fanny cannot see or even know about. Even little seventeen-year-old Catherine, in *Northanger Abbey*, conceived and written more than a decade earlier, moves swiftly to the centre of her novel and stays there, but Fanny, aged eighteen, takes a very long time to take up that position, and holds it more diffidently, though not *always* more diffidently. Trying to find Fanny's role in the novel, I felt a little like Mary Crawford when she asks the Bertrams, '"Pray, is she out, or is she not?"', a remark which, of course, Fanny does not hear (I v 56). Here, in the same paragraph in Chapter v, the omniscient narrator speaks of Fanny: 'And Fanny, what was *she* doing and thinking all this while? And what was *her* opinion of the new-comers? Few young ladies of eighteen could be less called on to speak their opinion than Fanny' (I v 56).

I think myself that Jane Austen is having a joke with us here about that silence I want us to talk about. Fanny does speak in the opening chapters, once to tell Edmund, and us, the pitiful fact that she believes, '"I can never be important to anyone"' (I iii 29), probably the only Jane Austen heroine who has felt that at eighteen! But as we read our way through the opening chapters we see and hear many things that Fanny does not. The tone in those chapters is of a novel of manners set in an English country house, without a central point of view, which tells us about Sir Thomas and Lady Bertram and their children, and Mrs. Norris, and the Crawfords, the young 'new-comers'. It is possible in those chapters to forget, as the Bertrams often do, that Fanny is there, and it is only, for most of us, on re-reading that she becomes the person we are most interested in—unless we have such tender hearts that we cannot forget the little girl sobbing on the attic stairs.

To establish the importance of Fanny's silence, and absence from the opening, let's look at some conversations Fanny does *not* hear, which occur in those chapters. I have in mind a rash of conversations which take place after the death of the (completely silent) Mr. Norris. One wonders if there were some clerical jokes on him that were crossed out, since the clergy are for the most part taken seriously here. There is Dr. Grant, the gourmand who dies after too many good dinners, but he hardly appears; there is no Mr. Collins or Mr. Elton to make Edmund's desire to be a clergyman look silly. By Chapter iii, Mr. Norris has gone to his reward, and Sir Thomas and Lady Bertram expect Mrs. Norris to take up her time-share option on Fanny, one promised years ago when the arrangement began:

> Lady Bertram soon brought the matter to a certainty, by carelessly observing to Mrs. Norris, –
>
> 'I think, sister, we need not keep Miss Lee any longer, when Fanny goes to live with you?'
>
> Mrs. Norris almost started. 'Live with me, dear Lady Bertram, what do you mean?'
>
> 'Is she not to live with you?—I thought you had settled it with Sir Thomas?'

'Me! Never. I never spoke a syllable about it to Sir Thomas, nor he to me. Fanny live with me! the last thing in the world for me to think of, or for any body to wish that really knows us both. Good heaven! what could I do with Fanny?—Me! a poor, helpless, forlorn widow, unfit for any thing, my spirits quite broke down, what could I do with a girl at her time of life, a girl of fifteen! the very age of all others to need most attention and care, and put the cheerfullest spirits to the test. Sure Sir Thomas could not seriously expect such a thing! Sir Thomas is too much my friend. Nobody that wishes me well, I am sure, would propose it. How came Sir Thomas to speak to you about it?'

'Indeed, I do not know. I suppose he thought it best.'

'But what did he say?—He could not say he *wished* me to take Fanny. I am sure in his heart he could not wish me to do it.'

[...]

'Then you will not mind living by yourself quite alone?'

'Lady Bertram, I do not complain. I know I cannot live as I have done, but I must retrench where I can, and learn to be a better manager. [...] I *must* live within my income, or I shall be miserable; and I own it would give me great satisfaction to be able to do rather more—to lay by a little at the end of the year.'

'I dare say you will. You always do, don't you?'

[...]

'Well, Lady Bertram,' said Mrs. Norris, moving to go, 'I can only say that my sole desire is to be of use to your family—and so, if Sir Thomas should ever speak again about my taking Fanny, you will be able to say that my health and spirits put it quite out of the question—besides that, I really should not have a bed to give her, for I must keep a spare room for a friend.'

Lady Bertram repeated enough of this conversation to her husband, to convince him how much he had mistaken his sister-in-law's views. (I iii 32–35)

I've chosen to look at this very typical exchange between the two sisters, so unalike in style and yet so alike in self-absorption, because I think it suggests something about the nature of dialogue in parts of Jane Austen's novels. The comedy here comes, and often comes in Jane Austen, from characters contradicting themselves. Here Lady Bertram—of whom I think it could be said that she is not a hypocrite, not *even* a hypocrite, perhaps, because her moral existence is not quite significant enough to attain to hypocrisy—does not generally contradict herself (it would take too much effort to play more than one part), though she is often absurd. Mrs. Norris, on the other hand, is one of Jane Austen's great comic creations, though Claire Tomalin says, with some justice, that she is 'almost too horrible to be comic'.[10] Both Mrs. Norris and her sister are revealed through characteristic dialogue in a way that Fanny, at least in the opening chapters, and perhaps altogether, is not. Here, dialogue and gesture give us Mrs. Norris's appalled reaction to the suggestion that she should share her bed and board with her teenage niece: 'Mrs. Norris almost started "Live with me, dear Lady Bertram, what do you mean?"' From Lady Bertram's wonderful, spaced-out rejoinders one would suspect, if there were an apothecary in attendance on Lady Bertram as there is on Mr. Woodhouse in *Emma*, substance abuse. Lady Bertram does not expect, or desire, to be kept informed of things, but she does know her husband and her sister are both always busy about something.

Then there is the rapid fire, the rat-tat-tat of Mrs. Norris at her most self-protective. My favourite images of her are perhaps of her making off with a few eggs in a basket or saving a few inches of fabric no one wants, but there is much to marvel over in her long, complicated passages of angry self-justification. Her speech here is rigid with exclamation points, they position themselves like fence pickets or sword points: it requires seven exclamations to get rid of the spectre of a long visit from Fanny. '"Me!"' she squeaks more than once, and more than once, too, she refers to the (surely unnecessary) 'spare bed for a friend'.

Lady Bertram's pace is altogether different, but she is, though less harshly, I think, being *exposed* to us by her speech in all her absurdity. I quoted the novel earlier to the effect that she is a 'woman of very tranquil feelings, and a temper remarkably easy and indolent', which the reader can corroborate as she spends much of the novel asleep, but her absorption in her pug and her 'work'—that wonderful Jane Austen word for needlework of all kinds, for what women did who didn't have to do anything—marks her, as Mrs. Allen's interest in clothes in *Northanger Abbey* will mark her, as something of a fool: '"I hope she will not tease my poor pug"', is all we hear her say on the subject of her little niece coming to live with them (I i 11). Later in the novel, when circumstances—the illness of her son, the disgrace of her daughter—require her to feel, she is shown as distinguished less by the depth of her feelings, than by their adaptability, their willingness to accept

---

10   Claire Tomalin, *Jane Austen. A Life* (London: Penguin, 1998; repr. 2000), p. 232.

substitutes. She does not, fortunately, lose her son, but when she to all purposes loses her daughter, Fanny becomes the substitute; then Susan becomes the substitute for Fanny; just as, presumably, in all these years, one pug must have given way to another.

I want to suggest that the hallmark of real feeling, of moral heroism, in this novel, the test of the strength of the capacity for attachment and therefore of one's moral life, is the refusal to accept substitutes. We might note in passing that this reflects better on Fanny than on Edmund. The little girl who loved her brother William, and was loved by him, can enlarge her heart for that sort of love just once, I think. Chapter ii ends, 'she loved him (Edmund) better than any body in the world except William; her heart was divided between the two' (I ii 25). When I reread this I can find it in my heart to pity Mr. Crawford.

Dialogue is used, in this novel, not only to *expose* as is the case with Mrs. Norris and Lady Bertram, but also to *reveal*. The opening chapters continue to enlarge the family circle with the introduction of Mr. Rushworth and his engagement to Maria—poor Mr. Rushworth! 'a heavy young man, with not more than common sense', and then the far from heavy, in every sense, Crawfords, the brother and sister who will cause all the trouble (I iv 44). I just want to point out that so far are we from being inside Fanny's head in these chapters (Chapters iv and v) that the conversations which introduce this attractive pair take place at the parsonage, where their half-sister lives with her piggy husband, while from the sections which follow, in which the two households of young people get to know each other, Fanny is almost eerily fenced off. But I think it is here, as Edmund and Mary Crawford begin to pair off (and, alas, Maria and Henry also, two pairs of doomed lovers in this novel which is full of doomed and illicit love affairs), that because, as Mary says about Fanny, '"she says so little"', it gradually comes to be *along with her* that we hear the others speaking, and Fanny begins to gain importance for the reader as a kind of co witness, and interpreter, of the events (I v 56). It is important that as she, with deep and unacknowledged sadness and, more painful, I think, unacknowledged *rage*, watches Edmund drifting toward Mary Crawford, that protective brother-circle around her is removed and we have a space to *be with her* and know her feelings.

I want to look now at a conversation which Fanny does hear, though she takes almost no part in it. This is in Chapter x, the day at Sotherton, after Fanny, exhausted by being an awkward third in the flirtatious conversation about distances (nicely complemented by the growing *lack* of distance between Edmund and Mary Crawford), is sitting pensively on a bench, only to be joined by Maria and Henry, another mismatched, erotically charged duo, and find herself once again, at barely eighteen, in a position halfway between chaperone and voyeur. As Edmund and Mary had made an allegory out of distance, Henry and Maria make one out of boundaries: '"I cannot get out"', Maria quotes, gesturing toward the locked park gate that points in the direction of her marriage to Mr. Rushworth (I x 116). '"And for the world you would not get out without the key and without Mr. Rushworth's authority and protection"', Mr. Crawford hums suggestively, '"with my assistance, I think it might be done"'. Maria passes round the edge of the gate to 'the other side' while Fanny objects, 'feeling all this to be wrong' and unconsciously grasping all the couple's *double entendres* (I x 116). And surely feeling that, while Mr. Crawford is trifling with Maria, he is treating Fanny as if she were of less consequence than a servant, as if she were *nothing*. This is so close to Fanny's own sense of herself that this moment, forgotten by him but not by her, is where her instinctive dislike of Mr. Crawford ripens into something very like hatred.

This moment is neatly, and painfully, paralleled with the later moment, in Chapter xviii, when, in the midst of the bustle of the theatricals, Fanny retreats to her beloved, if frigid, East Room to find herself followed there, first by Mary and then by Edmund, who are surprised and delighted to find each other! Once again, she is the unwilling third, the unhappy chaperone, in an unacknowledged love scene. In this section, in fact, she has to prompt the two lovers as they stumble through the scene in the play which does acknowledge their love. Fanny is by now very much the central point of view; let us see and hear the rich episode of the rehearsals of August von Kotzebue's *Lovers' Vows*, as translated by Elizabeth Inchbald.

The plot is as follows: Baron Wildenhaim has seduced and abandoned a young chambermaid called Agatha Friburg in his youth. When the story opens she is living in poverty, where she is found by her son, Frederick, who has been a soldier. When he learns the true story of his birth, he goes out to beg in order to support his mother. On the road he meets the Baron, his father, and tries to rob him. When he is taken by the police he reveals the identity of his mother, his father and himself. With the aid of the clergyman, Anhalt, he persuades the Baron to marry Agatha. The Baron also consents to the marriage of his daughter, Amelia, to Anhalt, instead of to Count Cassel, a rich but brainless fop he had in mind for her. The casting at Mansfield Park is as follows:

MEN

Baron Wildenhaim	Mr. Yates
Count Cassel	Mr. Rushworth
Anhalt	Edmund Bertram
Frederick	Henry Crawford
The Butler	Tom Bertram
Landlord	Tom Bertram
Cottager	Tom Bertram

WOMEN

Agatha Friburg	Maria Bertram
Amelia Wildenhaim	Mary Crawford
Cottager's Wife	Mrs. Grant (first, Fanny Price)

I think the wit with which Jane Austen accomplished the casting is very clear. Henry is Maria's *son*. This may license some touching, which Edmund would be more worried about if he weren't busily compromising himself with Mary while playing the clergyman who is to marry her character. Mr. Yates has all the lines, Tom is all over the place and poor Mr. Rushworth plays someone rich but brainless who gets written out of the story. Fanny writes herself out, too, but she stays to watch and listen to (and prompt—for she is always useful) the others.

Now, the issue of the moral dangers of private theatricals is always going to be a tough one for modern readers, but we should note it was an odd one for Jane Austen's contemporaries as well. The Austens performed plays at home themselves, Jane Austen as a teenager wrote plays for home performance, they attended many plays—even in the last year of her life, Jane Austen attended plays. She and Cassandra assisted, as women of nearly Lady Bertram's and Mrs. Norris's age, at the making of costumes—perhaps, who knows, the sewing of the curtain, too—in private theatricals at the house of her rich brother, Edward Austen Knight. The issue here seems not to be theatricals themselves, but both the absence of Sir Thomas and the presence of all of the strangers, though without Mr. Yates and the Crawfords, of course, the matter would never have arisen. That characteristic Bertram lack of *joie de vivre* means that, unlike the Austens, they have always confined themselves to occasional recitations from Shakespeare. Not only Jane Austen's audience in the wider public, but her first audience, her family, found the moral weight given to the theatricals a problem, and it was not the only problem that they found in the novel. They read in instalments, and Jane's beloved brother Henry, as soon as his namesake appeared, said to her, '"I see now how it will go"', but read the second half, he confessed, 'in *bafflement*'.[11] Jane told another correspondent, here showing less capacity for self-delusion than Fanny, I think, how much Henry liked *Mansfield Park* as a whole: 'Henry has finished Mansfield Park, & his approbation has not lessened. He found the last half of the last volume *extremely interesting*'.[12] Austen's biographer, Claire Tomalin, is not alone in pointing out how often we say that when we don't know what to say![13]

The family didn't like Fanny much, either, Mrs. Austen famously finding her 'insipid', the favourite niece Anna declaring she 'could not bear Fanny', and there is a long line of subsequent critics who have also found her insufferable.[14] Cassandra Austen was 'Fond of Fanny', and is reported to have 'tried to persuade [Jane Austen] to alter the end of

---

11   Ibid., p. 229. Austen wrote: 'Henry has this moment said that he like M.P. better & better;—he is in the 3d vol.—I believe now he has changed his mind as to foreseeing the end' (*Letters*, p. 258).

12   *Letters*, p. 261.

13   Tomalin, *Jane Austen*, p. 229: 'This is a remark so noncommittal that you suspect him too of reservations about the way she chose to end the story'.

14   'Opinions of Mansfield Park', in *Later Manuscripts*, ed. by Janet Todd and Linda Bree, The Cambridge Edition of the Works of Jane Austen (Cambridge: Cambridge University Press, 2008), pp. 230–31. Janet Todd writes that she was 'startled, then offended' by Fanny Price as a student, but offers a reconsideration of her in the light of later feminisms in Janet Todd, 'The Price is Right: Returning to *Mansfield Park* by Jane Austen', *TLS* (March 6, 2020), https://www.the-tls.co.uk/articles/re-reading-mansfield-park-jane-austen-janet-todd/

Mansfield Park and let Mr. Crawford marry Fanny Price'.[15] Why didn't Austen let this happen? Crucial here, it seems to me, is what Fanny sees when she is acting as impromptu prompter in *Lovers' Vows*. As readers we have to enjoy this part of the novel very much, as one thing it does is communicate the huge sense of fun and importance that surrounds almost all amateur dramatics: fun, importance, egoism, trickery, flirtation, disappointment, deception. And self-deception—even before the ghastly rehearsal in the East Room, Fanny has had the agony of listening—and trying to fill her required role sincerely—while Edmund talks himself into playing opposite Mary. '"It must be a great relief to her," said Fanny, trying for greater warmth of manner' (I xvi 182). Still, even Fanny has, through the play, reluctantly, some fun. She admires Mr. Crawford's acting, '"good hardened real acting"' as Edmund calls it (I xiii 146): 'She did not like him as a man, but she must admit him to be the best actor' (I xviii 193–94). She enjoys this, and enjoys prompting the others, listening to their complaints, sewing alongside her aunts, but she will not act, she will not even read the part, it is this fate from which Sir Thomas's startling return saves her.

And I would like to raise a question about that, and a suggestion. We know Jane Austen acted as a child and enjoyed acting as an adult, so it can't be *acting* that is wrong. But something about it is very wrong for Fanny, because although Edmund's request forces her to yield and say she will read the part, she never gets to do that. Why? We have seen this young woman suppressing, with mounting distress and nearly with anguish, her deepest feeling, the passion for Edmund, and her position at Mansfield Park has meant that she cannot at all hope to have what she wants, she can only refuse to take what she does *not* want. I wonder if it is not that, because we see her suppressing so much, it is perhaps terribly important, for our trust of her, that we not see her *pretending*? Is it perhaps that the novel does not—how could it?—condemn theatre, or acting—what it condemns is pretending?

---

15   *Later Manuscripts*, ed. Todd and Bree, p. 231. Louise Knight 'remembers their arguing the matter but Miss Austen stood firmly and would not allow the change'; quoted in Deidre Le Faye, *Jane Austen. A Family Record*, 2nd edn. (Cambridge: Cambridge University Press, 2004), p. 275. Jan Fergus suggests that this was 'almost certainly [...] a mock argument' (*Jane Austen: A Literary Life* (Basingstoke: Macmillan, 1991), p. 144).

I would like to close by returning to the contemporary 'Opinions of *Mansfield Park*', and in particular to the readers who thought that Fanny might marry Mr. Crawford.[16] I want to get there—if indeed I will get there—as Jane Austen did, via *Lovers' Vows.* If you glance at the plot summary, you will see that Baron Wildenhaim, when young, seduced Agatha, a servant in his mother's house. When young he was that stereotypical figure of Restoration and eighteenth-century drama, the rake. The play, like many others, gives him a second chance at love. He marries Agatha at the end, becoming 'the rake reformed', another stereotype. *I see how it will be*, Henry Austen, himself a bit of a charming chancer, if not exactly a rake, told his sister happily. *No you don't,* she must have been thinking, with that enigmatic smile we see in her portrait. There are such difficulties with Mr. Crawford: there is the scene which I have discussed, in which he and Maria behave so shamefully, and with so little care for Fanny's inexperience or her peace of mind. He pays dearly for that bit of indifference. Careless talk costs lives. And there is the heartless, unforgivable scheme he hatches with Mary in Chapter xxiv: '"my plan is to make Fanny Price in love with me"' (II vi 267). To which Mary's careless remonstrance is, '"I do desire that you will not be making her really unhappy"' (II vi 269). There is a BBC adaptation of the novel from the 1980s, which has many flaws, but which has hit upon a brilliant stroke of casting in that its Crawfords look like twins: here they are twins of evil. Though Fanny never hears what is being planned here, the reader cannot forget it.

But what the reader also cannot forget is the change which overtakes Henry Crawford, and I think the reader (this reader, anyway) does not recover from the moment in Chapter xxx when Henry, in love with Fanny Price, the nobody he thought to bowl over with his charm, says, and says truly, '"I could so wholly and absolutely confide in her [...] and *that* is what I want"' (II xii 341). It is surely very daring of Jane Austen to have a moment like this, when this rake longing to reform shows the sort of understanding of marriage that we attribute to the fortunate few who, in her other novels, triumph over the arduous process of courtship. This has echoes of Elinor and Edward in *Sense and Sensibility*—the foolish, erring man, the wise and understanding woman. Rational happiness. It

---

16   Mr. J. Plumptre: 'I had not an idea till the end which of the two wd. Marry Fanny, H.C. or Edmd.' *Later Manuscripts*, ed. Todd and Bree, p. 233.

takes perhaps many readings to note that she has staged this touching scene in the same room in the Parsonage, with the same *dramatis personae*, as the previous scene in which the Crawfords planned their assault on Fanny's innocence. We are not being allowed to forget Mr. Crawford's failings here, though we very nearly do forget them, in the scene in Portsmouth, another triangular scene, but here with Mr. Crawford attempting to undo the evils of those earlier triangles by his focus on Fanny without any discourtesy to Susan. No reader can ignore, I think, the way his quiet concern with Fanny resonates through his, '"I know Mansfield, I know its way, I know its faults toward *you*. I know the danger of your being so far forgotten, as to have your comforts give way to the imaginary convenience of any single being in the family"' (III xi 476). The terrible irony here is twofold: crudely, it seems that given sufficient distractions, Henry Crawford, too, can fall back into the Mansfield habit of forgetting Fanny. But the other forgetfulness, operating in these chapters set in Portsmouth, is Fanny's strange absent-mindedness about those Mansfield faults. In those chapters, as she realizes that her own mother really has no need of her—she was, remember, the child who could be spared—she begins to imagine that Mansfield Park, where she is 'useful', has been a refuge. But the reader was *there*, and knows what it was like for her. It is very disturbing for that remembering reader, to see Fanny recreate the East Room in miniature in the hideaway she makes for herself and Susan upstairs in the noisy Portsmouth house. And to see the alacrity with which she returns to Mansfield Park, 'in [...] danger of being exquisitely happy, while so many were miserable' (III xv 513).

There are lovely moments in the closing pages. The reader is electrified by Lady Bertram's coming 'with no indolent step' to greet her niece with the words, '"Dear Fanny! now I shall be comfortable"' (III xv 517). But the ending, Edmund's disillusionment with Mary, Fanny's efficient filling him in on the many faults he had missed, the vindictive completeness with which Maria and Mrs. Norris are packed off to 'another country' and, most of all, the cousin-marriage, with its suggestion of very quiet satisfactions indeed, seems deeply psychologically credible, rather than romantically satisfying (III xvii 538). Earlier I compared *Mansfield Park* with *Emma* and called it a psychological study. I would like to close by raising that comparison again and suggesting that both novels also, more daringly than the others, portray sexual passion, in particular, hidden passion. *Emma* gives us the extraordinary story of Jane Fairfax and Frank Churchill, and *Mansfield Park* gives us those theatricals, where we see, in a rather Shakespearean way, Mr. Rushworth who loves Maria who loves Henry Crawford, who is also loved by Julia; and Edmund, loving Mary, and also loved by Fanny, who will later be loved by Henry Crawford; and none of these people—the story is, as R. W. Chapman says, very near tragedy—none of these people will get what they want.[17] Except for Fanny. And that is, to quote Jane Austen's brother Henry, 'very interesting'. In the very last paragraph of the novel, as the young couple remove to Mansfield, which is defined there as 'thoroughly perfect', there is an undeniable sense of the drawbridge going up (III xvii 548). The reader can choose whether to be worried, or relieved, that Susan is also inside, 'the stationary niece', the explicit substitute for Fanny, but older, tougher, more vigorous—remember that she carries a knife! (III xvii 546). The two sisters have made their way into Mansfield as two earlier sisters did, and one, Fanny, has brought moral depth and moral meaning to the emptiness and silence she found there, but at such a cost. One remembers, almost too late, that these two sisters are called 'Price'. I draw from these disquieting events one consolation: Fanny and Edmund's children will love their parents and know themselves loved by them. Theirs will be a more blessed generation.

---

17 'In *Mansfield Park* alone does Jane Austen tread the confines of tragedy.' Chapman, *Facts and Problems*, p. 200.

11. Jane Austen and Grandparents

You could not with any confidence expect to see your grandchildren in the world we have lost.[1]

When Jane Austen was born in 1775, she had no grandparents living, her father having been orphaned young and her mother left parentless by 1768. From her teens, though, she lived with parents who were also grandparents, and her own talents as an aunt are testified to most convincingly in her nephew's *Memoir*—'"Aunt Jane" was the delight of all her nephews and nieces'—and elsewhere.[2] For this essay, the question I begin with, given the availability of the grandparent-grandchild relationship to her everyday experience, was why so few of her mature novels explore this relationship very fully. It is true that there are absurd grandparents in her juvenilia, like the mysterious stranger who comes and goes in a trice in *Love and Freindship*; after finding that he is grandfather to a mounting number of distinctly dodgy young people, he dispenses £50 notes and vanishes. And there are the long-suffering, letter-writing grandparents who battle with dignity against the threat posed to their children and their grandchildren by the insidious charms of Lady Susan in that savage, anti-filial little work.[3] But of the major novels, *Pride and Prejudice* is without depicted grandparents, and *Mansfield Park* with its disastrous marriage and its many thwarted marriages, almost seems—but only almost, as we shall see—designed to disappoint all hopes of parents to become grandparents.

In thinking Jane Austen gave little attention to realistic grandparental hopes, wishes and experiences, however, I was wrong, both from lack of alertness to the novels and from failing at first to realize that, though

---

1   Peter Laslett, *The World We Have Lost* (London: Methuen, 1965; repr. 1976), p. 103.
2   J. E. Austen Leigh, *A Memoir of Jane Austen by her Nephew* (London: Folio, 1989), p. 2.
3   For further discussion of *Lady Susan*, see Chapter 5.

    https://doi.org/10.11647/OBP.0216.11

the Austens were a multi-generation family, such a lucky experience, in a time of high infant mortality, late marriage and early death, was rare. As figures in Peter Laslett's *The World We Have Lost* show, before the economic transformations of the early-nineteenth century, less than 25% of the population of England was ever over forty: in Laslett's telling phrase, 'conversation across the generations must have been relatively rare, much more so than it is today'.[4] Although the conversation in *Emma* between Emma and Harriet about Robert Martin's prospects for marriage mimics the tone of an older, wiser woman advising a very young one and is not a reflection of Emma's serious thinking—indeed, like much of Emma's talk, it reflects no thought at all—it does show some knowledge of how her social and economic inferiors made decisions about marriage. Only at the more prosperous level, which Jane Austen usually concentrates on, could a Mrs. Bennet have been aiming for 'the marriage of a daughter, which had been the first object of her wishes, since Jane was sixteen' (III viii 342).

The Austens themselves were a long-lived family.[5] Even Jane survived her fortieth birthday, and her brothers were able to marry early, and to marry young women, some of whom had their first children while still in their teens. The brothers' marital experience also reflected the high rate of early death of first wives and the husbands' subsequent remarriage, a phenomenon also noted by Laslett.[6] With young children needing a mother's care, there would often be a remarriage. Of the five Austen brothers who married, four were married twice. The extensive grandparental experience testified to in the *Memoir* rested on these then-natural developments of family life, but even more it rested on the senior Austens' long and healthy—despite Mrs. Austen's claims to invalidism—lives, which were somewhat exceptional, since though the privileged could marry early they could not—despite their greater access to medical care—depend on that care to guarantee better health than lack of such care gave to the poor. Neither the richest of her brothers, nor the poorest, could keep his first wife alive, an experience

---

4   Laslett, *The World We Have Lost*, pp. 98; 108.

5   For a discussion of the implications of the longer life span in Austen's day, see Devoney Looser, *Women Writers and Old Age in Great Britain 1750–1850* (Baltimore: John Hopkin, 2008).

6   Laslett, *The World We Have Lost*, pp. 104–05.

perhaps reflected in the persistent family myth that *Emma's* Jane Fairfax, married into one of the richest families Jane Austen deals with, is to die in childbirth. It might be possible to see the novels as reflecting both the general experience, with not many grandparents about, and her own, with grandparents taking an active role in the upbringing of their grandchildren.

For, as we'll see, on careful examination, *Sense and Sensibility, Emma* and *Persuasion* turn out to be looking quite hard at grandparents and grandchildren. And *Persuasion,* in particular, uses the experience of the grandparent and the treatment of grandchildren, rather as some of the other novels use behaviour with money, to enable us to see deeply—though often in a quick, deft, sketch-fashion—into the moral and imaginative lives of Jane Austen's characters. So the question I started with—'why so few grandparents and grandchildren?'—has turned into 'why so many'!

If we run briskly through the novels in order of publication, and jettison *Northanger Abbey,* that late-published, early-written novel, as of no interest to the discussion because there is not a grandparent in sight, we see that *Sense and Sensibility* gives us two widowed grandmothers, Mrs. Jennings and Mrs. Ferrars, and one very funny scene in Volume II, Chapter xii, of these two nearly coming to blows over the relative heights of two of their grandchildren, only one of whom is present. For Mrs. Jennings, the affectionate grandmother, the novel also provides a new baby, a son and heir of the daughter to whom she is closer, Mrs. Palmer (Volume II, Chapter xiv). This also enables a plot-enhancing couple of weeks from home for her, looking after mother and baby and leaving the Dashwood sisters in the chilly company of Lady Middleton and the Steele girls. At the novel's end, there is also an almost coy nudge to the reader, an arch bit of indirection about Elinor's pregnancy, hinted at via their need for 'rather better pasturage for their cows' (III xiv 425). This child will have both Mrs. Dashwood and Mrs. Ferrars as grandmothers, and both women are widows. Thus, like the Middleton children and Harry Dashwood, Edward and Elinor's baby will have no living grandfather.

In *Pride and Prejudice,* we are spared seeing how either of the Bennet parents would anticipate either a Bingley, or a Darcy—or, horrors, a Wickham—baby. That is outside the book's scope. But there is the 'young olive branch' of Charlotte and Mr. Collins (III xv 403). One has great hopes for the humour and good sense with which any child of Charlotte's will be brought up; and that baby will have two grandparents, in the Lucases, presumably spending more time than ever calculating how long Mr. Bennet is likely to live.

Mansfield Park, as I've suggested, operates almost actively against a parent's natural wish for grandchildren: the wedding we see ends in bitterness and shame, and two prospective marriages between Bertrams (if Fanny here counts as a Bertram, as she seems to when her uncle is pressing for the marriage) and Crawfords fail to come off, and though the marriage between Mr. Yates and Julia turns out to be less catastrophic than circumstances suggested it might, one feels they both need to grow up themselves before any children would be a blessing.

But with the same coyness—or is it archness?—the sly indirection, the faint nudge, as in *Sense and Sensibility*, closes the novel as Fanny and Edmund 'had been married long enough to begin to want an increase of income, and feel their distance from the paternal abode an inconvenience' (III xvii 547). The plot—Dr. Grant's bathetic death from over-eating, and the expectation of a grandchild, never made explicit—moves them to Mansfield parsonage, so much easier for the new grandparents. Here is another living pair—this baby will have both grandfather and grandmother. We might note that the move closer to Mansfield is not a move closer to Portsmouth, where there will be another grandparental pair. It seems likely that Mrs. Price will content herself with a note saying she will knit something when she can find some time, and that the Bertrams, deprived of other grandchildren by their parental failings, will reap the grandparental benefits of their generosity in adopting Fanny.

Emma, on the other hand, could almost be thought to have been devised with the grandparental relationship in mind, as Mr. Woodhouse has five grandchildren. Unlike the other young mother of a large family whom we see in the novels, *Pride and Prejudice*'s Mrs. Gardiner, who is calm and confident, Isabella Knightley is forever anxious about her own and her family's health and takes them with her everywhere. Thus, Hartfield at Christmas, unlike Longbourne, is full of children. Here and later, when in the early summer Emma and her father are left in charge of the two eldest Knightley boys, we see Mr. Woodhouse in action as a grandfather—as much as we see him in action in anything!—mostly fretting about that holiday at the seaside and its threats, then fussing over Mr. Knightley's tossing the little boys high up into the air, but also enjoying the little word game Emma has made for them, at which he is probably pretty much at their skill level, or not so much below them that it is no fun for anyone but him. Just as he was an anxious father, he is an anxious grandfather, although he is a devoted, attentive one. Sadly, we see no scenes of his supervising their eating, which must require much sleight of hand on Emma's part to get the requisite calories into a pair of hungry and active boys.

Like many of Jane Austen's grandparents, Mr. Woodhouse is widowed, as is the novel's other grandparent, his worthy old friend, Mrs. Bates. The household over the shop in Highbury where so many of Frank Churchill's dreams and wishes are tending, is therefore all female, and includes three generations. I think we need to take some time to think about Jane Fairfax's difficult situation in that too-small house with the endlessly talking and thoroughly well-meaning Miss Bates. Mrs. Bates's deafness may be a trial to her daughter, though she does not complain, only describes: '"I say one thing and then I say another, and it passes off"', says Miss Bates, which the reader has no difficulty believing (II ix 255). But surely Mrs. Bates's great age and her extreme deafness may sometimes produce the blessed effect of total silence. Mrs. Bates seems quite content to be left out of things, and there must be times when Miss Bates is running errands, or talking to the servant Patty in the kitchen, and then one imagines Jane pressing her aching head, silently, to some cushion, and neither having to speak nor to listen. At times the deaf old lady may have been Jane's best friend and a desperately needed resource of silence.

There is, of course, no sly allusion at the end of *Emma* to possible babies—who, with Emma, would dare? Beyond the seaside honeymoon all else is outside the novel's scope; that is, all but perfect happiness. Perfect happiness is in store for the rather more deserving Anne Elliot, too, at the end of *Persuasion,* and, like *Emma, Persuasion* is a book about grandparents and grandchildren. The warm, unaffected Musgroves offer the reader the opportunity to observe a grandparent's trials, perhaps more than a grandparent's rewards. Parents themselves almost beyond count, the older Musgroves have not been prepared by their own (mostly) happy and contented children for dealing with the consequences of Mary's sulky, erratic mothering, as Anne learns on arrival at Uppercross: '"Oh! Miss Anne, I cannot help wishing Mrs. Charles had a little of your method with those children [...]—Bless me, how troublesome they are sometimes!"' (I vi 48). 'Troublesomeness', which the reader sees again and again, which steadily advances the plot and helps control the novel's action as it slowly turns and turns, returning Anne and Captain Wentworth to a right knowledge of their own feelings.

Many readers have been struck by the physical intensity of the scene in which the toddler is clinging stickily to Anne's neck until a whirling moment in which 'she found herself in the state of being released [...] some one was taking him from her [...] Captain Wentworth had done it' (I ix 86–87). Maria Edgeworth, for example, wrote to her aunt in 1818, so possibly during a first absorbed reading, 'Don't you see Captain Wentworth, or rather don't you in her place feel him taking the boisterous child off her back as she kneels by the sick boy on the sofa?'[7] *Persuasion* is the novel in which Jane Austen risks more of these high-intensity, shatter-the-surface moments. The last one in the White Hart Inn in Bath will leave Anne, in Charles Musgrove's honest affectionate words, 'rather done for' (II xi 261), as the moment of Anne's release from her nephew leaves most readers.

Another exceptionally rich moment that focusses on grandchildren is the Christmas scene at Uppercross Hall. This time, the grandparents are securely in control, and the scene has no role in the plot except to demonstrate to the reader how Anne has learnt, in the months at Uppercross, to relax and enjoy herself. The scene bears comparison, lean and concise though it is in style, with the glorious hyperbolic Christmas at old Fezziwig's that haunts Scrooge in Dickens's *A Christmas Carol*:

> There were more dances, and there were forfeits, and more dances, and there was cake, and there was negus, and there was a great piece of Cold Roast, and there was a great piece of Cold Boiled, and there were mince-pies, and plenty of beer. But the great effect of the evening came after the Roast and Boiled, when the fiddler (an artful dog, mind! The sort of man who knew his business better than you or I could

---

7   Quoted in Marilyn Butler, *Jane Austen and the War of Ideas* (Oxford: Clarendon Press, 1975; repr. 1989), p. 278.

have told it him!) struck up 'Sir Roger de Coverley.' Then old Fezziwig stood out to dance with Mrs. Fezziwig. Top couple too; with a good stiff piece of work cut out for them; three or four and twenty pair of partners; people who were not to be trifled with; people who *would* dance, and had no notion of walking.[8]

This section is about a page long; Uppercross Christmas, so trim it is easy to miss, is a paragraph in Chapter ii of Volume II, and depicts the visiting Harville children, the Musgrove children home from school. The girls gather around the table, 'chattering' and 'cutting up silk and gold paper', while at a host of other tables 'bending under the weight of brawn and cold pies [...] riotous boys were holding high revel', and the scene is 'completed by a roaring Christmas fire' (II ii 145).

Without the sensory overload—the 'more' and 'more' of the Fezziwig scene—there is nevertheless a quality of perfectly judged sensory delight here: one hears the 'chatter', and almost hears the scissors snipping, sees the pleasurable flimsiness and flash of gold and silver, smells those pies, and all is brought together with care by the solidity of the tables and trestles, and the sound of the fire, which gives the reader gratifyingly more than just enough, but never too much.

But we would want to note that even in the midst of this idyll there is grandparental labour to be done, the '[sedulous] guarding' of the well-brought up young Harvilles 'from the tyranny of the two children from the Cottage, expressly arrived to amuse them' (II ii 145). As with the list of pleasures, every word here describing the pains of family life is placed with care, and the irony of 'tyranny' juxtaposed with 'amuse' speaks very clearly to the reader who has paid attention to those unruly young boys. Affection and fun—Mr. Musgrove bellowing into Lady Russell's ear while small children clamour on each of his knees—but 'guarding', too. This 'a fine family-piece', as the paragraph concludes, is also a fine grandparental piece (II ii 146).

If this is an almost symbolic moment, renewing the early admiring tones about the elder Musgroves being formed in 'the old English style' (I v 43), the famous picture with which the novel opens, of Sir Walter Elliot gratifying himself with his own entry in the Baronetage, has its symbolic aspect, too. From the image of Sir Walter reading we are moved

---

8　Charles Dickens, *A Christmas Carol* (London: Champan and Hall, 1843), https://www.gutenberg.org/files/46/46-h/46-h.htm, pp. 60–61.

right into looking over his shoulder to read exactly what he is reading, and also to see what, in the past, he has written into this moveable feast of a book. And if we see the Musgroves through their commonplace everyday pleasures, we see Sir Walter through his—and through the pleasures and pains he has avoided.

Sir Walter has amended the entry—'improved it by adding, for the information of himself and his family, these words, after the date of Mary's birth—"married, Dec. 16, 1810, Charles, son and heir of Charles Musgrove, Esq. of Uppercross, in the county of Somerset," and by inserting most accurately the day of the month on which he had lost his wife' (I i 3). One feels intuitively that Sir Walter would have beautiful penmanship. There are no blots or splodges here. And well-known though it is, the paragraph—the corrected version in particular—gives us much to think about. Sir Walter has not added the births of his grandsons, who, of course, do not carry the Elliot name. They are not in line to inherit the baronetcy, or Kellynch-hall. Neither will they be dependent on the shaky Elliot finances for their own start in life. Whatever of '"the Elliot pride"' (I x 95) Mary manages to pump into her sons will not be enhanced by their grandpapa's efforts.

His total silence here about the grandchildren is echoed throughout the novel, as Sir Walter nowhere—nowhere—acknowledges that he is a grandfather. Can it be his vanity, his unwillingness to consider himself old enough for the grandfather role? Possibly. But possibly it is something even less active, and more repellent: Sir Walter does not seem to remember that his grandsons exist. The messages sent to Mary by Sir Walter and Elizabeth do not mention the boys—something which the narrative highlights by contrasting Mrs. Clay's 'more decent attention, in an inquiry after Mrs. Charles Musgrove, and her fine little boys' (II vi 180). In every inquiry after the Cottage household it is only Mary—the Elliot—who is mentioned, though even there neither father nor sister waits to hear the answer. When Mary and Charles arrive in Bath the boys are not mentioned. Since we have no quoted or reported speech from the two little Cottage boys—or any other child in *Persuasion*—it isn't really possible to estimate the importance the Elliot side of the family has in their imaginations. It feels as if Sir Walter may have as little presence in their lives as they have in his.

Neither side could play the role the cultivated Austens played in their own grandchildren's lives, of inspiring reading and writing. The male Musgroves cheerfully accept their limitations, to 'sport [...] without benefit from books, or any thing else' (I vi 47), while the ladies focus on household matters: 'neighbours, dress, dancing, and music' (I vi 46). But despite all the pride, we are assured that Sir Walter never reads anything but the Baronetage, every time we see Elizabeth with a book she is closing it. And I think we can feel reasonably sure that Mary's delight with the Lyme circulating library is not caused by her finally being able to get hold of Mary Wollstonecraft's *A Vindication of the Rights of Woman*! Where the depiction of grandparents may reflect Jane Austen's own experience, though, is in the Musgroves, however commonplace and rough-hewn they are, because they are shown, as the Austens are in the letters and the family *Memoir*, in loving connection with their grandchildren, not just at Christmas, but every day. The chilly blank of Sir Walter's lack of connection with his grandsons thus has in the Musgroves a moral yardstick—but also something more.

For one thing of which Sir Walter is not accused by the world who would call him a 'foolish, spendthrift baronet' (II xii 270) is a lack of family pride. Yet, just as the novel shows from the outset that his pride in Kellynch-hall is something of a delusion (as he deserts it at the first opportunity), it also shows him—and it is in the treatment of his living descendants that it shows him—essentially without the real family pride that keeps the Baronetage going.

The 'book of books' is steeped in dynastic drive (I i 7). Those marriages to 'Marys' and 'Elizabeths' that made and marred fortunes and futures in the past, the 'exertions of loyalty', the mention in Dugdale, though set in the past, were made by men and women who thought not only of their family name but about the future of that name—about their legacy, their descendants (I i 4).[9] Some of the Elliots of the past must have been violent men and determined women, carving out a dynasty, not a race of courtiers and fops gazing into an endless series of mirrors. Sir Walter cannot be blamed for—like Mr. Bennet—failing to produce a male heir (the reader feels sure poor Lady Elliot, leaving three daughters, bore

---

9   For the importance of dynastic names in Austen's fiction, see Margaret Doody, *Jane Austen's Names: Riddles, Persons, Places* (Chicago and London: Chicago University Press, 2015), https://doi.org/10.7208/chicago/9780226196022.001.0001

the brunt of that blame) but he can be blamed, and is, in the novel, both by his own grandparental indifference and the Musgroves' steady exertions: their undemonstrative energy—they are an old county family that is rising in the world, not falling—is contrasted with Sir Walter and Elizabeth's stasis.

In the White Hart scene which gives so much warmth and bustle, chatter and action to the second volume of the novel, there is the memorable eruption—missile-like—of Sir Walter and Elizabeth which effects a physical drop in temperature, 'a general chill [...] an instant oppression' of the happy group spirit which is felt by and simultaneously shames Anne (II x 245). Throughout the novel we see her, though a dutiful and loyal, uncomplaining daughter and sister to these worthless people, shamed by their callousness and irresponsibility. Anne, that thoughtful Anne—and, like Jane Austen, Anne is a loving aunt, who even in her darkest hours can take some pleasure in having been of use in caring for the little boys—does not reflect, as far as the reader knows, on her father's shortcomings as a grandparent. She is aware of his failings in upholding the values of 'an ancient and respectable family' (I i 4), and sadly certain the Elliot tenants and other dependants will be better looked after by the incoming Crofts: she 'felt the parish to be so sure of a good example, and the poor of the best attention and relief, that however sorry and ashamed for the necessity of the removal, she could not but in conscience feel that they were gone who deserved not to stay, and that Kellynch-hall had passed into better hands than its owners' (II i 136). And, of course, the childless Admiral Croft, in a scene with the little boys, behaves much more like an indulgent grandfather with them, than even Mr. Musgrove does: 'he was cut short by the eager attacks of the little boys, clinging to him like an old friend, and declaring he should not go' (I vi 53).

At the opening of Volume II, the little boys at the Cottage—left to the care of servants as the family from the big house leave to support Louisa at Lyme—are presented in an almost symbolic way, an analogue to Anne's own neglect. In reality, of course, elements are already in motion which will transform her condition, in a few months she will be a sailor's wife, who 'gloried' in her situation (II xii 275). And the boys at the Cottage—one imagines them stuffed with cake while the servants gossip and flirt—probably enjoy the license of their temporary situation, which Christmas, as we've seen, will transform. It doesn't seem likely that they suffer from the temporary neglect here anymore than from the steady neglect by their maternal grandfather. But, like the one-book reading list and the mirrored dressing room and the reduction of meaningful connections to the family member who most resembles that dressing room, the grandparental inertia defines Sir Walter's character, and shows him failing not only as a paterfamilias—that would mean nothing to him—but as an Elliot. And that would shame even Sir Walter.

12. Jane Austen and Burns

The immediate stimulus for my discussion today, of Jane Austen and Robert Burns, two writers whose lives overlapped but who are seldom brought together by literary critics, is a passage in a novel which Jane Austen sadly did not live to finish, *Sanditon*, which survived in manuscript and was first published on its own in an earlier period of Jane Austen fever, the 1920s. The passage was first drawn to my attention at, appropriately, a Burns supper. I will first give you a little of the plot context. *Sanditon* tells the story of a sensible, pretty, rather wry young woman, called Charlotte Heywood (she always puts me in mind of a slightly younger and prettier version of Charlotte Lucas, Elizabeth Bennet's friend from *Pride and Prejudice*). Charlotte is paying a visit to the Parkers, a pleasant but rather eccentric family. Mr. Parker, the head of the family, who has inherited a middling sort of fortune, is trying to turn the eponymous village of Sanditon into a seaside holiday town in the mould of Weymouth. Under Charlotte's mildly satirical eye, the locals are shown trying to lure summer visitors with such novelties as a lending library, fashionable medical practitioners, a spanking new hotel, etc. The conversation about Robert Burns that I will come to takes place between Charlotte and a personable but rather silly young man, a baronet whose stepmother is one of the most important of the local entrepreneurs. But all you really need to know is that it takes place between a marriageable young man and a young woman who, like all of Jane Austen's heroines, is in need of, but not in quest of, a husband. So the conversation is between two people who could, though probably won't, fall in love. That gives it its particular flavour.

Like the rest of the draft, which is about sixty pages long, what we're reading is stopped forever at an early point in the composition process. Jane Austen was ill, indeed, though she did not know it, dying, all through the writing, so it is interesting and perhaps poignant that

 https://doi.org/10.11647/OBP.0216.12

among the novel's preoccupations, illness and hypochondria, medical cures and quack practices, loom large. In the following passage, the topic of poetry is treated satirically and the suggestion is that the subject of Burns is a fashionable one. This is the young baronet speaking:

> 'But while we are on the subject of poetry, what think you, Miss Heywood, of Burns's lines to his Mary?—Oh! there is pathos to madden one!—If ever there was a man who *felt*, it was Burns.—Montgomery has all the fire of poetry, Wordsworth has the true soul of it—Campbell in his pleasures of hope has touched the extreme of our sensations—"Like angel's visits, few and far between." Can you conceive anything more subduing, more melting, more fraught with the deep sublime than that line?—But Burns—I confess my sense of his pre-eminence, Miss Heywood.—If Scott *has* a fault, it is the want of passion.—Tender, elegant, descriptive—but *tame.*—The man who cannot do justice to the attributes of woman is my contempt.—Sometimes indeed a flash of feeling seems to irradiate him—as in the lines we were speaking of—"Oh! Woman in our hours of ease" —. But Burns is always on fire.—His soul was the altar in which lovely woman sat enshrined, his spirit truly breathed the immortal incense which is her due.—'

The buoyancy of tone alters markedly in Charlotte's reply:

> 'I have read several of Burns's poems with great delight,' said Charlotte as soon as she had time to speak. 'But I am not poetic enough to separate a man's poetry entirely from his character;—and poor Burns's known irregularities greatly interrupt my enjoyment of his lines.—I have difficulty in depending on the *truth* of his feelings as a lover. I have not faith in the *sincerity* of the affections of a man of his description. He felt and he wrote and he forgot.' (vii 175–76)

This would seem to be a very damning critique of Robert Burns, but we'll see whether, by the end, we think it really is.

Burns was sixteen when Jane Austen was born in 1775, and interestingly, only a year earlier he had first committed what he called 'the sin of Rhyme', writing some lines as part of a campaign to, of course, woo a local beauty.[1] Robert Crawford, author of a notable biography

---

1   'This kind of life—the chearless gloom of a hermit, with the unceasing moil of a galley-slave, brought me to my sixteenth year; a little before which period I first committed the sin of Rhyme'. Letter to Dr John Moore (August 2, 1787), in *The Works of Robert Burns, containing his Life by John Lockhart* (New York: Pearson, 1835), p. 283.

of Burns, and himself a good love poet, comments about this phrase, and these early poems, that it is worth noting both how closely Burns connects the poetic and the erotic impulses, and also that the word 'sin' should attach itself not only to love but to rhyme. He thinks of Burns as having, along with his renowned sense of the pleasures offered by the world, the flesh and the devil, a pervasive sense of sin.[2] My own thought here is that Burns has a sense, as Keats does, of the earthly pleasures, and indeed of sexual attraction and sexual pleasure, as fleeting.[3] 'My luve is like a red, red rose', in the famous late lyric, written only two years before his death, is not initially very promising—how long does a rose last? Yet in the same poem, he promises also to love, to feel what it is to love the girl (which is not the same thing as marrying her, or committing to her for life, as we'll see) 'till a' the seas gang dry [...] And the rocks melt with the sun'.[4] Here, and we'll see this again, images of fleetingness rub against, are haunted by, images of a deeper, longed-for, permanence—'till rocks melt with the sun'. A tough, even a harsh image. To bring to life the cliché 'till the end of time', forever.[5]

Burns's short life, early and late, was marked by sexual liaisons, mostly brief, with a number of women for whom he wrote songs, and though the important relationship is with Jean Armour, whom he eventually married, I want to look at two other relationships which produced songs. But I will start by looking at an imaginary relationship that, as we'll see, eventually produced an alteration in one of Burns's songs, and the paragraph in the unfinished novel that we have already looked at: the relationship between Robert Burns and Jane Austen.

---

2   Robert Crawford, *The Bard: Robert Burns, A Biography* (London: Pimlico, 2010), pp. 63–65.

3   For a discussion of Austen's relationship with Romantic poets, see William Deresiewicz, *Jane Austen and the Romantic Poets* (New York: Columbia University Press, 2005), https://doi.org/10.7312/dere13414

4   *The Works of Robert Burns*, p. 191

5   As fair art thou, my bonie lass,
    Sae deep in luve am I;
    And I will luve thee still, my dear,
    Till a' the seas gang dry.
    Till a' the seas gang dry, my dear,
    And the rocks melt wi' the sun;
    I will luve thee still, my dear,
    While the sands o' life shall run. (Lines 5–12; *The Works of Robert Burns*, p. 191)

Let's do some comparisons first. When Jane Austen was born in December 1775, Burns was, as I've said, sixteen and a budding poet and a precociously sexual, hardworking farmer. His father had already taken on a second farm, and the crushing debt that would mar all their fortunes, but the Burns family never tried to save money by stinting their sons' education (as, decades later, Charles Dickens's hard-pressed family would try to save money). Burns, the farmer's son, who drove a plough and worked with his hands, actually received a more intensive education in mathematics, English, French and Latin, and, I should add, was a much better speller (he won a prize for spelling) than the parson's daughter Jane Austen. However, both were precocious writers. Flash forward to 1787. Burns, after a season of litigation with Jean Armour's parents as to whether he would marry the mother of his children, or whether, indeed, he had already married her, had published the Kilmarnock volume of *Poems, Chiefly in the Scottish Dialect*, and was in Edinburgh receiving the star treatment, enjoying conversations with Edinburgh's great literary men, and having at least one affair and fathering at least one illegitimate child. Hundreds of miles to the south, Jane Austen was perhaps reading aloud to her family from her first 'novel', the eight-page *Frederic and Elfrida*. From the lofty viewpoint of a twelve-year-old genius, she looked down on the sentimental literature of the day, of which she seems to have read, and relished, even at that age, a great deal, having characters fall in love, fall out of love, and die for love with a rapidity that would have astonished even the fast-moving Burns. Into the novel's prose and conversation she also interweaves some verse, songs and an epitaph for one of these passionate creatures, a young woman who, in a predicament Burns would have understood, has entered into two simultaneous engagements and chooses suicide as a way out:

> Here lies our friend who having promis-ed
> That unto two she would be marri-ed
> Threw her sweet Body and her lovely face
> Into the Stream that runs thro' Portland Place. (*Juvenilia* 9)

This is what the author of *Pride and Prejudice* was writing at the age of twelve. This burlesquing, cheerfully heartless attitude to love and death is characteristic of her juvenile work, more mature in its brilliant style perhaps than in its emotion. Adult lives and feelings seem merely

absurd to the brilliant, precocious little girl. Since these early writings
were among the few original manuscripts that were saved, and exist
today, we can assume, I think, that the Austen family supported and
encouraged her efforts. A few years later, at fifteen (the age at which
Burns committed 'the sin of Rhyme' for the first time) she wrote her
wonderful eleven-page *History of England*, whose heroine is, fascinatingly,
Mary, queen of Scots: 'this amiable Woman [...] abandoned by her Son,
confined by her Cousin [...] firm in her Mind; Constant in her Religion;
and prepared herself to meet the cruel fate to which she was doomed,
with a magnanimity that could alone proceed from conscious Innocence'
(*Juvenilia* 184). So, Jane Austen's attentions were on matters Scottish in
that year, 1791, just five years before his death, when Burns wrote some
of his most beautiful verses, including 'Ae Fond Kiss', which I will look
at in a moment. These will take us back to *Sanditon* and *Persuasion* and
Jane Austen's incursions into Burns territory.

But first I want to look at the moment in Burns's writing which
brings him, I think, deepest into the kind of world we associate with
Jane Austen—the world of men and women and manners—and that
is the wonderful, funny, touching poem 'To a Louse', set in a church
(we might pause here to note that no long scene in the novels of Jane
Austen, the parson's daughter, is set during a church service). Burns's
poem depicts a moment between a young man and a young woman of
which the young woman is completely unaware (like Elizabeth under
Mr. Darcy's surreptitious gaze). Seated in church behind a pretty girl in
a fancy hat, the poet notices a head louse in action on the hat:

> Ha! whare ye gaun, ye crowlin' ferlie?
>
> Your impudence protects you sairly,
> I canna say but ye strunt rarely,
> Owre gauze and lace,
> Tho' faith! I fear ye dine but sparely
> On sic a place.[6]

The poem is often described as a satire, and the young lady's pretensions
to glamour are lightly mocked: 'sae fine a lady!' (line 10). The fat grey
louse is told firmly to 'crowl' on 'some poor body' (line 12), and the

---

6   Lines 1–6; *The Works of Robert Burns*, p. 42.

famous last stanza would seem to reprimand the young lady for not having 'the giftie/ To see oursels as ithers see us!' (lines 43–44), or the gift to see the back of her head! But assigning the poem solely to satire is missing its tenderness, a tenderness emphasized, I think in works where Burns uses the 'standard Habbie' stanza with its gentle dragging close: the double effect, the combination of sympathy and mockery in 'sae fine a lady' and 'O' Miss's bonnet' (line 24). Who can, after all, see the back of her own head? This is the kind of very complex attention to absurdities that begins to appear in Jane Austen's writing in the novels she started working on in the year Burns, of whom by then she was aware, as we'll see, died, 1796.

In *Pride and Prejudice*, and especially in *Sense and Sensibility*, her richest characters are both absurd and touching: Mrs. Jennings in *Sense and Sensibility*, with her infuriating matchmaking and her devoted nursing; Jane, Elizabeth's sister, in *Pride and Prejudice*, who frustrates clever Lizzy with her absurd inability to see wrong in anyone and who, in the end, is proved to be right about Mr. Darcy. Both these great writers, both Burns and Jane Austen, in their mature work, display qualities of attention that enable them to see human lives as complicated, as not simply tragic nor simply comic, as both foolish and moving in their self-deceptions and their desires. Both also, and this is noted more often in the case of Burns than in Jane Austen, are curious about how people behave, how they manage their bodies, in public. 'O Jenny, dinna toss your head' (line 37), the poet warns the poor young lady—and surely, sitting near someone of Burns's class in church in Scotland in 1786, this cannot be other than quite a poor young lady, dressing herself as fine as she can manage? And body-conscious Jane Austen notes with scorn Mrs. Bennet's winks and fidgets and Lydia Bennet's 'violent yawn' (I xviii 115), but also, more sympathetically, Marianne in *Sense and Sensibility*, broken-hearted after Willoughby's desertion, 'perfectly indifferent' to her toilette (II xiv 282)—not caring at all, at this stage of her young life, how 'others see us'.

Where Burns and Jane Austen come together most closely, even before those words in *Sanditon* quoted above, among the last which Jane Austen wrote, is in Jane Austen's music. During the years that she and her family were without a permanent home, living in rented rooms in Southampton and Bath, she was separated from her beloved piano. Unlike the Burns family, the Austens on the whole were not very musical; she was the musician among them. The pieces played by young ladies in those times were not often pieces by composers we now consider great. She does not seem to have played Mozart. But she did play at least one Burns song. Recent scholarly examination of a cache of musical manuscripts which are known to have been in her possession reveals that she had a copy of Burns's 1795 song 'Their Groves o' Sweet Myrtle':

> Their groves o' sweet myrtle let foreign lands reckon,
> Where bright-beaming summers exalt the perfume;
> Far dearer to me yon lone glen o' green breckan,
> Wi' the burn stealing under the lang, yellow broom.
>
> Far dearer to me are yon humble broom bowers
> Where the blue bell and gowan lurk, lowly, unseen;
> For there, lightly tripping, amang the wild flowers,
> A-list'ning the linnet, aft wanders my Jean.
>
> Tho' rich is the breeze in their gay, sunny valleys,
> And cauld Caledonia's blast on the wave;
> Their sweet-scented woodlands that skirt the proud palace,
> What are they?—the haunt o' the tyrant and slave.
>
> The slave's spicy forests, and gold-bubbling fountains,
> The brave Caledonian views wi' disdain;
> He wanders as free as the winds of his mountains,
> Save Love's willing fetters—the chains of his Jean.[7]

What is most striking about Jane Austen's relationship with this song is that in her copy 'Jean' is replaced by 'Jane' and 'the chains of his Jean' becomes 'the charms of his Jane'.[8] Since her manuscript is not the

---

7   *The Works of Robert Burns*, p. 196.

8   For accounts of Jane Austen's music collection, see Mollie Sands, 'Jane Austen and Her Music books', in *Collected Reports of the Jane Austen Society 1949–65*, ed. by Jane Austen Society (London: Dawson, 1967), pp. 91–93; Diana Shervington, 'Jane Austen's Music Books', in *Collected Reports of the Jane Austen Society 1966–75*, ed. by Jane Austen Society (London: Dawson, 1977), pp. 149–51; Robert K. Wallace, 'Jane Austen's Neglected Song Book', in *Collected Reports of the Jane Austen Society 1976–85*, ed. by Jane Austen Society (Overton: Jane Austen Society, 1989), pp. 121–25. For a discussion of Austen's musical manuscripts, see Linda Zionkowski and Mimi

only one to have this variant, too much should not be made of it, but one wonders with what emotions she sang those words: with a sense of the absurd, or with a sense of admiration both for the poet and for the nature of this feeling. Reading the song, with its equation of love of a woman with the love of a country, one thinks of the passage in *Northanger Abbey* when Henry Tilney chides Catherine for thinking that the sort of murderous goings-on she is imagining, and which of course would be run of the mill in Italy, could happen in England: '"Remember that we are English, that we are Christians!"' (II ix 203). Perhaps Jane Austen was thinking of the contrast between those 'spicy forests, and gold-bubbling fountains' (line 13) where dark, Gothic doings occurred, and the 'cauld' if not 'Caledonian' (line 10) blast with which Henry blows Catherine's imaginings away.

In 1791 Burns had written another and more famous song, which we don't know if Jane Austen read or not, though she could easily have done so, and that is the great—for some the greatest of his lyrics—'Ae Fond Kiss', and it is this song which echoes most hauntingly the question which Jane Austen's heroine raises in *Sanditon*: the connection between feeling and forgetting:

> Ae fond kiss, and then we sever;
> Ae farewell, alas, for ever! [9]

The song was written, most likely, for the woman called 'Clarinda', with whom Burns had a fleeting affair, and who, lest we become too tender-hearted towards the Bard, considered suing him when she heard he was married to Jean Armour. Their actual affair seems to have been measured in weeks, and this was possibly true of a number of his dalliances. In some cases, he surely felt, and forgot. But the words of this song are about that very forgetting, and about the tug of memory when it persists beyond forgetting:

> Had we never loved sae kindly,
> Had we never loved sae blindly;

Hart, '"Aunt Jane Began Her Day with Music": Austen and the Female Amateur', *Persuasions*, 17 (1995), 165–85. Digitised copies of the songbooks themselves are available on the internet archive of the Hartley Library, University of Southampton (https://archive.org/details/austenfamilymusicbooks).

9   Lines 1–2; *The Works of Robert Burns*, p. 188.

Never met—or never parted,
We had ne'er been broken-hearted.[10] (lines 13–16)

All the doubleness of feeling which is, at once, for him, overpowering
and fleeting, is summed up in the wonderful haunting rhyme of 'sever'
with 'forever'.

To return now at last to *Sanditon*, the woman in Burns's life to
whom the young man who admires Burns so much is referring is
neither 'Clarinda' nor Jean Armour but the legendary 'Highland Mary',
Margaret Mary Campbell, the young servant girl who came briefly into
Burns's life and flickered there briefly in 1786, and to whom Burns, at
that time in a kind of marriage or betrothal with Jean Armour, seems
to have proposed. He seems to have proposed to one woman while
promised to another. But sometime in the autumn of that year Margaret
Mary Campbell died, and she is memorialized in the poems 'Highland
Mary', 'Mary in Heaven', 'My Highland Lassie' and probably in 'Sweet
Afton':

My Mary's asleep by thy murmuring stream;
Flow gently, sweet Afton, disturb not her dream.[11]

'Highland Mary' was a subject of much speculation in the years after
Burns's death, and it is deeply appropriate that that such a silly young
man as the baronet in *Sanditon* should be concerned with the heroine
of what was even then known as 'the mysterious episode' in Burns's
life. We might want to compare this to some of the speculation about
whether Jane Austen had her heart broken by any of a series of young
men whose names appear in her letters. Readers love a mystery.

But let us end by revisiting those passages from Jane Austen with
which we started. I'll just repeat the criticism from Charlotte with its
lovely, rather Burnsian, rhythm: 'he felt, and he forgot'. What I would like
to point out in this statement is that though she does question his truth,
there is no suggestion in the comment of Burns having been deceitful.
'Truth' and 'sincerity' here seem to be more like loyalty, perhaps, close
to what today is known as 'commitment'. Burns is not being called a
Wickham, nor a Willoughby, just someone whose feelings were stronger

---

10 Lines 13–16; ibid.
11 Lines 23–24; *The Works of Robert Burns*, pp. 188–89.

than his memory. And if Jane Austen did know, which she easily could have known, 'Ae Fond Kiss', she might on reflection have added, 'He felt, and he forgot, but sometimes he remembered what he had forgotten'.

I said earlier that Jane Austen's heroines, though sympathetically presented, and important viewpoints through which we can see most of the story, are not identical with Jane Austen, or with her narrators. The young girl who wrote those stinging satires had grown into an adult young lady, a tireless dancer and party-goer, who was, as Mary Russell Mitford said, 'a husband-hunting butterfly', then into the spinster author of a number of brilliant novels.[12] That's a path none of her heroines takes. The one who goes farthest down it, simply by growing older, reaching the advanced age of twenty-seven, is that great lover of poetry (though she never mentions Burns) Anne Elliot in *Persuasion*, whose words I also looked at earlier. Let's look at them in greater detail now before we close. To remind you of the context, Anne is here talking to the retired sailor Captain Harville, who, stung by the fact that his friend Captain Benwick, who was once engaged to his sister, has very quickly after her death met someone else and asked her to marry him. '"she would not have forgotten him so soon!"', he says of his sister, and Anne replies feelingly that no woman would forget a man she loved (II xi 252). Captain Harville says, in some surprise, that women are always— it's a cliché—known for their fickleness, their changeability.

So what does Anne, twenty-seven years old, suffering from eight aching years of silent love for Captain Wentworth, what does she reply? '"All the privilege I claim for my own sex (it is not a very enviable one, you need not covet it) is that of loving longest, when existence or when hope is gone"' (II xi 256). When Burns felt spurned by Jean Armour, he turned to Highland Mary; when Mary died, back to Jean; in Jean's many pregnancies, he turned to other women, like Clarinda; then back to Jean, who, 'loving longest', survived him by many years, bringing up her own children, and some of those he fathered on other women. In Jane Austen's novels depth of feeling is most often indicated by the refusal to accept substitutes. Elinor in *Sense and Sensibility* remains true to her first love, as does Anne, and Fanny in *Mansfield Park*. The thoughtful heroines, like Jean Armour, 'love longest' even when they think 'existence and hope'

---

12   Rev. A. G. L'Estrange, ed., *The Life of Mary Russell Mitford*, 3 vols, 2nd edn (London: Bentley, 1870), I, p. 306.

are gone. But the heroes, or some of them? Captain Wentworth flirts, almost disastrously, with two teenage girls he meets in a country house; Edward in *Sense and Sensibility* falls in love first with the scheming Lucy Steele, and then with Elinor, with seemingly little sense that this is a problem; and, also in *Sense and Sensibility*, Colonel Brandon, that deep, that serious man, who has loved and lost in his youth, learns to love again with Marianne. And we ought to spend some time with Marianne, that heroine most likely to have sung Burns's songs. Marianne, who so scorns the idea of second attachments, at fifteen thinks she will never meet anyone up to her high standards, at sixteen falls in love with a deceiving scoundrel, and at nineteen marries Colonel Brandon, who becomes the love of her life, but who is undoubtedly a second attachment. What are we to think of such apparent self-contradiction? Let me remind you once again that Jane Austen knows more than any of her heroines, and take one last flash back to the opening of *Persuasion*, that 300-page hymn to first attachments, where we read some words no one ever talks about, in which the wise narrator says, of Anne's first broken engagement and its painful aftermath, 'No second attachment, the only thoroughly natural, happy, and sufficient cure, at her time of life, had been possible to the nice tone of her mind, the fastidiousness of her taste, in the small limits of the society around them' (I iv 30–31). Many things are possible in human life, Jane Austen would seem to be suggesting here, among them feeling, forgetting, remembering, and feeling again. Her final heroine in the tragically unfinished *Sanditon* may not be able to love Burns's poetry when she thinks about the man, but I think Jane Austen could.

13. *Sanditon* and Suspense

I will be talking to you today about *Sanditon*, the novel which Jane Austen started in the last year of her life but was unable to finish because she was too ill. *Sanditon* was read by very few people before 1925 when the great Jane Austen scholar R. W. Chapman edited it for publication and gave it its title. And because many people, even those who love Jane Austen's novels, have not read it, or don't know it well, I will also be talking about the novels everyone will know, and in particular the two that were published and read in the year of her death, *Northanger Abbey* and *Persuasion*, brought out in a single volume as neither was quite long enough to suit the expectations of the readers of 1817. Both of these novels, *Persuasion* which is so many people's favourite, and *Northanger Abbey*, which has fewer adherents, but very fanatical ones, have things which poor little *Sanditon* does not, and I will be talking first about what it does *not* have, cannot have, at this stage of production, which is: rich and rounded characters, and that hard-to-define 'air of reality' which marks the great finished novels. Then I want to talk about what it does have and since my title is about suspense, I will leave you in suspense for a while about those qualities.

Sanditon is one of the few works which survive in manuscript in Jane Austen's handwriting, but I'll talk first about another surviving fragment, also in her own hand. Everyone will know that among the tantalizingly random scraps of Jane Austen's writing is a chapter she wrote for the close of *Persuasion* and then dropped, replacing it with two more chapters which give us the end as we now have it. The survival of the cancelled chapter of *Persuasion* always makes me feel some of the woe that Mrs. Smith, late in that novel, expresses over the scanty paper trail left by her beloved husband on his death: "'this [...] happened to be saved [...] while many letters and memorandums of real importance had been destroyed"'(II ix 219). Here Mrs. Smith prefigures the

    https://doi.org/10.11647/OBP.0216.13

emotions of Jane Austen scholars over the centuries when faced with her fragmentary manuscript legacy.

In the case of the cancelled chapter, it is thought that, as with her proposal of marriage from Harris Bigg-Wither in 1802, Jane Austen said one thing, tossed and turned, and waked to change her mind. Or maybe it took a few sleepless nights, not just one, but it happened over a very short time in July of 1816, just a year before her death, and somehow that 'cancelled' version remained in physical existence, when every other manuscript trace of the six mature novels has vanished.[1] There is some fascination in the fact that it is *Persuasion* that leaves this physical trace, since *Persuasion* begins with the unliterary Sir Walter Elliot poring over a book, and ends, in the final version, with Anne being wooed and won by a *letter* slipped to her by Captain Wentworth. Lots of reading and writing in *Persuasion*.

In the cancelled chapter, though, the one that didn't make it past the final cut, Jane Austen has Anne and Captain Wentworth united in what can only be described as a *slapstick* style by Admiral Croft, who flings them alone together into a room in his rented house in Bath to have an awkward exchange about whether or not Anne is going to marry the man Wentworth thinks is his rival, Mr. Elliot:

> 'The Adm. Madam, was this morning confidently informed that you were—upon my word, I am quite at a loss, ashamed—(breathing & speaking quick)—the awkwardness of *giving* Information of this sort to one of the Parties. You can be at no loss to understand me.' (Appendix 1, p. 317)

Here, Captain Wentworth reverts to calling her 'Madam' as he did at Uppercross, and we watch the two of them blushing, stammering and 'breathing quick'. It is possible to see that this scene was great fun for Jane Austen to write, and that it was necessary for her to jettison it after she had put them through such agonies and a long awkward speech from Captain Wentworth—which would have been his longest speech in the book had it remained, full of 'it was said [...] it was added', until

---

1   For two different fine analyses of Austen's manuscript of the cancelled chapters, see Kathryn Sutherland, *Jane Austen's Textual Lives: from Aeschylus to Bollywood* (Oxford: Oxford University Press 2005; repr. 2007), pp. 148–68; Jocelyn Harris, *A Revolution Almost beyond Expression: Jane Austen's Persuasion* (Detroit: University of Delaware Press, 2007), pp. 63–72.

finally Anne puts an end to both their miseries by mumbling almost inaudibly, '"There is no truth in any such report"' (Appendix 1, p. 318).

'"No truth!"' Captain Wentworth replies twice. It feels as if he is trying out for a scholarship to RADA, as it does when a moment later he takes her hand and murmurs, '"Anne, my own dear Anne!"' (Appendix 1, p. 318). The tone of exaggeration is palpable, and must have been, almost immediately, apparent to Jane Austen. Where else in her mature work would a hero say, while pressing the heroine's hand, 'My own dear Anne!' Nowhere in Jane Austen's finished novels would this sort of male hysteria flourish, although we saw lots of it in the youthful *Love and Freindship*, and in the phony emotionalism of Mr. Elton's drunken pass at Emma in the snowbound carriage: the seized hand, the clumsy grope and the exclamation points: '"Charming Miss Woodhouse! allow me to interpret this interesting silence"' (I xv 142).[2] This sort of effusion has little in common with the restrained, embarrassed, deep feeling (also of course in *Emma*) of Mr. Knightley's much later and more successful proposal, or with the final version of *Persuasion*. It is wonderful what a few sleepless nights can do for one's prose!

In the rewritten denouement of *Persuasion* there is, instead, the infinitely subtler walk through Bath which Anne and Captain Wentworth take after ditching Charles Musgrove: 'smiles reined in [...] spirits dancing in private rapture [...] words enough [...] passed between them' (II xi 261). As usual with the profound mutual recognition of love which characterizes her happy endings, we don't hear those words, we imagine them, we invent them. The cancelled chapter, though, whatever its weaknesses, never fails to charm me, because I feel as if Jane Austen, in writing it, was falling victim to her own talent and to the power of her imagination. Having got rid of the threat of Mr. Elliot in Chapter xxii she simply, at first, could not wait to bring the right pair of lovers together. So—slam! Bam! She gets Admiral Croft to shut them up in a room together to fight it out.

Soon, though, she regained her perspective, and rather than succumbing to the desire for instant gratification in this swift reunion of her young lovers—after all, they had waited eight years, they could wait a little longer—she describes this process of delay: not Anne stumbling

---

2   For further discussion of this scene, see Chapter 9.

immediately into Captain Wentworth reading by the fire and resolving the situation in minutes as happens in the cancelled chapter, but two chapters and almost three whole days in which a jaded Anne endures one more evening of Mr. Elliot's now utterly unwanted attentions, and a morning in which a desperate, but surprisingly scheming and artful, Anne elaborately demonstrates her indifference to her cousin before the party assembled at the Musgroves' inn, then one last, long morning in the same room, filled with people, during which she and Captain Wentworth manage to find intricate and complicated ways to make their simple feelings known to one another. The delay deepens the meaning of what happens, keeps *us* waiting along with the lovers, as the short perspective is abandoned, in keeping with this love story's unequalled eight-year trajectory, for the long.

And when we turn to discuss this fragmentary novel *Sanditon*, in which all of the action we have takes place over less than a month, it is valuable to note that the foreshortened perspective, the haste, the rapid-fire breathless *telling*, which characterizes that cancelled, abandoned chapter of *Persuasion*, is a central characteristic of *Sanditon* throughout. And *Sanditon* is a work which, like that chapter, comes from the last year of the life of a great author, but it is still the *first part* of a *first draft* of a never-to-be-completed seventh novel. Comparing this to the two different versions of *Persuasion's* end enables us to note two things. First, that Jane Austen did not produce perfection every time she put pen to paper. Marilyn Butler perhaps goes too far when she says of *Sanditon*, 'it is surprising that even a first draft by the author of *Emma* would be quite like this'—I think we should be more impressed, as I hope to demonstrate.[3] But, second, as the *rewriting* of that chapter of *Persuasion* shows, when she was able to flesh out something that even to her most passionate admirers looks crude and sketchy, as the cancelled chapter does, she could swiftly produce something very like perfection. In the case of *Sanditon* that perfection is something that will hang forever out of our reach. There are completions of *Sanditon*. I don't like completions. I don't want to know what any 'other lady' will do with Jane Austen's book. Let's see what Jane Austen did with it in the little time she had.

---

3   Marilyn Butler, *Jane Austen and the War of Ideas* (Oxford: Clarendon Press, 1975; repr. 1989), p. 288.

But first, something she didn't do: and I will start with what I take to be the main problem with the novel fragment, which is that we don't have a rich enough relationship with the central figure, Charlotte Heywood. It is not that Charlotte is not a promising character, though she is a new type of young woman for Jane Austen to place right at the heart of a story. It is often pointed out that, in nature as well as in name, she resembles the 'unromantic' Charlotte Lucas of *Pride and Prejudice*. Like many readers of that novel, I have always had a soft spot for Charlotte, who is clever and funny and kind—and a loyal friend to Elizabeth, ever her well-wisher, 'rejoicing in the match' to Mr. Darcy whatever the wrath of Lady Catherine or the tut-tutting of Mr. Collins (III xviii 425). And I would suggest that the problem with Charlotte Heywood is not so much those sober, level-headed, Charlotte Lucas-like qualities, her primness, her impatience with others' absurdities; indeed, it seems to me a bold move on Jane Austen's part to focus on the experience of such a downright, feet-on-the-ground young woman. No. The problem is that the point at which the writing has stopped is a point where we don't have Charlotte Heywood's experience in the powerful way in which other heroines' is given to us.

Jane Austen did not have time or energy, in the six or eight weeks of deteriorating health which she had to give to this novel, to give us what in a film would be called 'reaction shots': we never really *see* Charlotte blink, or start, or blush in response to others. In all of the finished novels, and even in the unfinished novel *The Watsons*, the absurdity of characters, or their shallowness, or their moments of grace, are borne witness to by the instinctive reactions of the heroine, in little physical symptoms, often, but largely in her thoughts, in Jane Austen's use of what has come to be called free indirect discourse, the duets between narration, and the thoughts of a character, which gives us the unparalleled sensation of knowing her. In *Sanditon*, except for tiny moments, we don't have this. Instead we have a sketch of Charlotte's reactions *summarized* in ordinary direct discourse, flat and somewhat toneless, as here when we are told in Chapter vii about the opinion she is forming of mercenary Lady Denham:

> Charlotte's feelings were divided between amusement and indignation—
> but indignation had the larger and the increasing share.—She kept
> her countenance and she kept a civil silence. She could not carry her

forbearance farther; but without attempting to listen longer, and only conscious that Lady Denham was still talking on in the same way, allowed her thoughts to form themselves into such a meditation as this:–

'She is thoroughly mean. I had not expected any thing so bad.' (vii 180–81)

Here we know what Charlotte thinks and feels, and we respect her qualities of discernment by this time enough to feel she is probably right, but we are not *with her* as we are with Elizabeth Bennet as she forms a similarly negative opinion of the Bingley sisters in Chapter vi of *Pride and Prejudice*: 'Elizabeth still saw superciliousness in their treatment of every body, hardly excepting even her sister, and could not like them' (I vi 23). One feels the weight on that 'she *still* saw' and 'she *could not* like them', that is Elizabeth's inner voice mingling with the narrator's, and there is little of that distinctive ventriloquism, little of that variety of tone in Charlotte's reported indignation or in her quoted thoughts.

Jane Austen has not had time to invent a way of writing Charlotte which will give us full access to her, though the amused speaking voice in her dialogue with others is promising: one relishes her exchange with the hypochondriac Mr. Arthur Parker as he describes the effects on him of a single dish of strong green tea in the evening:

'it would act on me like poison and entirely take away the use of my right side, before I had swallowed it five minutes.—It sounds almost incredible—but it has happened to me so often that I cannot doubt it.— The use of my right side is entirely taken away for several hours!'

'It sounds rather odd to be sure'—answered Charlotte coolly—'but I dare say it would be proved to be the simplest thing in the world, by those who have studied right sides and green tea scientifically, and thoroughly understand all the possibilities of their action on each other.' (x 199)

'Scientifically' is a gem, I think, and this grave drollery, something like the tone of the juvenile *History of England*, and perhaps of some of the letters to Cassandra, has appeal. I will come back to Charlotte just before I close: to me it seems unarguable that she is not yet a lovable heroine; yet it is not her 'character' that is the problem, but the stage of writing at which her character has been necessarily abandoned.

Charlotte's cool, wry comment—and, even more, the reason for the abandonment of Charlotte's story, in Jane Austen's fatal illness— should draw us on to the important topic of 'those who have studied

[...] scientifically', and the treatment throughout, *throughout*, the novel, of illness—so courageous in someone herself so ill! But before we look at that great positive quality of *Sanditon*, let us look briefly at another aspect, which is the vividness of the setting, and the nature of the setting, which has frequently and rightly been described as something new in Jane Austen, a new experimental direction her writing would have taken had she not fallen ill and died. I am speaking particularly of the depiction of the village of Sanditon itself, in a novel which, like *Emma* and *Persuasion*, shows that in these closing years of her life Jane Austen's thoughts were running very much on the sea: Emma's honeymoon spot, Anne Elliot's reverence for the Navy and, of course, her visit to Lyme but that visit was out of season. Now, finally, we have an up-to-the-minute depiction of a fashionable seaside town, or a would-be fashion spot, and in season, the middle of July.

But let's pause for a moment, before we dive in, at the slightly dry-land opening at Willingden (which turns out to be 'the wrong Willingden') and is an opening unlike any other in Jane Austen's novels: 'A gentleman and lady travelling from Tunbridge towards that part of the Sussex coast which lies between Hastings and Eastbourne [...] were overturned in toiling up its long ascent—half rock, half sand' (i 137). To begin *not* with a self-mocking aphorism ('a truth universally acknowledged') nor with a family history ('Sir Walter Elliot'; 'the family of Dashwood') but with an *accident* to unknown persons, 'A gentleman and lady', whose names we don't learn for three pages—this suggests the experimental sparseness of this narrative, its almost harsh quality, lacking the reticence of the finished novels, and its location in a vividly sketched, sharply contemporary setting. It introduces the 'very quiet, settled, careful' Heywood family of Willingden to the Parkers of Sanditon, who are anything but quiet and settled (ii 149).

What is fascinating in the picture we have will soon have of Sanditon is that unlike rut-roaded, rural Willingden with its one gentlemanly house, Sanditon is so evidently a place in the process of transformation, but, like Willingden where Mr. Heywood is first seen making hay, it is a location for work, a distinctive kind of work, one intricately linked to commerce, in a village that revolves explicitly around economic expansion, rather than implicitly revolving around money by means of courtship and class, as every other village in Jane Austen does.

The windows in Sanditon's houses are full of bills—rooms to let—the library sells parasols, we rapidly hear the names of local farmers, market gardeners, shopkeepers, all of whom seem to have been drawn into the speculative bubble which is most fully embodied by the ebullient boosting of Mr. Thomas Parker who has introduced himself to the bemused Heywoods as follows:

> '*My* name perhaps—though I am by no means the first of my family, holding landed property in the parish of Sanditon, may be unknown [...] but Sanditon itself—everybody has heard of Sanditon—the favourite— for a young and rising bathing-place, certainly the favourite spot of all that are to be found along the coast of Sussex;—the most favoured by Nature, and promising to be the most chosen by man.' (i 142)

We might want to note that Mr. Parker, who is really a very sweet man, is ready to transfer any significance which might adhere to his own family name, to transfer importance to the name of Sanditon (compare this with Sir Walter Elliot and how little he thinks of the importance of place in comparison to that of the Elliot family name!) and also note the place-name's importance for the novel. Though it seems to have been the editor, R. W. Chapman, who named it *Sanditon*—the intended title appears to have been *The Brothers* and the Austen family referred to it as 'the Last Work' in the 1870 *Memoir*—the concern here does seem to be with place, with atmosphere, with the ethical consequences of this type of public, fast-moving setting, rather than with any of the characters, even the heroine.

There is a moment towards the end of *Northanger Abbey*, which Jane Austen was revising for publication in the same period, when Catherine's patroness, Mrs. Allen, who is really too stupid to be insensitive, does manage to say an insensitive thing: reflecting with Catherine on their 'forlorn' and friendless early days in Bath, she recalls how much meeting with the Thorpes had rescued them, and this in front of both Catherine and Mrs. Morland, apparently forgetting that Isabella Thorpe has only a few weeks earlier jilted James Morland, their son and brother, and 'made [him] miserable for ever' (II xiv 247; II x 207). But I want us to keep not only those shallow friends, the Thorpes, those drifters from Putney to Tonbridge to Bath, in mind, but also Mrs. Morland's comments on friendships made in such fashionable watering places—'"soon made and soon ended"' (I xiv 244)—and to remember Mr. Knightley's comment about the kind of places Frank Churchill frequents: "'the idlest haunts in the kingdom'" (I xviii 157). This gives us a perspective on the viewpoint of the 'steady' and 'sensible', a pair of adjectives Jane Austen likes to ring the changes on, about such fast-moving public places as Bath or Brighton or Weymouth—or Sanditon, though unlike long-fashionable Bath, the aspiring-to-fashion Sanditon is a queer combination, isn't it, of a public place, a backwater and a building site?

But the most important thing about Sanditon, as Mr. Parker tells the healthy Heywoods, is its healthfulness: "'finest, purest sea breeze on the coast [...] no mud—no weeds—no slimy rocks'" (i 143). The Parkers overturn their carriage in search of a surgeon to treat the illnesses that the sea breeze can't take care of, many of which we will see even in the narrow compass of *Sanditon*'s sixty pages. I have already looked at the marvellous Arthur Parker, confining himself at twenty-one to the delights of cocoa and rheumatism. I won't spend time with his poor sister Susan, who when we meet her has just had three teeth removed for what one suspects are largely whimsical reasons. But I think we all want to look at Diana, Diana who is marvellously introduced in a kind of slapstick race with Charlotte, which Diana, the thirty-two-year-old invalid, wins, of course, outrunning the healthy twenty-two-year-old farmer's daughter. Charlotte has been walking by the sea when she sees a carriage arrive at the hotel:

> Delighted to have such good news for Mr. and Mrs. Parker [...] she proceeded for Trafalgar House with [...] alacrity [...] but she had not reached the little lawn, when she saw a lady walking nimbly behind her [...] she resolved to hurry on and get into the house if possible before her. But the stranger's pace did not allow this to be accomplished. (ix 185)

Strait-laced Charlotte sticks to the path but Diana takes a short cut across the lawn! And, perhaps like the Parkers' overturning carriage— for almost everyone who has read *Sanditon* feels a little gloomy about the Parkers' financial prospects—this speedy determination of Diana's to get in first is symbolic. Though no one is more ill than she is, as she is fond of proclaiming, no one has more energy. Her style of invalidism is very different from Mary Musgrove's plangency and whining. Diana, who proudly claims the title of invalid, is enjoying herself to the hilt: "'my dear Miss Heywood, we are sent into this world to be as extensively useful as possible, and where some degree of strength of mind is given, it is not a feeble body which will excuse us"' (ix 189).

I do not know whether I prefer Diana's insomnia—'"[Susan] had not a wink of sleep either the night before we set out [...] and as this is not so common with her as with *me*, I have a thousand fears for her"' (ix 191)—or her lack of appetite—'"I never eat for about a week after a journey"' (ix 186)—but I think I admire her most for her ready skills as a masseuse:

> 'nothing would have been so judicious as friction, friction by the hand alone [...] Two years ago I happened to be calling on Mrs. Sheldon when her coachman sprained his foot [...] and could hardly limp into the house—but by the immediate use of friction alone, steadily persevered in (and I rubbed his ancle with my own hand for six hours without intermission)—he was well in three days.' (v 163)

I won't comment as I think that speaks for itself, though we might want to note that here we have another instance of the novel's cheerful inclusiveness about class. Possibly too cheerful an inclusiveness for the peace of mind of the coachman.

Jane Austen is interested in wild imaginations, and one form this takes is her fascination with hypochondriacs, with *malades imaginaires*. I've already mentioned Mary Musgrove, and we'll all remember many others, but in *Sanditon* we have a steady dissection of the condition of invalidism and its invention in relation to a consumer culture.[4] This motif is present from the very start, when Charlotte's father, Mr. Heywood, is described as someone who is 'well-looking' and 'hale' and a chapter later as someone rich enough 'to have indulged [...] in symptoms of the gout and a winter at Bath', but who is too busy, with his farm and his 14 children, to have realized what an opportunity he is missing (i 138; ii 149). It is as if the norm, once a certain social and financial status has been reached, is invalidism. In *Sanditon* the imaginary invalid constitutes an absurd, nonsensical kind of norm: people in this little novel use their bodies to tell the world something about themselves that they just cannot wait for others to find out.

In the earlier, rampantly burlesque *Love and Freindship*, a satire on the novel of sensation and sensibility, written when Jane Austen was a

---

4   For further discussion of hypochondria, see Chapter 6.

teenager, a carriage accident kills off half the characters in one fell swoop; the milder one which opens *Sanditon* kills no one, but produces two weeks of intensive nursing. Here it is not so much a literary phenomenon which is being lampooned but a social one, the explosion of health resorts, and the preoccupation with health, in Georgian England. Now, nursing moves the plot in her other novels, too: Elinor and Mrs. Jennings nurse Marianne back to health in *Sense and Sensibility*. Edmund nurses Tom in *Mansfield Park*. Elizabeth would never have been *invited* to spend five nights at Netherfield—she goes there to nurse Jane. Mrs. Smith in *Persuasion* would never have found out so much about Mr. Elliot's schemes for Anne had it not been for her friend Nurse Rooke, and in the same novel everyone agrees that they 'love [Louisa] the better for having nursed her'—even those who, like Mary Musgrove, have never nursed her at all (II vi 179).

But there is something peculiar about *Sanditon* as far as nursing goes, and I cannot help thinking the imaginary surgeon—the doctor who never comes—is a wonderful match for this little novel's huge cast of imaginary invalids—these strange, strange people who live to nurse, and doctor, themselves. I've mentioned Mary Musgrove, and everyone must be thinking, of course, not only of *Persuasion* and Mary Musgrove, but of *Emma*, and Mr. Woodhouse and Mrs. Churchill, those twin hypochondriacs sadly doomed never to meet. In *Sanditon* this condition has expanded with the same soap-bubble preposterousness that may be at work in the economy of this little not-quite-boom-town itself. Mr. Parker is surprised and delighted when he returns after a few weeks away from home to look into a shop window and find blue shoes, but there are characters in *Sanditon* in whom it would not surprise the reader, to find blue *feet*.

This propensity for exaggeration of symptoms is most notable of course in the three Parker siblings, but as the narrative tells us, their invalidism is an aspect of the enthusiastic temperament they share with their eldest brother, the Mr. Thomas Parker we meet in Chapter i. Perhaps, in these similar siblings, it should make us worry even more about Sanditon's real prospects for economic survival when we note the capacity Diana Parker demonstrates to turn one small family of holiday-makers into two large ones, and her insouciance about the mistake, the generosity she shows in cheerfully apportioning blame to others, 'the trifle' she bestows on herself. We are in a world which must make us think of the nonsense and exaggeration of *Love and Freindship*, where the two heroines travel huge distances by hackney coach—for no reason—rob, and are robbed, of large sums of money, and blithely and inconsequentially ruin the lives of many of those they meet. Jane Austen is certainly working here in this last fragment with some of the same qualities, including the prodigious, free-wheeling imagination, which gave her juvenile novels such verve and snap and wildness. And she also seems to be working within the great English nonsense tradition which stretches back to medieval riddles and forward to Lewis Carroll and Oscar Wilde.[5]

The 'great' Lady Denham, certainly, with her determination not to be 'had' even over the price of butcher's meat, and her barefaced admission to a complete stranger that she married one husband for money and another for a title, looks forward both to Lady Bracknell and to the Red Queen in *Alice*. But—to end as I began—Lady Denham would be funnier if she had someone we knew better than Charlotte to watch her with. More needs to be done perhaps with Charlotte's situation. She is not vulnerable, not trapped in London like Marianne or in Portsmouth like Fanny Price. If sturdy Charlotte wearies of Sanditon, she only needs to write home, and that lumbering old carriage, with its faded upholstery, will be sent to pick her up. In the version of Charlotte we have now, she is a little like a grown-up Alice in Wonderland, one who doesn't eat the wrong things, doesn't weep floods of tears, doesn't get called a 'serpent'. Pert and cool, she walks about observing the grotesque antics of others. As experienced readers of Jane Austen we struggle with Charlotte; we need to invent a complicating, endangering situation for her, and we need to see her respond to it.

And here is where the zany, dreamlike world of *Sanditon* has to be examined for the signs of that quality so important in Jane Austen's finished novels, and that is *suspense*. The aspect of Jane Austen which resembles Agatha Christie and resembles Alfred Hitchcock: suspense not so much of plot but of style. Earlier, in discussing the rewriting of *Persuasion's* finale, I mentioned her use of *delay*, something she learned from the sentimental novel and from the Gothic novel, from *Pamela* and

---

    5   See Elizabeth Sewell, *The Field of Nonsense* (London: Chatto and Windus, 1952); Neil
        Malcolm, *The Origins of English Nonsense* (London: Harper Collins, 1997).

Evelina and the *Mysteries of Udolpho*, where characters dawdle and dither and hesitate far beyond the limits of the reader's patience but which Jane Austen honed in her own writing into a taut, sharpened tool. And delay is only part of it: Jane Austen's imaginary worlds are ordered by the elements of suspense. Think of the dramatic crises of all the finished novels and how they leave us in dreadful doubt, each time we read them: will Elizabeth marry Mr. Darcy or will she never see him again? Will Edmund propose to Mary Crawford? Will Captain Wentworth stop behaving like an idiot with Louisa Musgrove? We know, but we need to prove it to ourselves with another reading. This is technical suspense. As with Hitchcock, one aspect is the precise distance created by the uneasy layering of wit and deeper feeling, so that every time we tear open those two misdirected letters from Jane Bennet along with Elizabeth in the inn at Lambton and shake our heads over the muddle of Jane's thoughts and even of her handwriting, our hearts are still in our mouths—'"Oh! where, where is my uncle?"' AND the door opens—AND it is not her uncle (III iv 304).

And there is concealment: who is that riding toward Barton Cottage? It should be Colonel Brandon—but it has not his height—it is Edward, whom we have been told is tragically mismarried to Lucy Steele. Concealment *and* delay: '"Is Mrs. Ferrars at Longstaple?"' asks Elinor, resorting to the good manners which help to get through but also prolong those agonising pauses (III xii 407). Wit and feeling, concealment and delay, and shift of perspective: Mrs. Morland goes up into the attic to get an essay to cure her daughter of the affliction into which she has apparently fallen at Northanger Abbey, of being a spoiled brat, but there are interruptions, 'family matters [...] to detain her', and then she has to find the blooming book—and when she comes downstairs, sermon in hand, there is a stranger in the parlour with Catherine (II xv 250). And Catherine is no longer inexplicably morose.

In detective fiction, in Hitchcock films, we know it's all about something we call pace: in Jane Austen's fiction we are so aware of the power and truth of the emotion and the dazzle of the comedy, that we don't notice it is all about pace, until the pace starts killing us. When Jane Austen began *Sanditon,* she was already ill, and she was writing, though we don't know how fully she knew it, against time, like T. S. Eliot in *The Waste Land,* shoring these fragments against her ruin. So if we look over the events of this strange, event-filled, sixty-page novel, if it has aspects of nonsense, and aspects of classic suspense, it also has aspects of science fiction: what strange things happen when you transplant a healthy young woman into a world, in which everyone is ill! If we look at it again, we see it begin with an accident, introduce a mysterious surgeon, who is what Hitchcock might have called 'a MacGuffin'—a plot device that goes nowhere—and then uproot its young heroine as *Northanger Abbey* uprooted Catherine, and place her, like Catherine, in an environment that stands in vivid contrast to her own family's rural retirement, knowing, as Mrs. Allen is probably aware that 'if adventures will not befal a young lady in her own village, she must seek them abroad' (I i 9). And unlike Catherine, whom it takes several yawning days to meet with any adventures, Charlotte has plenty from the start— she encounters a great lady, a romantic orphan and many other strange figures, including a number of possible suitors, though her good sense, and ours, too, rules out most of them.

Until the vertiginous close of the fragment, halfway through Chapter xii, which leaves us gasping to know: will Lady Denham ever come into the drawing room? (is she upstairs with her throat cut?); why is Miss Brereton sitting alone with Sir Edward, that would-be rake (is she falling for his charms or giving him a swift tutorial about eighteenth-century poetry?). And that very last page that lies open before the end of the book introduces Sidney Parker, the man 'with a decided air of ease and fashion, and a lively countenance' who has been trailed enough to interest us, though we don't know enough about Charlotte yet to know if he interests her (xii 207). I'll just close with that scene, because it is charming, including one of the very few moments in Jane Austen when a child speaks. First there is the nice—suspenseful—approach of a carriage through the mist, and then the cheerful anti-climax of little Mary Parker's pleased recognition of a favourite (well, how could he not be, given the competition?) relative:

> It was a close, misty morning, and when they reached the brow of the hill, they could not for some time make out what sort of carriage it was, which they saw coming up. It appeared at different moments to be everything from the gig to the phaeton,—from one horse to four; and just as they were concluding in favour of a tandem, little Mary's young eyes distinguished the coachman and she called out, ''Tis Uncle Sidney, mama, it is indeed.' And so it proved. (xii 206)

We leave Sidney a moment later, though first we do see him behave, unlike the wolfish Sir Edward or the piggy Arthur, in a gentlemanly fashion to Charlotte, with a 'very well-bred bow and proper address [...] on her being named to him' (xii 207). 'First impressions' are important in Jane Austen, aren't they? But as with Charlotte herself, we don't know what is going to be done with Sidney: will he break hearts, or mend them, and whose heart will it be?

Because of course the ultimate element of suspense about *Sanditon*, which nothing we can possibly find out will alter, is one which will go on forever. We are left forever clinging to *Sanditon's* cliffs by our fingertips.

Bibliography

d'Ancourt, Abbé. *The Lady's Preceptor or A Letter to a Lady of Distinction* (London: J. Watts, 1743).

Anderson, Beatrice. 'The Unmasking of Lady Susan', in *Jane Austen's Beginnings: The Juvenilia and Lady Susan*, ed. by J. David Grey (Michigan: Ann Arbor, 1989), pp. 193–203.

Aspinall, A., ed., *Letters of the Princess Charlotte 1811–1817* (London: Home and Van Thal, 1949).

Austen, Henry, 'Biographical Notice of the Author', in *Jane Austen: Critical Assessments*, ed. by Ian Littlewood, 4 vols (Mountfield: Helm, 1998), I, p. 38.

Austen Leigh, J. E., *A Memoir of Jane Austen by her Nephew* (London: Folio, 1989).

Bartlett, Nora, 'An Excerpt from my Unpublished Writing', in *On Gender and Writing*, ed. by Michelene Wandor (Boston: Pandora, 1983), pp. 10–16.

——, 'Deaths and Entrances: The Opening of *Sense and Sensibility*', *Persuasions On-line*, 32.2 (2012), http://jasna.org/persuasions/on-line/vol32no2/bartlett.html?

——,'Mary Ellmann', *The Independent* (June 7, 1989), 18.

——,'Silence as a Weapon of Self-Defence in *Sense and Sensibility*', in *Emotion, Violence, Vengeance and Law in the Middle Ages: Essays in Honour of William Ian Miller*, ed. by Kate Gilbert and Stephen D. White (Leiden: Brill, 2018), pp. 344–50, https://doi.org/10.1163/9789004366374_019

Benedict, Barbara M., and Deirdre Le Faye, eds, *Northanger Abbey*, The Cambridge Edition of the Works of Jane Austen (Cambridge: Cambridge University Press, 2006).

Beresford, John, ed., *The Diary of a Country Parson: The Reverend James Woodforde*, 5 vols (London: Oxford University Press, 1924–31).

Bloom, Harold, *How to Read and Why* (New York: Touchstone, 2000).

Bray, Joe, *The Epistolary Novel: Representations of Consciousness* (London and New York: Routledge, 2003), https://doi.org/10.4324/9780203130575

——, *The Female Reader in the English Novel from Burney to Austen* (London and New York: Routledge, 2009), https://doi.org/10.4324/9780203888674

Brown, Julia Prewitt, 'Private and Public in *Persuasion*', *Persuasions,* 15 (1993), 131–38, http://www.jasna.org/persuasions/printed/number15/brown.htm?

Burney, Fanny, *Diary and Letters of Madame D'Arblay*, 7 vols (London: H. Colburn, 1854), https://catalog.hathitrust.org/Record/000323685

——, *Evelina*, ed. by Edward A. Bloom (Oxford and New York: Oxford University Press, 1968; repr. 1990).

Burns, Robert, *The Works of Robert Burns, containing his Life by John Lockhart* (New York: Pearson, 1835).

Butler, Marilyn, *Jane Austen and the War of Ideas* (Oxford: Clarendon Press, 1975; repr. 1989).

——, *Jane Austen* (Oxford: Oxford University Press, 2007).

Bynum, Caroline Walker, *Dissimilar Similitudes: Devotional Objects in Late Medieval Europe* (New York: Zone Books, 2020), https://doi.org/10.2307/j.ctv15r5dvj

Bynum, W. F., Roy Porter and Michael Shepherd, eds, *Anatomy of Madness: Essays in the History of Psychiatry*, 3 vols (London and New York: Tavistock, 1985).

Byrne, Paula, *Jane Austen and the Theatre* (New York and London: Hambledon, 2002).

Chapman, R. W., ed., *The Works of Jane Austen*, 6 vols (Oxford and New York: Oxford University Press, 1923; repr. 1967).

——, *Jane Austen: Facts and Problems* (Oxford: Clarendon Press, 1948; repr. 1949).

Cheyne, George, *The English Malady or, a Treatise of Nervous Diseases of all Kinds; as Spleen, Vapours, Lowness of Spirits, Hypochondriacal, and Hysterical Distempers, Etc.* (London: Strahan, 1733), https://archive.org/stream/englishmaladyort00cheyuoft?ref=ol

Cope, Zachary, 'Jane Austen's Last Illness', *British Medical Journal*, 2 (1964), 182–83, https://doi.org/10.1136/bmj.2.5402.182

Copeland, Edward, ed., *Sense and Sensibility*, The Cambridge Edition of the Works of Jane Austen (Cambridge: Cambridge University Press, 2006).

Crawford, Robert, *The Bard: Robert Burns, A Biography* (London: Pimlico, 2010).

Cronin, Richard, and Dorothy McMillan, eds, *Emma*, The Cambridge Edition of the Works of Jane Austen (Cambridge: Cambridge University Press, 2005).

Davidson, Jenny, *Reading Jane Austen* (Cambridge: Cambridge University Press, 2017), https://doi.org/10.1017/9781108367974

Deresiewicz, William, *Jane Austen and the Romantic Poets* (New York: Columbia University Press, 2005), https://doi.org/10.7312/dere13414

Dickens, Charles, *A Christmas Carol* (London: Chapman and Hall, 1843), https://www.gutenberg.org/files/46/46-h/46-h.htm

Doody, Margaret. *Jane Austen's Names: Riddles, Persons, Places* (Chicago and London: Chicago University Press, 2015), https://doi.org/10.7208/chicago/9780226196022.001.0001

Drabble, Margaret, ed., *Lady Susan, The Watsons, Sanditon, by Jane Austen* (London: Penguin, 1974).

Duckworth, Alistair M., *The Improvement of the Estate: A Study of Jane Austen's Novels* (Baltimore: Johns Hopkins Press, 1971).

Eliot, T. S., *The Waste Land and Other Poems* (London: Faber and Faber, 1985).

Forster, E. M., *Abinger Harvest and England's Green and Pleasant Land* (London: Andre Deutsch, 1996).

Fraiman, Susan, 'The Liberation of Elizabeth Bennet', *Persuasions On-line*, 31.1 (2010) http://www.jasna.org/persuasions/on-line/vol31no1/fraiman.html.

Fergus, Jan, *Jane Austen: A Literary Life* (Basingstoke: Macmillan, 1991).

——, '"My Sore Throats, You Know, Are Always Worse than Anybody's": Mary Musgrove and Jane Austen's Art of Whining', *Persuasions* 15 (1993), 139–47, http://www.jasna.org/persuasions/printed/number15/fergus.htm?

Fowler, Karen Joy, *The Jane Austen Book Club* (London: Penguin, 2005).

Galperin, William, '*Lady Susan*, Individualism and the (Dys)functional Family', *Persuasions*, 31 (2009), 47–58, http://jasna.org/publications/persuasions/no31/lady-susan-individualism-and-the-dysfunctional-family/

Gay, Penny, *Jane Austen and the Theatre* (Cambridge: Cambridge University Press, 2002).

——, '*Sense and Sensibility* in a Postfeminist World: Sisterhood Is Still Powerful', in *Jane Austen on Screen*, ed. by Gina Macdonald and Andre F. Macdonald (Cambridge: Cambridge University Press, 2003), pp. 90–110.

Gérin, Winifred, *Emily Bronte. A Life* (Oxford: Oxford University Press, 1971).

Graham, Peter W., 'Born to Diverge: An Evolutionary Perspective on Sibling Personality Development in Austen's Novels', *Persuasions On-line*, 25.1 (2004), http://www.jasna.org/persuasions/on-line/vol25no1/graham.html

Greenfield, Susan C., *Mothering Daughters: Novels and the Politics of Family Romance, Frances Burney to Jane Austen* (Detroit: Wayne State University Press, 2001).

Grey, J. David, ed., *Jane Austen's Beginnings: The Juvenilia and Lady Susan* (Michigan: Ann Arbor, 1989).

Halsey, K., 'The Blush of Modesty or the Blush of Shame? Reading Jane Austen's Blushes', *Forum for Modern Language Studies*, 42 (2006), 226–38, https://doi.org/10.1093/fmls/cql015

Harding, D. W., 'Regulated Hatred: An Aspect of the Work of Jane Austen', in *Jane Austen: Critical Assessments*, ed. by Ian Littlewood, 4 vols (Mountfield: Helm, 1998), II, p. 292.

Harris, Jocelyn, *A Revolution Almost beyond Expression: Jane Austen's* Persuasion (Detroit: University of Delaware Press, 2007).

Heilbrun, Carolyn G., *Writing A Woman's Life* (London: The Woman's Press, 1988).

Johnson, Claudia L., *Equivocal Beings: Politics, Gender, and Sentimentality in the 1790s* (Chicago and London: University of Chicago Press, 1995).

——, *Jane Austen: Women Politics, and the Novel* (Chicago and London: Chicago University Press, 1988).

Kaplan, Deborah, 'Female Friendship and Epistolary Form: "Lady Susan" and the Development of Jane Austen's Fiction', *Criticism*, 29.2 (1987), 163–78.

Kermode, Frank, 'Too Good and Too Silly', *London Review of Books*, 31.8 (2009), https://www.lrb.co.uk/the-paper/v31/n08/frank-kermode/too-good-and-too-silly

Lascelles, Mary, *Jane Austen and Her Art* (Oxford and New York: Oxford University Press, 1939; repr. 1983).

Laslett, Peter, *The World We Have Lost* (London: Methuen, 1965; repr. 1976).

Landry, Donna, *The Invention of the Countryside: Hunting, Walking, and Ecology in English Literature, 1671–1831* (Basingstoke: Palgrave Macmillan, 2001).

Lane, Maggie, *Jane Austen and Food* (London: The Hambledon Press, 1995).

Le Faye, Deirdre, *Jane Austen's Letters*, 3rd edn. (Oxford and New York: Oxford University Press, 1995; repr. 1996).

——, *Jane Austen. A Family Record*, 2nd edn. (Cambridge: Cambridge University Press, 2004).

L'Estrange, Rev. A. G., ed., *The Life of Mary Russell Mitford*, 3 vols, 2nd edn. (London: Bentley, 1870).

Leighton, Angela, 'Sense and Silences: Reading Jane Austen Again', in *Jane Austen: New Perspectives*, ed. by Janet Todd (New York and London, Holmes and Meier, 1983), pp. 128–41.

Liddell, Mark, 'Nora Bartlett', *Mark Liddell* (November 24, 2016), https://liddellmark.wordpress.com/2016/11/24/nora-bartlett/

Littlewood, Ian, ed., *Jane Austen: Critical Assessments*, 4 vols (Mountfield: Helm, 1998).

Looser, Devoney, *Women Writers and Old Age in Great Britain 1750–1850* (Baltimore: John Hopkin, 2008).

Macdonald, Gina, and Andrew F. Macdonald, eds, *Jane Austen on Screen* (Cambridge: Cambridge University Press, 2003).

Malcolm, Neil, *The Origins of English Nonsense* (London: Harper Collins, 1997).

McMaster, Juliet, 'Hospitality', *Persuasions*, 14 (1992), 26–33.

——, 'Jane Austen's Children', *Persuasions On-line*, 31.1 (2012), https://jasna. org/persuasions/on-line/vol31no1/mcmaster.html?_

Miller, D. A., *Jane Austen, or The Secret of Style* (Princeton and Oxford: Princeton University Press, 2003).

Morgan, Susan, *In the Meantime: Character and Perception in Jane Austen's Fiction* (Chicago: University of Chicago Press, 1980).

——, 'Adoring the Girl Next Door: Geography in Austen's Novels', *Persuasions On-line*, 21.1 (2000), http://www.jasna.org/persuasions/on-line/vol21no1/ morgan.html

Murphy, Olivia, 'Jane Austen's "Excellent Walker": Pride, Prejudice, and Pedestrianism', *Eighteenth Century Fiction*, 26.1 (2013), 121–42, https://doi. org/10.3138/ecf.26.1.121

Pride and Prejudice, dir. by Joe Wright (United International Pictures, 2005).

Richardson, Alan, *British Romanticism and the Science of Mind* (Cambridge: Cambridge University Press, 2001).

Ricks, Christopher, 'Jane Austen and the Business of Mothering', in *Essays in Appreciation* (New York and Oxford: Oxford University Press, 1998), pp. 90–113.

Roberts, Michele, 'When Jane Austen Describes Meals, They Are Never Innocent', *New Statesman*, 132 (July 21, 2003), p. 56.

Rogers, Pat, ed., *Pride and Prejudice*, The Cambridge Edition of the Works of Jane Austen (Cambridge: Cambridge University Press, 2006).

Sabor, Peter, ed., *Juvenilia*, The Cambridge Edition of the Works of Jane Austen (Cambridge: Cambridge University Press, 2006).

Sales, Roger, *Jane Austen and Representations of Regency Society* (London: Routledge, 1994; repr. 1996).

Sands, Mollie, 'Jane Austen and Her Music books', in *Collected Reports of the Jane Austen Society 1949–65*, ed. by Jane Austen Society (London: Dawson, 1967), pp. 91–93.

Sense and Sensibility, dir. by Ang Lee (Sony Pictures Releasing, 1995).

Sewell, Elizabeth, *The Field of Nonsense* (London: Chatto and Windus, 1952).

Shervington, Diana, 'Jane Austen's Music Books', in *Collected Reports of the Jane Austen Society 1966–75*, ed. by Jane Austen Society (London: Dawson, 1977), pp. 149–51.

Southam, Brian, *Jane Austen and the Navy* (London: Hambledon and London, 2000).

Spacks, Patricia, 'Female Resources: Epistles, Plot and Power', *Persuasions*, 9 (1987), 88–98, http://www.jasna.org/persuasions/printed/number9/spacks.htm

Spring, David, 'Interpreters of Jane Austen's Social World', in *Jane Austen: New Perspectives*, ed. by Janet Todd (New York and London, Holmes and Meier, 1983), pp. 53–72.

Stovel, Bruce, and Lynn Weinloss Gregg, eds, *The Talk in Jane Austen* (Edmonton: University of Alberta Press, 2002).

Sutherland, Eileen, 'Dining at the Great House: Food and Drink in the Times of Jane Austen', *Persuasions*, 12 (1990), 88–98, http://www.jasna.org/persuasions/printed/number12/sutherland2.htm

Sutherland, Kathryn, *Jane Austen's Textual Lives: from Aeschylus to Bollywood* (Oxford: Oxford University Press, 2005; repr. 2007).

Tanner, Tony, *Jane Austen* (Houndmills: Macmillan, 1986).

Todd, Janet, ed., *Jane Austen: New Perspectives* (New York and London: Holmes and Meier, 1983).

——, *The Cambridge Introduction to Jane Austen* (Cambridge: Cambridge University Press, 2006), https://doi.org/10.1017/cbo9780511607325

——, 'The Price is Right: Returning to *Mansfield Park* by Jane Austen', *TLS* (March 6, 2020), https://www.the-tls.co.uk/articles/re-reading-mansfield-park-jane-austen-janet-todd/

Todd, Janet, and Antje Blank, eds, *Persuasion*, The Cambridge Edition of the Works of Jane Austen (Cambridge: Cambridge University Press, 2006).

Todd, Janet, and Linda Bree, eds, *Later Manuscripts*, The Cambridge Edition of the Works of Jane Austen (Cambridge: Cambridge University Press, 2008).

Tomalin, Claire, *Jane Austen. A Life* (London: Penguin, 1998; repr. 2000).

Trotter, Thomas, *A View of the Nervous Temperament* (Newcastle: Longman, Hurst, Rees, Orme, 1807), https://archive.org/stream/viewofnervoustem00trot?ref=ol

Trusler, John, *The Honours of the Table or, Rules for Behaviour during Meals with the Whole Art of Carving* (London: Literary-Press, 1788), https://wellcomecollection.org/works/qszhwdv8/items?canvas=1&langCode=eng&sierraId=b21526199

Twain, Mark, *The Adventures of Tom Sawyer*, ed. by Peter Stoneley (Oxford: Oxford University Press, 2007).

Vickery, Amanda, *The Gentleman's Daughter: Women's Lives in Georgian England* (New Haven and London: Yale University Press, 1998).

Wallace, Robert K., 'Jane Austen's Neglected Song Book', in *Collected Reports of the Jane Austen Society 1976–85*, ed. by Jane Austen Society (Overton: Jane Austen Society, 1989), pp. 121–25.

Wiltshire, John, *Jane Austen and the Body* (Cambridge: Cambridge University Press, 1992; repr. 2004).

——, ed., *Mansfield Park*, The Cambridge Edition of the Works of Jane Austen (Cambridge: Cambridge University Press, 2005).

——, *The Hidden Jane Austen* (Cambridge: Cambridge University Press, 2014), https://doi.org/10.1017/cbo9781107449435

Yelland, Cris, *Jane Austen: A Style in History* (London: Routledge, 2018), https://doi.org/10.4324/9780429486067

Zionkowski, Linda, and Mimi Hart, '"Aunt Jane Began Her Day with Music": Austen and the Female Amateur', *Persuasions* 17 (1995), 165–85.

Index

About the Team

Alessandra Tosi was the managing editor for this book.

Adèle Kreager performed the copy-editing, proofreading and indexing.

Anna Gatti designed the cover using InDesign. The cover was produced in InDesign using the Fontin font.

Melissa Purkiss typeset the book in InDesign and produced the paperback and hardback editions. The text font is Tex Gyre Pagella; the heading font is Californian FB.

Luca Baffa produced the EPUB, MOBI, PDF, HTML, and XML editions — the conversion is performed with open source software freely available on our GitHub page (https://github.com/OpenBookPublishers).

This book need not end here...

Share

All our books — including the one you have just read — are free to access online so that students, researchers and members of the public who can't afford a printed edition will have access to the same ideas. This title will be accessed online by hundreds of readers each month across the globe: why not share the link so that someone you know is one of them?

This book and additional content is available at:

https://doi.org/10.11647/OBP.0216

Customise

Personalise your copy of this book or design new books using OBP and third-party material. Take chapters or whole books from our published list and make a special edition, a new anthology or an illuminating coursepack. Each customised edition will be produced as a paperback and a downloadable PDF.

Find out more at:

https://www.openbookpublishers.com/section/59/1

Like Open Book Publishers

Follow @OpenBookPublish

Read more at the Open Book Publishers BLOG

You may also be interested in:

Prose Fiction
An Introduction to the Semiotics of Narrative
Ignasi Ribó

https://doi.org/10.11647/OBP.0187

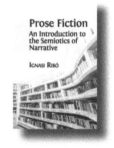

Tennyson's Poems
New Textual Parallels
R. H. Winnick

https://doi.org/10.11647/OBP.0161

Love and its Critics
From the Song of Songs to Shakespeare and Milton's Eden
Michael Bryson and Arpi Movsesian

https://doi.org/10.11647/OBP.0117

Lightning Source UK Ltd.
Milton Keynes UK
UKHW020714290622
405079UK00002B/8